AMP: Building Accelerated Mobile Pages

Create lightning-fast mobile pages by leveraging AMP technology

Ruadhan O'Donoghue

BIRMINGHAM - MUMBAI

AMP: Building Accelerated Mobile Pages

First published: September 2017

Production reference: 1270917

Published by Packt Publishing Ltd.
Livery Place
35 Livery Street
Birmingham
B3 2PB, UK.

ISBN 978-1-78646-731-7

www.packtpub.com

Credits

Author
Ruadhan O'Donoghue

Reviewer
Jeff Deskins

Commissioning Editor
Amarabha Banerjee

Acquisition Editor
Siddharth Mandal

Content Development Editor
Arun Nadar

Technical Editor
Shweta Jadhav

Copy Editor
Safis Editing

Project Coordinator
Ritika Manoj

Proofreader
Safis Editing

Indexer
Mariammal Chettiyar

Graphics
Jason Monteiro

Production Coordinator
Shantanu Zagade

About the Author

Ruadhan O'Donoghue is a web and mobile developer based in Ireland. He has worked in web development since 1999, and developed his first mobile web application back when the mobile web was built on WAP and WML and was browsed on tiny monochrome phone screens.

Since then, he has gained experience in many different roles, including as Head of Engineering at dotMobi (Afilias), where he created mobile solutions for companies worldwide. He has been an editor with and contributor to the mobile technology site `mobiForge.com` for over 10 years, and publishes articles on mobile web development regularly.

He currently runs his own web development agency, Western Technological.

You can contact Ruadhan by any of the following means:
Email: `ruadhan@westerntechnological.ie`
Twitter: `@rodono` (`https://twitter.com/rodono`)
Personal site: `https://ruadhan.com`

Acknowledgements

I'd like to thank my partner, Eadaoin, who, with her big heart, has kept me fed over the past seven months, and with her big brain, has added valuable contributions to this book.

Also to Ronan Cremin, James Pearce, and Jo Rabin, all former work colleagues and mentors to me back in the dotMobi days when every year was going to be the year of the mobile web.

To the AMP Project and its contributors, without whom there would only be empty space where this book is now.

To Arun, Siddharth, and the team at Packt, who gently kept the pressure on to bring this book to completion.

To the Superfriends, who provided the comic relief.

Finally, to my mum, who has always been supportive of whatever I've chosen to do in life.

Thank you!

About the Reviewer

Jeff Deskins has been building commercial websites since 1995. He loves to turn ideas into working solutions. Lately, he has been working with Docker and Kubernetes and is continuously learning best practices for high-performance sites.

Prior to his internet development career, he worked for 13 years as a television news photographer, including shooting live satellite shots for CBS News and CNN during breaking news events. Jeff continues to provide internet solutions for television stations through his TVstats.com website.

> *I would like to thank my wife for her support and patience through the many hours of me sitting behind my laptop learning new technologies. Love you the most!*

www.Packtpub.com

For support files and downloads related to your book, please visit www.PacktPub.com. Did you know that Packt offers eBook versions of every book published, with PDF and ePub files available? You can upgrade to the eBook version at www.PacktPub.com and as a print book customer, you are entitled to a discount on the eBook copy. Get in touch with us at service@packtpub.com for more details.

At www.PacktPub.com, you can also read a collection of free technical articles, sign up for a range of free newsletters and receive exclusive discounts and offers on Packt books and eBooks.

https://www.packtpub.com/mapt

Get the most in-demand software skills with Mapt. Mapt gives you full access to all Packt books and video courses, as well as industry-leading tools to help you plan your personal development and advance your career.

Why subscribe?

- Fully searchable across every book published by Packt
- Copy and paste, print, and bookmark content
- On demand and accessible via a web browser

Customer Feedback

Thanks for purchasing this Packt book. At Packt, quality is at the heart of our editorial process. To help us improve, please leave us an honest review on this book's Amazon page at http://www.amazon.in/dp/1786467313.

If you'd like to join our team of regular reviewers, you can email us at customerreviews@packtpub.com. We award our regular reviewers with free eBooks and videos in exchange for their valuable feedback. Help us be relentless in improving our products!

Table of Contents

Preface

Why did I write this book? Back in 2006, I was working with a company called dotMobi. I had the wonderful opportunity of working with some super-smart people--Ronan Cremin, Jo Rabin, and James Pearce--who were trying to make the mobile web happen (every year, according to James, was going to be the year of the mobile web, until 2008, when it eventually was).

One of the things that the team at dotMobi was doing was working with the W3C to help draft the Mobile Web Best Practices (MWBPs). We had already built the mobiReady mobile web checker, and the W3C was building its own Mobile Web Best Practices checker that, with my experiences with mobiReady under my belt, I was able to help out with. It was around this time, too, that we launched mobiForge; this was an educational site for web developers getting into mobile web development.

The point of all these initiatives? To give web developers and site owners the tools and knowledge they needed to build sites that performed acceptably under the constraints of the devices and cell networks of the day. This was 10 years ago, pre-iPhone, and the challenges for mobile web developers were considerable. Slow devices, slow networks, and small screens were the order of the day.

When the AMP project was launched, the similarities with the W3C MWBPs struck a chord with me. For one thing, the general goal was the same: follow good development practices, make the mobile web faster, and deliver a better user experience. However, even more than this, the AMP restrictions echoed very much the MWBPs, and the rules we'd built into mobiReady, even if some of the exact details had changed during the intervening 10 years. These were things like not using JavaScript, limiting the number of external resources and HTTP requests, and keeping the page size down. I could be talking about AMP, or the MWBPs.

So, AMP was a project I could identify with, even if some parts of it (such as the AMP cache URLs) are controversial, and I embraced what--as Alex Russell described it at the first AMP conference--has become "the most successful component library in the world." I understand the criticisms of the project, but coming from a background where web performance and user experience goals are important, I believe that, right now, the benefits outweigh the drawbacks.

Even without the cache, AMP is a fast, easy-to-use, and versatile component library. I hope that this book will help you see it the way I do.

What this book covers

Chapter 1, *Ride the Lightning with AMP*, introduces AMP, why it's needed, and what it brings to the mobile web. It describes how performance affects user behavior on the web, and its effect on conversions. It explains, at a high level, how AMP solves the problem of performance. Basic AMP concepts are introduced, and AMP boilerplate code is demonstrated in this chapter.

Chapter 2, *Building Your First AMP Page*, builds on the boilerplate code from the last chapter. The reader will see how to build a simple blog/article content page, while highlighting the similarities and differences between AMP-HTML and regular HTML. It demonstrates what happens when you use HTML tags that aren't allowed, to introduce AMP validation. The reader will learn how to develop and debug AMP pages, making use of the AMP validator and browser console as indispensable tools. Also, custom elements are introduced in the chapter.

Chapter 3, *Making an Impression - Layout and Page Design in AMP*, improves on the article-style page we built in the last chapter. The reader will learn about layout support and responsive design in AMP, and styling using CSS.

Chapter 4, *Engaging Users with Interactive AMP Components*, looks at how to deliver better user experiences via enhanced interaction mechanisms available in AMP. Building upon the prototype from the previous chapters, the reader will learn how to develop a side-drawer navigation menu, collapsible accordion content containers, and dismissible user notifications, as well as other techniques designed to make the most of limited screen space on mobile devices.

Chapter 5, *Building Rich Media Pages in AMP*, shows how to add rich media to AMP pages by building out an e-commerce product page prototype, which includes product image galleries and lightboxes, as well as audio and video components.

Chapter 6, *Making Contact - Forms in AMP*, shows what support there is for forms and form submission in AMP. A signup form, a product search form, and a basic shopping cart are developed that will demonstrate client-side validation and error handling, as well as how to build an endpoint to process form submissions.

Chapter 7, *Dynamic Content and Data-Driven Interaction*, explains how to automatically populate AMP pages with data retrieved by the JSON API. The product page is improved by dynamically adding related content data retrieved this way, and the shopping cart is enhanced to allow removal of items.

Chapter 8, *Programming in AMP - amp-bind*, introduces a programming paradigm offered in AMP via the amp-bind component.

Chapter 9, *When AMP Is Not Enough - Enter the iframe*, talks about workarounds for the limitations imposed by AMP. While it provides many custom elements to provide extended behavior, there are times when AMP can't provide the functionality you need. In these cases, the desired behavior can often be achieved with iframes, using amp-iframe.

Chapter 10, *Ads and Analytics in AMP*, introduces the reader to the different ways in which ads can be integrated into AMP pages. Different ad types and styles are reviewed and implemented. Analytics solutions are also implemented, demonstrating how to track user visits and other trackable events.

Chapter 11, *AMP Deployment and Your Web Presence*, outlines a number of options to deploy your AMP pages, whether standalone or as part of a bigger web presence.

Chapter 12, *AMP - Where It's at and Where It's Going*, reflects on what has been achieved. It covers the recent and under-development features in AMP, and where the project is going.

Appendix A, *AMP Components*, provides a reference list of all AMP components.

Appendix B, *Actions and Events*, provides a reference list of actions and events that can be used for interactions in your AMP pages.

Appendix C, *amp-bind Whitelisted Functions*, provides a reference list of whitelisted JavaScript functions that can be used in amp-bind expressions

Appendix D, *amp-bind Permitted Attribute Bindings*, provides a reference of element attributes that support data binding

What you need for this book

The requirements for this book are straightforward for AMP, and are similar for every chapter:

- Webserver such as Apache, NGINX, or NodeJS
- Web browser (such as Chrome or Firefox)
- Text/HTML editor (such as SublimeText)
- A web-connected mobile device, such as an Android or iOS phone, is recommended but not required

Additionally, some examples require the following. Where required, this is noted along with the example:

- HTTPS.
- Server-side technology--some examples require a server-side component to deliver data. PHP was chosen for its wide availability, but any server-side language could be used.
- Access to an alternative domain--this can simply be a domain alias that points to the same application directory on your server. For example, some files must be accessible at `example.com`, and another part of the example must be available at `alt.example.com`.

Who this book is for

This book is for experienced web developers who are seeking to serve content to their end users in a rich and enticing way using Accelerated Mobile Pages. You need to be familiar with HTML5, CSS3, JavaScript, and JSON, and be aware of the impact of slow-loading web pages and performance on conversion rates and user engagement.

Conventions

In this book, you will find a number of text styles that distinguish between different kinds of information. Here are some examples of these styles and an explanation of their meaning.

Code words in text, database table names, folder names, filenames, file extensions, pathnames, dummy URLs, user input, and Twitter handles are shown as follows: "Just add `<meta charset="utf-8">` immediately after the opening `<head>` tag."

A block of code is set as follows:

```
<script async src="https://cdn.ampproject.org/v0.js"></script>
```

Any command-line input or output is written as follows:

```
npm install -g amphtml-validator
```

New terms and **important words** are shown in bold. Words that you see on the screen, for example, in menus or dialog boxes, appear in the text like this: "Select **System info** from the **Administration** panel."

Warnings or important notes appear in a box like this.

Tips and tricks appear like this.

Reader feedback

Feedback from our readers is always welcome. Let us know what you think about this book-what you liked or disliked. Reader feedback is important for us as it helps us develop titles that you will really get the most out of.

To send us general feedback, simply e-mail feedback@packtpub.com, and mention the book's title in the subject of your message.

If there is a topic that you have expertise in and you are interested in either writing or contributing to a book, see our author guide at www.packtpub.com/authors.

Customer support

Now that you are the proud owner of a Packt book, we have a number of things to help you to get the most from your purchase.

Downloading the example code

You can download the example code files for this book from your account at http://www.packtpub.com. If you purchased this book elsewhere, you can visit http://www.packtpub.com/support and register to have the files e-mailed directly to you.

You can download the code files by following these steps:

1. Log in or register to our website using your e-mail address and password.
2. Hover the mouse pointer on the **SUPPORT** tab at the top.
3. Click on **Code Downloads & Errata**.
4. Enter the name of the book in the **Search** box.
5. Select the book for which you're looking to download the code files.
6. Choose from the drop-down menu where you purchased this book from.
7. Click on **Code Download**.

Once the file is downloaded, please make sure that you unzip or extract the folder using the latest version of:

- WinRAR / 7-Zip for Windows
- Zipeg / iZip / UnRarX for Mac
- 7-Zip / PeaZip for Linux

The code bundle for the book is also hosted on GitHub at `https://github.com/PacktPublishing/AMP-Building-Accelerated-Mobile-Pages`. We also have other code bundles from our rich catalog of books and videos available at `https://github.com/PacktPublishing/`. Check them out!

Downloading the color images of this book

We also provide you with a PDF file that has color images of the screenshots/diagrams used in this book. The color images will help you better understand the changes in the output. You can download this file from `https://www.packtpub.com/sites/default/files/downloads/AMPBuildingAcceleratedMobilePages_ColorImages.pdf`.

Errata

Although we have taken every care to ensure the accuracy of our content, mistakes do happen. If you find a mistake in one of our books-maybe a mistake in the text or the code-we would be grateful if you could report this to us. By doing so, you can save other readers from frustration and help us improve subsequent versions of this book. If you find any errata, please report them by visiting `http://www.packtpub.com/submit-errata`, selecting your book, clicking on the **Errata Submission Form** link, and entering the details of your errata. Once your errata are verified, your submission will be accepted and the errata will be uploaded to our website or added to any list of existing errata under the Errata section of that title.

To view the previously submitted errata, go to
`https://www.packtpub.com/books/content/support` and enter the name of the book in the search field. The required information will appear under the **Errata** section.

Piracy

Piracy of copyrighted material on the Internet is an ongoing problem across all media. At Packt, we take the protection of our copyright and licenses very seriously. If you come across any illegal copies of our works in any form on the Internet, please provide us with the location address or website name immediately so that we can pursue a remedy.

Please contact us at `copyright@packtpub.com` with a link to the suspected pirated material.

We appreciate your help in protecting our authors and our ability to bring you valuable content.

Questions

If you have a problem with any aspect of this book, you can contact us at `questions@packtpub.com`, and we will do our best to address the problem.

1
Ride the Lightning with AMP

Web performance is immensely important. Especially on mobile. According to recent research by Google, 53 percent of your visitors will leave your site if it takes longer than three seconds to load. Let that sink in: Over half of your visitors won't get to see your message or what you have to offer if your web pages are slow. The **Accelerated Mobile Pages** (**AMP**) project exists because performance is so important. With AMP, you don't have to miss out on that 53 percent.

By constraining the HTML, CSS, and JavaScript that you can use in your web pages, along with optimized resource management and smart caching, AMP solves the performance problem on mobile, while at the same time providing a framework for delivering engaging, media-rich, and lightning-fast web pages.

The AMP project has a lightning bolt as its logo for good reason: AMP pages are lightning fast. In this book you'll learn how to ride the lightning with AMP.

In the following sections, we'll look at:

- What AMP pages look like
- Why the time is right for AMP
- How AMP solves performance on mobile
- What the basic AMP building blocks are
- How to build your first AMP page

What do AMP pages look like?

AMP pages are often indistinguishable from non-AMP mobile pages. To get you excited before we dive in, let's take a look at some real-world examples to see the kinds of rich web experiences possible with AMP.

In the following images, note the Guardian's use of some common AMP components: the hamburger menu activates an *animated sidebar menu,* and the sidebar menu includes an *expandable accordion* sub-menu.

The Guardian's AMP pages include a dynamic hamburger menu with collapsible accordion sub-menu

In the next image, we see how ebay is using AMP for e-commerce: a *horizontally scrolling carousel* is used to promote products. Each item of the carousel contains image and text components.

In the final image, we see how Genius (`genius.com`) uses *embedded videos* within a carousel. (Incidentally, the aging rockers in this example sure knew how to turn their amps up to ride the lightning!)

Ebay and Genius.com AMP pages showing image and video carousels, and embedded videos

These examples were chosen to show that AMP isn't limited to static text and blog type pages, but that rich, interactive experiences can be built. AMP pages can include animated menus, accordions, carousels, image galleries, light boxes, embedded videos, and more. They support analytics and ad providers, and there is even an embeddable virtual reality component in development. In the following chapters, we'll see how to implement features like these and more.

Why now?

The importance of web performance is clear to most web developers today. Intuitively, nobody likes waiting around watching progress bars and spinners while pages load. The abundance of performance-testing services, such as `webpagetest.org`, Pagespeed Insights, and `mobiReady.com`, highlights the widespread emphasis and interest in making the web fast. But *why* is web performance so important on mobile?

Why performance is important on mobile

A steady stream of data has surfaced over the past few years that highlights the correlation of performance with user engagement. For example:

- Walmart found that each one second decrease in page load time resulted in a 2 percent increase in conversions (`slideshare.net/devonauerswald/walmart-pagespeedslide`)
- Amazon reported that a 100 ms increase in latency resulted in a 1 percent reduction in sales (`blog.gigaspaces.com/amazon-found-every-100ms-of-latency-cost-them-1-in-sales/`)
- Barack Obama's US presidential campaign saw a 14 percent increase in donations with a 60 percent increase in site speed (`kylerush.net/blog/meet-the-obama-campaigns-250-million-fundraising-platform`)
- Google found that a half second longer search page generation time caused traffic to drop by 20 percent (`glinden.blogspot.gr/2006/11/marissa-mayer-at-web-20.html`)

Clearly, performance has an impact on conversions. While the exact numbers will vary from study to study, any research you see on the subject will confirm the trend: *as page load time increases*, *bounce rate increases*, and *conversion rate decreases*. If your site is slow, you're going to lose out.

Mobile technology advances won't make websites fast

A commonly held view is that, as mobile technology improves, the performance problem will solve itself. On the face of it, this seems like a reasonable assumption. It's been 10 years since the original iPhone was unveiled. Back then, it had only a 2G network connection and a 412 MHz ARM CPU to deliver the web to its owner. Today, the newest iPhone model comes with a high-speed LTE network connection, and Apple's newest multi-core A11 CPU with a clock-speed of several GHz. The latest Android devices run on octa-core CPUs.

With these advances, the mobile devices in our pockets have evolved into super-computers. Surely then, mobile web performance is not a problem for these little power-houses. So why does the world need AMP now?

Unfortunately, these technology advances don't always translate into performance improvements for a number of reasons:

- **The performance gap is getting wider**: While newer, faster, and better mobile devices are shipping every month, only a portion of these will ever be used by your audience. The rest of your visitors will be relying on older and slower devices. Recent research from DeviceAtlas indicated that the original iPhone 2G is still being used to browse the web. This means that on average, the performance gap between low-end and high-end devices is increasing.
- **Physical limitations of mobile technology**: Device specifications aren't everything. Faster CPUs run hotter, and there is no active cooling in mobile devices. They have to dissipate heat through layers of plastic, the battery, electronics, and the screen. When they get too hot, they have to throttle down and shut off cores. So even if a user has the newest, fastest iPhone, there's no guarantee it will be running all its cores when they're needed.
- **Lie-Fi and slow cell networks**: Wi-Fi networks are often oversubscribed or backed by a poor internet connection: the user's device might have full signal bars, but really the connection sucks! The same goes for cell networks. Just because a device reports that it has an LTE connection, doesn't mean it's a fast connection.

Despite technology advances, unless you take great care, your web pages can end up being slow and frustrating on mobile devices.

AMP exists because of the realization that faster devices and networks are not going to fix performance on mobile. Instead, the problem needs to be fixed from the other end: websites need to be faster. But this is only half the story.

Business cases behind AMP

Google is a business, and as such, strategic business pressures lie behind much of its activity. The AMP project is no exception.

- **Facebook Instant Articles and Apple News**: Facebook and Apple launched similar technologies in the months before AMP was announced. Compared to AMP's open, web-based approach, the Apple; and Facebook services are more closed, in-app experiences focused on the presentation of static news-type content. Despite this, Google would have seen them as a competitive threat on a new front in the battle for publishers' content and readers' eyeballs. Indeed, AMP was originally viewed as a direct response to these services, although now the range of content it supports has moved beyond the capabilities of the competition.
- **Ad technology**: Google makes a lot of money from ads. Ads have a notoriously bad reputation for slowing pages down, to the point that ad-blockers are now commonplace, and even come bundled with browsers. If users block ads, or leave slow sites without viewing ads, then Google doesn't make money. If Google can improve the ad experience for users, as it does in AMP, then the threat to its ad revenue stream is mitigated.

So, the AMP project was born out of a need for faster websites, the need to answer competitor threats, and the need to maintain ad revenue. Performance underpins all these reasons, and AMP is about bringing web performance to the masses.

Web performance - why are web pages slow?

Web development is difficult to get right. The web technology stack is complex, and there are many things between the web server and the user's device that can contribute to poor performance.

There are some things that you have no control over, such as the user's network quality or device grade. But there are plenty of things that affect performance that you *do* have control over. Some of the most significant of these factors are *page size, resource loading, number of HTTP requests,* and *slow JavaScript execution*:

- **Page size**: In 2016, mobiForge (`mobiforge.com`) reported a sobering statistic: the average web page, at 2.3 MB, had grown as large as the original PC game, DOOM. Something is wrong when a web page needs to be the same size as a multi-level first-person shooter with an advanced 3D graphics engine. Many things can contribute to page size, including images, videos, ads, and third-party libraries (which themselves can include further third-party code).
- **Resource loading**: The order in which a page's resources are loaded can significantly affect the performance of the page. A naive approach to resource loading would be to just queue up all resources and download them as the page loads. But then network bandwidth and CPU resources are wasted on downloading and rendering items that may never be seen by the user. A smarter approach is to only load items as they are needed.
- **Number of HTTP requests**: Each external resource in a web page requires an HTTP request to fetch it. HTTP requests are slow, especially on mobile. HTTP requests can be reduced by inlining CSS and images where appropriate, and by including fewer external resources.
- **Slow JavaScript execution**: Today, there are JavaScript libraries for just about any task you can think of. Including and using JavaScript libraries has never been easier. But this poses problems on mobile, where every library chews through precious CPU cycles, contributing to laggy and unresponsive pages.

What exactly is AMP?

AMP is essentially a performance optimized HTML and JavaScript framework designed to deliver content quickly. It was originally conceived as a delivery format mostly for static, news-type content. But AMP has already evolved beyond its original static content aspirations, and now rich, interactive, and engaging pages can be built. Indeed, the range of user experiences possible was underscored at the first ever AMP conference in NYC in March 2017, where a fully functional messaging app was demonstrated, as well as an e-commerce app complete with payment capabilities.

There are three main components of AMP: **AMP-HTML**, **AMP-JS**, and **AMP Cache**. Let's take a look at them next.

AMP-HTML

AMP-HTML is an HTML5-based markup language that's used to write AMP content. It's basically a flavor of HTML5 designed with performance in mind. It both restricts *and* extends the HTML tags you can use in your pages. It restricts the HTML tags you can use to ensure reliable performance, and it provides a set of custom HTML tags--AMP components--to deliver rich but constrained functionality on top of the permitted HTML tags.

Because they are HTML-based, AMP pages will run in any web browser, out of the box. Additionally, AMP-HTML is designed so that it can also be served from the AMP Cache, and when it is, further optimizations can be automatically applied.

AMP-JS

AMP-JS is a JavaScript library that powers AMP pages. It's a runtime that orchestrates the optimized loading and rendering of AMP content. To achieve lightning-fast page loads, AMP-JS follows strict web performance best practices.

AMP-HTML restricts the tags you can use so that the exact layout needed to render the page can be known in advance. The AMP-JS runtime calculates page size and converts your custom AMP-HTML tags into HTML that the browser understands. It also assumes control of the loading of resources from the browser, so that it can prioritize resources that are above-the-fold or likely to be viewed by the user.

AMP Cache

Sometimes referred to as **AMP-CDN**, this is the caching component of AMP. It's a free-to-use **content delivery network** (**CDN**), for caching AMP pages so that they can be rendered instantly. Anyone is free to implement and use their own CDN. AMP Cache is a key component in delivering AMP's instant-loading experience.

When AMP pages are served from the cache, they can be optimized even further. These optimizations include:

- Resizing images to match the user's viewport (reduces page size)
- Inlining images that are above-the-fold (reduces HTTP requests)
- Inlining CSS (reduces HTTP requests)
- Preloading of extended components (reduces perceived page load time)

- Minification of HTML and CSS (reduces page size)
- Pre-rendering of web pages in the background (reduces perceived page load time)

AMP URLs

It's worth noting that a side-effect of the AMP Cache is that AMP documents will have a separate URL for the cached version. In fact, AMP documents have *three* different kinds of URL. For domain `example.com`, these will be:

- Original URL:
  `https://example.com/amp_doc.html`

- AMP Cache URL:
  `https://example-com.cdn.ampproject.org/c/s/example.com/amp_doc.html`

- AMP Viewer URL (when viewing AMP pages from Google search results):
  `https://www.google.com/amp/example.com/amp_doc.html`

Having three URLs might be a little confusing, but they're necessary for caching and pre-rendering in AMP.

Preparing your web server environment

Time to roll up our sleeves and get our hands dirty with some code. First we'll need to set up a web server. Since AMP is built on standard web technologies--HTML, JavaScript, and CSS--there are no special hosting requirements. To run the examples in this book, you'll need to host the example files on a web server such as Apache, NGINX or NodeJS; any web server will do. We won't go into how to set up a web server in this book, but you should have a basic understanding of working with the web server of your choice. In particular:

- You should be able to deploy HTML files to the correct location on the server
- In some cases AMP requires files to be served from an alternative domain or subdomain, so you should have a way to achieve this, whether it's via a virtual host or domain alias on the same server, or hosted on another server altogether

- Unless you are working on the `localhost` domain, AMP requires HTTPS in some cases, so it's a good idea to have this set up too

Alternatively, if you just want to follow along without hosting the files yourself, the examples are all hosted on `theampbook.com`. The source code is also available on github at `github.com/ruborg/amp`.

AMP Hello World - your first AMP page

Let's take a look at the most basic AMP page possible. It consists of the AMP boilerplate code that will be used in every AMP page you write. You can find this code at `/ch1/amp.html`.

```
<!doctype html>
<html ⚡>
  <head>
    <meta charset="utf-8">
    <script async src="https://cdn.ampproject.org/v0.js"></script>
    <link rel="canonical" href="https://theampbook.com/ch1/amp.html" />
    <meta name="viewport" content="width=device-width, minimum-scale=1,
initial-scale=1">
    <style amp-boilerplate>body{-webkit-animation:-amp-start 8s
steps(1,end) 0s 1 normal both;-moz-animation:-amp-start 8s steps(1,end) 0s
1 normal both;-ms-animation:-amp-start 8s steps(1,end) 0s 1 normal
both;animation:-amp-start 8s steps(1,end) 0s 1 normal both}@-webkit-
keyframes -amp-start{from{visibility:hidden}to{visibility:visible}}@-moz-
keyframes -amp-start{from{visibility:hidden}to{visibility:visible}}@-ms-
keyframes -amp-start{from{visibility:hidden}to{visibility:visible}}@-o-
keyframes -amp-
start{from{visibility:hidden}to{visibility:visible}}@keyframes -amp-
start{from{visibility:hidden}to{visibility:visible}}</style><noscript><styl
e amp-boilerplate>body{-webkit-animation:none;-moz-animation:none;-ms-
animation:none;animation:none}</style></noscript>
  </head>
  <body>Hello World!</body>
</html>
```

 Note when copying the boilerplate code: the `<style amp-boilerplate>...</noscript>` markup **must all be on a single line**. If copying from the ebook version of this book, you may run into issues with unwanted line-breaks, so it's recommended to copy the source code from the github repository for this book, or from `theampbook.com`.

Save this file as `amp.html` on your web server, and open it up in your browser (any browser will do, even a desktop browser). You should see **Hello World!** printed to the browser. Well done, you've created your first AMP page!

Nearly every line you see in this example is required in every AMP page you will write. Let's walk through the code and use it to highlight the minimum requirements of all AMP pages:

- AMP pages must start with `<!doctype html>` followed by `<html amp>` or `<html ⚡>`
- AMP pages must contain `<head>` and `<body>` tags
- The opening `<head>` tag must be immediately followed by:

      <meta charset="utf-8">

- Next it must include the AMP JS library, with:

      <script async src="https://cdn.ampproject.org/v0.js"></script>

- It must contain a canonical tag pointing to its associated desktop HTML version, or pointing to itself if there is no associated page:

      <link rel="canonical" href="amp.html" >

- It must include a viewport meta tag:

      <meta name="viewport" content="width=device-width,minimum-scale=1">

  (`initial-scale=1` is also recommended)

- AMP pages must include the following `style` boilerplate within the `<head>`:

      <style amp-boilerplate>body{-webkit-animation:-amp-start 8s
      steps(1,end) 0s 1 normal both;-moz-animation:-amp-start 8s
      steps(1,end) 0s 1 normal both;-ms-animation:-amp-start 8s
      steps(1,end) 0s 1 normal both;animation:-amp-start 8s steps(1,end)
      0s 1 normal both}@-webkit-keyframes -amp-
      start{from{visibility:hidden}to{visibility:visible}}@-moz-keyframes
      -amp-start{from{visibility:hidden}to{visibility:visible}}@-ms-
      keyframes -amp-
      start{from{visibility:hidden}to{visibility:visible}}@-o-keyframes -
      amp-start{from{visibility:hidden}to{visibility:visible}}@keyframes
      -amp-
      start{from{visibility:hidden}to{visibility:visible}}</style><noscri
      pt><style amp-boilerplate>body{-webkit-animation:none;-moz-

```
animation:none;-ms-
animation:none;animation:none}</style></noscript>
```

Ironically, the AMP lightning bolt symbol ⚡ is slow to type, since you won't find it on your keyboard. It's the unicode *high voltage sign* character, code point U+26A1. Using *copy-paste* is the easiest way to get it into your documents.

Optional but recommended boilerplate

The following items are not required in AMP pages, but are recommended so that you get the most SEO benefit from your web pages:

- **Title tag**: Title tags are used as a ranking signal in search engines, and are useful to users in identifying pages. You can add the title tag right after the AMP-JS `<script>` tag:

  ```
  <title>Hello World!</title>
  ```

- **Structured metadata**: Adding structured metadata allows third-party services to more efficiently index and preview your pages. For example, Facebook uses the *Open Graph Protocol*, while Twitter uses *Twitter Cards*, to extract images and specific data about your page. Additionally, Google's *Top Stories Carousel* supports the `schema.org` *Article* and *Video* categories to generate article previews such as the ones shown in the next section.

  To get a structured metadata preview of your page in Google search results, you need to add code similar to this to the `head` of your page:

  ```
  <script type="application/ld+json">
  {
   "@context": "http://schema.org",
   "@type": "NewsArticle",
   "headline": "Article headline",
   "image": [
   "thumbnail1.jpg"
   ],
   "datePublished": "2017-03-01T08:00:00+08:00"
   }
  </script>
  ```

Structured metadata and the AMP carousel

While structured metadata is not generally AMP specific, a significant AMP-only benefit of adding structured metadata to your page is the *AMP Top Stories carousel*. This is a horizontal carousel of relevant search results featured prominently on the Google search results page. Having your content featured in this carousel brings obvious SEO benefits, and so including structured meta data is highly recommended.

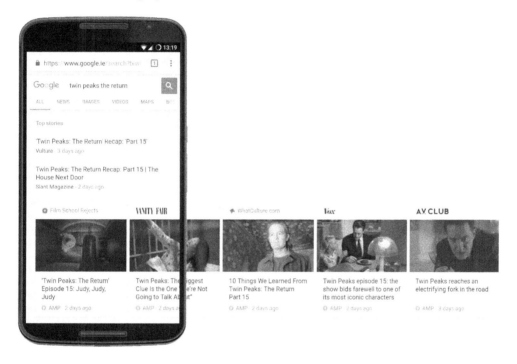

AMP Top Stories carousel

Validating your AMP pages

We'll be seeing more about validation in the next chapter. For now, you just need to know that your AMP pages must validate before they will be added to the AMP Cache. The easiest way to check if your page is valid is to append `#development=1` to the URL of the page in the browser address bar, and open up the Developer Tools (*Cmd + Opt + I* on Mac, *Ctrl + Shift + I* on Windows), and navigate to the **Console** tab. You'll then get a report for your page, indicating if it's valid. The page we just created should validate as follows:

Successful AMP validation in Chrome developer console

If it's not valid, you'll get some helpful error messages for any failures. To see this in action, remove the line that begins with `<link rel="canonical"...>` from your code and reload the page with `#development=1` at the end of the URL. This time the validator informs us that the mandatory canonical tag is missing:

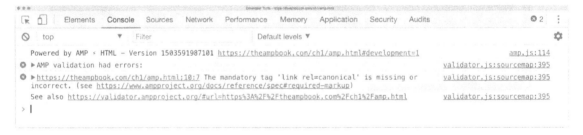

AMP validation reports an error for an invalid page

You'll need to add that line back in before the page validates again. But even if it doesn't validate, it *will* still render in most modern web browsers, since AMP is HTML-based. You *will* lose out on the benefits of the AMP Cache however.

What's with the <style amp-boilerplate> code?

You might be wondering why you need to include the `<style amp-boilerplate>` code in every page. Even AMP's creator and tech lead, Malte Ubl, described this code as an atrocity! Unfortunately, it's a necessary evil; a hack developed by the AMP project team to avoid the infamous flash of unstyled content while the AMP page is loading.

It works like this. First, the AMP page content is hidden while it loads. Then, when the AMP-JS library has loaded, it will unhide the page after it has finished rendering it. This presents a problem, however. If the AMP-JS library was ever unavailable when a user requested the page, then the page would stay blank forever. This would be an unacceptable user experience, even if it happened only rarely.

The trick, then, is to use a CSS keyframe animation as a timeout function: if the AMP-JS library fails to make the content visible, then the CSS animation will make it visible automatically after a few seconds, and the user will still get to see some content. A simplified version of this trick, without the vendor prefixes, is shown as follows:

```
body {
  animation: amp-timeout 0s 8s 1 normal forwards;
}
@key-frames amp-timeout {
  0%    {opacity: 0;}
  100%  {opacity: 1;}
}
```

How AMP solves mobile web performance

There are many factors that can contribute to poor web performance. AMP is able to solve performance issues and deliver pages instantly because it follows web performance best practices. But AMP is not magic: anyone can build fast pages without AMP if they follow web development best practices. This is a point that the AMP team has made on several occasions: *an AMP page won't be faster than a hand-tooled page*, if you know what you're doing. It will be faster than the average mobile webpage, however: AMP is about bringing best practices to the masses.

In addition to the best practices that it implements, AMP imposes restrictions that developers must follow to guarantee a certain baseline performance.

Optimizations that make AMP fast

- **JavaScript**: All JavaScript is loaded asynchronously and is non-blocking. No user JavaScript is allowed in the main page (although you *can* include JavaScript in iframes that can't block the main page render).
- **Static resource sizing**: External resources such as images, videos, and ads must specify their sizes statically. This means that AMP can calculate the position of all elements and page layout before anything is downloaded.
- **CSS inlining and limitations**: CSS must be inlined in the head of the AMP page and is limited to 50 KB per page. Some CSS is restricted, including the `*` `selector`, the `not selector`, the `filter` property, and the `!important` declaration. Only GPU-accelerated CSS animations and transitions are permitted. If the GPU can't handle an effect, then the browser must perform the required computation instead, slowing down the page render. Specifically, only `transform` and `opacity` properties can be animated.
- **Web fonts**: Web fonts can only be loaded from white-listed providers.
- **Optimized resource loading**: AMP takes control of resource downloading from the browser. Only items that are above-the-fold, or that are likely to be seen by the user, are fetched.
- **Efficient pre-rendering**: When possible, AMP pages are pre-rendered in the background. This is where things get really interesting!

AMP pre-rendering

AMP pre-rendering deserves a special mention here. It's used to boost the loading time of pages in the AMP cache. With AMP-HTML and AMP-JS, you get *fast* web pages. But with pre-rendering, you get *instant* pages.

Pre-rendering works by using a hidden iframe to download and render AMP pages in the background, even before the user has decided to visit them. The embedding page loads a hidden iframe with the AMP page content. The browser then loads the AMP runtime and starts to render the page. Since the AMP runtime manages resource loading, nothing else is loaded by the browser at this point (although the AMP runtime might decide to download necessary *above-the-fold* resources).

If the user clicks a pre-rendered AMP link, all the work to render the page has already been completed, so it can be displayed instantly simply by making the iframe visible. The JavaScript component that manages the pre-rendering iframe is called the **AMP Viewer**.

Controversy and criticisms of AMP

To achieve its performance, the AMP team have made design decisions that have resulted in aspects of AMP that seem incompatible with a distributed and open web. The most contentious of these are outlined as follows:

- **The AMP cache is owned and run by Google:** With the performance optimizations of AMP-HTML and AMP-JS you get *fast* web pages. Add pre-rendering and you get *instant-loading* pages. But pages are *only* pre-rendered when they are served from the Google controlled AMP Cache. And you only get the AMP lightning badge if your pages are pre-rendered via the cache.
  So this leads to an uncomfortable situation, where you only get the benefits if you agree to have your pages hosted and served from Google's servers. The URL of the cached page is not the original URL, but instead it's served from a Google domain, for example:
  ```
  https://www.google.com/amp/theampbook.com
  ```
  instead of
  ```
  https://theampbook.com
  ```
  This is somewhat misleading for the user: it looks like you are on one site, but really you are still on Google's servers. Additionally for publishers, using a Google URL dilutes their brand.

- **Preferential treatment of AMP pages in search results:** Google gives special treatment to AMP pages in its search results:
  - AMP pages are annotated with the AMP lightning badge and the text "AMP", to indicate that they are fast. However, fast pages that *don't* use AMP *don't* get the lightning badge. Some argue here that Google is taking advantage of its dominant position in search to push its own technology.

- Only AMP pages can be promoted to the AMP carousel. Given its prominent position on the results page, this offers a clear SEO advantage to AMP pages over alternatives. If you are competing for positioning, then you can't afford to be outside the AMP tent. Again, it can be argued that Google is giving preferential treatment to its own technology.

- **Centrally hosted JavaScript:** Every AMP page must include the AMP-JS library from a central location by including this line:
```
<script async src="https://cdn.ampproject.org/v0.js"></script>
```
You are not allowed to download the library and host it yourself. This means there is a central point of failure: if the library is unavailable, broken or hacked, then every AMP site will have problems.

While these are valid concerns, they have all been robustly defended by the AMP team. Take the AMP cache. According to the AMP team, the pre-render can only happen when a page is served directly from the AMP Cache, and not from the original URL. This is because Google *knows* that pages in the AMP Cache conform to the AMP specification, so it can guarantee that it can be efficiently pre-rendered in the background. It cannot make this guarantee about pages not served from the cache.

Likewise, the annotation of AMP pages in the search results. In the same way that it's good practice to annotate a download link with its type and size (for example **download [pdf 5 MB]**), isn't it acceptable to prime a user's expectation that a link will be fast and from the AMP Cache?

Benefits of AMP

There are many benefits to using AMP. First, AMP addresses the biggest web performance issues, which means that your pages will load more quickly. Since page speed affects user engagement, having a faster page means that you're engaging your visitors more. If you implement AMP, you're likely to see an increase in conversions. There are more success stories than can be listed here; these are just a few:

- The Guardian reported that its *AMP traffic has overtaken its non-AMP mobile traffic*, and observed *8.6 percent more clicks* on related content links
- LinkedIn reported a *10 percent increase in time spent on AMP pages* over non-AMP pages

- Gizmodo reported a *3x increase in mobile page speed* and a *50 percent increase in impressions*
- WompMobile reported a *105 percent increase in conversions* on AMP pages and a *31 percent decrease in bounce rate*

Next is the AMP Cache. If your pages are valid AMP, then they will be added to the AMP Cache automatically, and you will see further performance gains.

Then there's the AMP lightning badge of trust. Again, if your pages validate, then they will be annotated with the AMP lightning badge in Google's search results pages. With this badge, users can be confident of a speedy page load if they click your link.

Finally there is the AMP Top Stories carousel. As we saw earlier, this is a horizontally scrollable results carousel, displayed prominently, with images, early in the Google search results page. So, while Google has stated that AMP is not a ranking signal for its indexing algorithms, there is a definite SEO benefit to having your pages included in the carousel.

AMP adoption

AMP was first announced in August 2015, and launched in February 2016. At first, in Google's search results pages, AMP results were limited to the AMP carousel. But by March 2016 AMP results were being surfaced along with normal, non-AMP results. Since then AMP has seen massive adoption among publishers and search engines. The first AMP conference was held in March 2017, where the scale of its adoption became apparent, and it was reported that AMP was already the *largest web components library in the world*.

At the time of writing, with behemoth web services such as Pinterest and Tumblr on board, there are *billions* of AMP pages live on the web already. Bing is also working with Google on the project, and reportedly saw AMP adoption rates rise from 8 percent to 62 percent in one year. Baidu and Sogou, the two largest search engines in China have adopted AMP, and Yahoo Japan is also signed-up. There is an audience of billions for AMP pages.

So, do you need AMP?

At the first AMP conference, one of the panelists, Jeremy Keith, was asked why he implemented AMP on his site. He didn't know. After some consideration, he said it was another distribution format, like RSS, so why not?

For some, it's about reach. AMP can be thought of as another distribution format, as Keith pointed out. To maximize your reach, you should embrace as many distribution channels as you can. As noted, some of the biggest search engines in the world, including Google, Bing, and Baidu and Sogou, are indexing and surfacing AMP pages in their search results. That's an audience of billions. And if your content is featured in the AMP carousels, that's even more eyeballs for you.

For others, it's about performance. Malte Ubl reported that the Guardian's regular mobile website was faster than its AMP page. So why did the Guardian implement AMP? Despite having an already fast site, there were still performance gains to be made via the AMP Cache and its instant pre-rendering.

If your competitors are using AMP, and are featured in the AMP carousel, then they have a competitive edge on you, and it could be worth your while investigating it.

Ultimately, if your site is not performing as well as it could be and this is affecting user engagement or revenue, then you should address this. AMP is about improving performance, so it could be part of your solution. Even if you have a hand-crafted super-fast site, like the Guardian, you might still have something to gain by adopting AMP.

Summary

We've covered a lot of ground in this first chapter. You should now have a good idea of what AMP is and what it's capable of, the problems that it solves and how it solves them, and how it might be able to help you. In particular, you should now know:

- What AMP is and why it exists
- The factors that affect web performance and why it's important
- The components that make up AMP
- How AMP addresses web performance issues
- How to build a basic AMP page

In the next chapter, we'll move beyond the AMP boilerplate code. We'll see how AMP custom elements and CSS are used as we start to build our own experiences. Let's go ride the lightning!

2
Building Your First AMP Page

In this chapter, we're going to build on the boilerplate code from the previous chapter. We'll see how to build a simple news article page, while highlighting similarities and differences between AMP-HTML and regular HTML.

We'll also learn about AMP validation. Validation is a key step in the AMP development workflow. We'll see what happens when you use HTML tags that aren't permitted and we'll learn how to develop and debug AMP pages, making use of the AMP validator and browser developer console as indispensable tools. What AMP takes with one hand in restricting HTML tags, it gives with the other, in providing custom elements. We'll see how custom elements can be used in your AMP pages to add functionality otherwise unavailable.

So, in this chapter we'll be covering:

- How to develop pages in AMP, and how to convert a non-AMP HTML page to AMP-HTML
- Restricted HTML tags in AMP
- How to validate and debug your AMP pages
- What AMP custom elements are
- How to use `amp-img`
- How to measure web page performance

Going from HTML to AMP-HTML

Assuming that you have a basic familiarity with HTML, we'll use a simple HTML5 news page as our jump-in point, and we'll convert it to AMP-HTML. Unless you are building a *canonical AMP page*, that is, a standalone AMP page that doesn't have a desktop counterpart, then a common task you may find yourself doing is converting a full HTML page to AMP-HTML. That's what we're going to do now.

Below is a screenshot of the page we'll be working with. It's a simplified version of a typical news article page. It includes some key items that we'll convert to AMP-HTML in this chapter. These are the *header, logo, nav menu, article title, feature image, article content,* and *footer.* In subsequent chapters we'll refine and improve the AMP page as we go along.

Our first AMP page!

The HTML behind this page is listed below, and can also be found at `/ch2/news.html`. There's nothing difficult here, but if you don't understand this markup, now would be a good time to brush up on your HTML and CSS skills before proceeding further:

```html
<!doctype html>
<html lang="en">
  <head>
    <title>The AMP Book News Daily</title>
    <link href="style.css" rel="stylesheet" />
    <script type="text/javascript" src="script.js"></script>
  </head>
  <body>
    <header>
      <div class="logo">theampbook</div>
      <nav>
        <ul class="primary-nav">
          <li>news</li>
          <li>sports</li>
          <li>arts</li>
        </ul>
      </nav>
    </header>
    <article>
      <h1>Breaking: AMP is fast</h1>
      <img class="feature-img" src="lightning.jpg" />
      <p>Lorem ipsum dolor sit amet, consectetur adipiscing elit. Etiam
egestas tortor sapien, non tristique ligula accumsan eu.</p>
    </article>
    <footer>
      privacy policy
    </footer>
  </body>
</html>
```

It also includes a CSS file (`/ch2/style.css`) that contains the following CSS rules:

```css
html, body, ul {
  margin:0;
  padding:0;
}

header {
  background-color: #005689;
  padding:0.5rem;
}

.logo {
  text-align: right;
```

```
    font-size:2.5rem;
    color:#fff;
    font-weight:bold;
  }

  header li {
    display: inline-block;
    color: #fff;
    font-size: 1.5rem;
    line-height: 2.625rem;
    padding-right: 10px;
  }

  h1 {
    background-color: #eee;
    color: #005689;
    margin: 0;
    padding:1rem 0.5rem;
  }

  img.feature-img {
    width: 100%;
  }
  p {
    padding:0.5rem;
  }

  footer {
    color: #dcdcdc;
    background: #484848;
    padding:0.5rem;
  }
```

Since we'll be converting this HTML file to AMP-HTML, we'll save it as news.amp.html and make our changes in this file.

Including the AMP-JS library

The very first step in converting any page to AMP will be to include the AMP-JS library in the page. This is an important first step since the AMP library includes development tools that will guide us as we build our AMP pages.

To include the AMP-JS library, simply add the following line within the `<head>` tag of your markup:

```
<script async src="https://cdn.ampproject.org/v0.js"></script>
```

If you open your developer tools console in any modern browser, you should see a line of AMP-specific output:

Powered by AMP ⚡ HTML

This means the AMP-JS library has loaded and our journey to ride the AMP lightning has truly begun!

Validating your AMP pages

Now that we've included the AMP-JS library we have access to a very important component of AMP that comes bundled with the library: the AMP validator. We briefly touched on AMP validation in the last chapter. Let's look at it in a bit more detail now.

Validation is useful because it will tell us when there are issues with our AMP pages, and it will report which part of a page has caused a problem. If an AMP page doesn't validate, it won't be included in the AMP Cache, and while it will still generally load quickly, it won't enjoy the benefit of instant loading that the cache brings.

Time to validate! If there's one thing that AMP is not short on, it's validation tools. There are a few different ways we can validate our pages.

Developer tools console

The browser developer console is probably the easiest way to start validating your pages. Since the validator is included in the AMP-JS library, you can validate every page out of the box. To validate an AMP page, open the page in your browser, and add `#development=1` to the URL. Your URL will look something like this:

```
https://theampbook.com/ch2/news.amp.html#development=1
```

Or, if you're working locally, then your URL will look something like this:

```
http://localhost/news.amp.html#development=1
```

Now, with the developer console open, reload the page. You should see some validator output in the console that looks like this:

AMP validation errors in browser developer console

Ouch! Look at all those red error messages. Each one is telling us about some issue with the AMP page. To get all the benefits of AMP, we will need to address each of these errors to fix our page so that it validates. This will become an important part of your AMP workflow.

Online validator

There is an online AMP validator available at `validator.ampproject.org`. It works much like the browser console validator, indicating if your pages validate and listing errors when they don't. An advantage of the online validator is that it displays validation errors right next to the markup that caused the error, as shown in the following image:

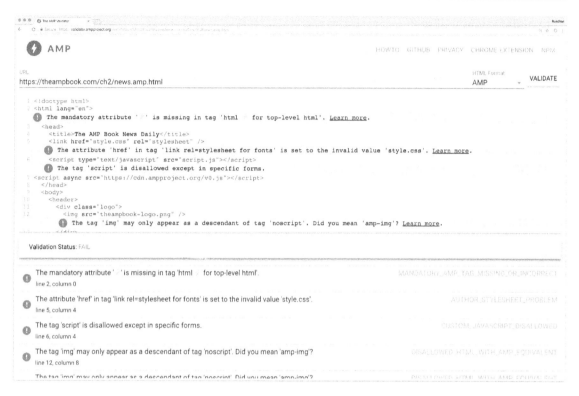

AMP validation with online validator

Command line validation

If you have Node.js installed on your machine, you can use the command line validation tool to validate both local and remote files. An advantage of this tool is that it can be included in your workflow and deployment process to automatically validate pages, and alert you when unexpected validation failures occur. A process like this will help to ensure that you don't accidentally deploy invalid pages and lose AMP badges and positioning in AMP search results carousels.

You can install the command line validator with the following command:

```
npm install -g amphtml-validator
```

To validate a page, use:

```
amphtml-validator https://theampbook.com
```

If it validates you will see:

```
https://theampbook.com: PASS
```

If there are any validation failures, they are listed just like in the developer console tool:

AMP validation with command line tool

Fixing AMP validation errors

To keep things simple, we'll use the developer console validator for most of this book because it works without having to install anything. This makes it the easiest approach to get started with.

If you haven't already activated the AMP validator, then do it now by adding the fragment `#development=1` to the end of your URL and reload the page with the developer tools console open. Your URL will be something like this:

```
https://theampbook.com/ch2/news.amp.html#development=1
```

You should see a list of errors similar to those in the previous images. Each validation error includes three important pieces of information:

- The filename in which the error occurred
- The line number and character number of the error
- A description of the error

We can use this information to pinpoint in the AMP-HTML markup where the error occurred.

Although it looks like we have a lot of errors, most of these are related to the required boilerplate we saw in the last chapter, so we know how to fix them already.

AMP boilerplate validation errors

Let's quickly go through the errors related to the AMP boilerplate. Errors related to AMP boilerplate are usually reported as occurring at the end of the document, and usually begin with text: "**The manadatory tag...**", like in the following two messages:

news.html:2:0 The mandatory attribute ' ⚡ ' is missing in tag 'html ⚡ for top-level html'. (see https://www.ampproject.org/docs/reference/spec#required-markup)

news.html:30:7 The mandatory tag 'html ⚡ for top-level html' is missing or incorrect. (see https://www.ampproject.org/docs/reference/spec#required-markup)

These two error messages relate to the opening HTML tag. One occurs at line 2, character 0, and the second occurs at line 30, character 7 (that is, the end of the document). We see at line 2, we have `<html lang="en">` but we know that our AMP documents should start with `<html ⚡ >` or `<html amp>`. So make this change and reload. This error should be resolved.

 Don't worry if the line numbers in the examples here don't match up exactly with what you see. As you fix the errors by making changes to the HTML, the line numbers may change. We'll omit the line numbers for the remainder of the examples unless they are needed.

The next error is:

The mandatory tag 'link rel=canonical' is missing or incorrect. (see https://www.ampproject.org/docs/reference/spec#required-markup)

We know how to fix this! Just add a canonical tag pointing to itself or its desktop counterpart:

```
<link rel="canonical" href="https://theampbook.com/ch2/news.html" />
```

If you are using a local web server, then your canonical tag will look something like this:

```
<link rel="canonical" href="http://localhost/news.html" />
```

Next is:

The mandatory tag 'meta charset=utf-8' is missing or incorrect. (see https://www.ampproject.org/docs/reference/spec#required-markup)

We can fix this too: Just add `<meta charset="utf-8">` immediately after the opening `<head>` tag.

Next we have:

The mandatory tag 'meta name=viewport' is missing or incorrect. (see https://www.ampproject.org/docs/reference/spec#required-markup)

For this one, we need to add the following to our AMP page:

```
<meta name="viewport" content="width=device-width,minimum-scale=1,initial-scale=1">
```

Then we have three related errors:

The mandatory tag 'noscript enclosure for boilerplate' is missing or incorrect.
The mandatory tag 'head > style[amp-boilerplate]' is missing or incorrect.
The mandatory tag 'noscript > style[amp-boilerplate]' is missing or incorrect.

We can take these three errors together since they are all caused by the same issue: the missing mandatory `<style amp-boilerplate>` tag. Add the following:

```
<style amp-boilerplate>body{-webkit-animation:-amp-start 8s steps(1,end) 0s
1 normal both;-moz-animation:-amp-start 8s steps(1,end) 0s 1 normal both;-
ms-animation:-amp-start 8s steps(1,end) 0s 1 normal both;animation:-amp-
start 8s steps(1,end) 0s 1 normal both}@-webkit-keyframes -amp-
start{from{visibility:hidden}to{visibility:visible}}@-moz-keyframes -amp-
start{from{visibility:hidden}to{visibility:visible}}@-ms-keyframes -amp-
start{from{visibility:hidden}to{visibility:visible}}@-o-keyframes -amp-
start{from{visibility:hidden}to{visibility:visible}}@keyframes -amp-
start{from{visibility:hidden}to{visibility:visible}}</style><noscript><styl
e amp-boilerplate>body{-webkit-animation:none;-moz-animation:none;-ms-
animation:none;animation:none}</style></noscript>
```

 As noted in the last chapter, the `<style amp-boilerplate>` code **must be on a single line**, so if you copy from the PDF or eBook versions of this book, you may run into problems with unwanted line-breaks. It's therefore recommended to copy the code from the github repository at `github.com/ruborg/amp`, or from `theampbook.com`.

With each error you fix, hit reload and examine the developer console. You should see the list of errors getting smaller. Good work! You're making progress. So far, we've dealt only with the validation errors related to the mandatory AMP boilerplate code. You should only have the following validation errors remaining:

The tag 'script' is disallowed except in specific forms.
The tag 'img' may only appear as a descendant of tag 'noscript'. Did you mean 'amp-img'?
The attribute 'href' in tag 'link rel=stylesheet for fonts' is set to the invalid value 'style.css'.

Using JavaScript in AMP pages

Let's deal with our first non-boilerplate error message:

The tag 'script' is disallowed except in specific forms.

In AMP, to guarantee performance, the use of JavaScript is greatly restricted. You can't write your own scripts, or include non-AMP JavaScript code. To fix this error, just remove the following line from your AMP document.

```
<script type="text/javascript" src="script.js"></script>
```

Don't worry, it's not needed. It was only included to demonstrate what the validator thinks of you including your own JavaScript!

Using CSS in AMP pages

We're not finished converting our page to AMP just yet; let's deal with the validation error that mentions the style sheet next:

The attribute 'href' in tag 'link rel=stylesheet for fonts' is set to the invalid value 'style.css'.

One of the ways that AMP achieves its speed is by forbidding linked external style sheets. This means that all CSS must be inlined in the <head> of your AMP page. Open up the style sheet, and copy-paste all of the CSS rules you find into the AMP document. You'll need to wrap this CSS in a <style amp-custom> tag like this:

```
<style amp-custom>
  html, body, ul {
    margin:0;
```

```
    padding:0;
  }
  ...
</style>
```

 You can only have one `<style>` tag in your AMP document, and it must include the `amp-custom` attribute.

Inlined CSS is limited to 50 KB per page, which is considered enough to style a single page

If you reload the page now, you should see that the CSS validation error message is now resolved.

Your first AMP component - <amp-img>

The next validation error message is interesting:

The tag 'img' may only appear as a descendant of tag 'noscript'. Did you mean 'amp-img'?

This error deserves special attention: it's the first error that's complaining about what looks to be standard use of an HTML tag. It's basically telling us that the HTML `<img>` tag is not permitted in AMP, and it's suggesting an alternative `<amp-img>`.

Let's try to swap in `<amp-img>` in place of our `<img>` tag. Copy this line in instead:

```
<amp-img src="https://theampbook.com/ch2/lightning.jpg"></amp-img>
```

Note the closing `</amp-img>` tag. The HTML `img` tag is a **void** tag, which means that it doesn't need to be explicitly closed. However, the same does not hold for `amp-img`; so you must close it explicitly. Hit reload and check the developer console.

So that didn't work out so well: the image isn't displaying and the validator is reporting the following messages:

The implied layout 'CONTAINER' is not supported by tag 'amp-img'.
The mandatory attribute 'height' is missing in tag 'amp-img'.

The first error is complaining about *layout,* and the second is about a missing `height` attribute. Let's specify both the `width` and `height` attributes (if we omit `width` we'll see an error about that the next time we validate):

```
<amp-img src="https://theampbook.com/ch2/lightning.jpg"
         width="768"
```

```
        height="305">
</amp-img>
```

 You must always specify `width`, and `height` for `amp-img` tags.

That fixed one of the errors, but we still need to deal with the layout error. Add the attribute `layout="responsive"` to the `amp-img` tag, so it now looks like this:

```
<amp-img src="https://theampbook.com/ch2/lightning.jpg"
        width="768"
        height="305"
        layout="responsive" >
</amp-img>
```

When you reload the page, you should now be able to see the image, and the validation errors should be gone.

Layout in AMP

The reason we must provide `width`, `height`, and `layout` attributes for images is to do with how AMP calculates the layout of the page. AMP uses a *static layout system* so that it can render pages more quickly. If the AMP runtime has this information upfront, in the markup, then it can always know how much space any element will take up. This means it can calculate the layout of the page efficiently even before external resources are loaded, and without having to reflow the page as they are loaded. We'll look at the AMP `layout` attribute in more detail in the next chapter.

We've just had our first encounter with HTML tag restrictions in AMP. Now's a good time to take a look at what tags are or aren't permitted.

HTML tags that aren't allowed in AMP

You're free to use most HTML elements in your AMP pages. Some are restricted however. Generally, elements that have a performance impact, for example, elements that involve external HTTP requests, are forbidden. For some of these, replacement AMP tags provide similar functionality but in a performance-optimized way.

In general, you can use any HTML tag as usual if it is not listed in the following sections in the *forbidden* or *has-an-AMP-alternative* tag lists.

Forbidden HTML tags

The following tags are outright banned in AMP pages:

`base`, `frame`, `frameset`, `object`, `param`, `applet`, and `embed`.

HTML tags with AMP-HTML replacements

The following table shows HTML tags that are forbidden and for which there are AMP alternatives:

HTML tag	AMP-HTML version
`img`	`amp-img`
`video`	`amp-video`
`audio`	`amp-audio`
`iframe`	`amp-iframe`

HTML tags that are allowed, but with restrictions

These are HTML tags that are allowed in AMP pages, but which have some special requirements:

HTML tag	Conditions
`script`	To ensure that third-party JavaScript does not interfere with AMP performance `script` tags are allowed in under certain circumstances: • To load the AMP-runtime • To include AMP components • To load JSON data, with type set to `application/ld+json` Additionally, all script tags must be declared `async` so that they won't block the main render.
`meta`	Allowed, except for the attribute `meta-quiv`

form, input	Allowed with `form-extension` except for `<input[type=image]>`, `<input[type=button]>`, `<input[type=password]>`, and `<input[type=file]>`.
style	Only one user `style` tag is permitted. It must appear in the head of the document, it must contain the attribute `amp-custom`, and it must contain less than 50 KB of CSS.
link	Allowed to include fonts from white-listed origins only, or with `rel` attribute values for metadata registered at `microformats.org`.

See the AMP-HTML specification for more details: `https://www.ampproject.org/docs/reference/spec#html-tags`.

AMP components

We've seen how AMP restricts HTML. It's not all bad though: AMP also extends HTML with replacement tags that provide similar behavior to the forbidden tags, but in a constrained and performance-optimized way. These are known as **AMP components** or **AMP custom elements**.

There are three types of AMP component:

- **Built in/core components**: These components are ready to use in your AMP-HTML page right away. They are distributed with the core AMP-JS library, so you don't need to explicitly include them in the head of your document. These include the most commonly used tags, such as `amp-img`, `amp-video`, and `amp-pixel`.

- **Extended components**: These components extend the functionality beyond the most common core components. You need to include them explicitly before you can use them on your page. For example, to use form elements, you need to include the form extension in the head of your AMP document:

```
<script async custom-element="amp-form"
src="https://cdn.ampproject.org/v0/amp-form-0.1.js"></script>
```

- **Experimental components**: These are components that have been released to the public but are not yet finalized and don't validate yet. Experimental features are *opt-in*, and can be activated at the document or the feature level. We'll see more on these features later. AMP experimental features are described online here: `github.com/ampproject/amphtml/tree/master/tools/experiments`.

Measuring AMP page performance

AMP is a performance framework, but is it worth it? You could just take Google's word that it is, and that would be enough for some people. But if you're curious, you can measure the performance of your AMP and non-AMP pages. Depending on how well-built your original page is, you can expect to see performance gains in your AMP pages. And even if your non-AMP page is already fast-loading, you should still see improvements when it's served from the AMP cache.

Measuring mobile web performance

Measuring web performance is a whole subject in itself, with a wide range of dimensions to measure and tools to measure them. We can only scratch the surface here, but it will be enough for you to do basic performance measurement of your web pages.

What is "good" web performance?

Measuring web performance is complicated. Since we are interested ultimately in providing a good user experience, this means we are interested in optimizing for the user's perception of how quickly the page loads, rather than an absolute, objective measure of how fast the entire page actually loads. You can think of it as building an illusion for the user: use a bunch of tricks to get just enough of the page rendered so the user thinks it has loaded, and in the meantime finish the job in the background.

When performance-tuning a web page, we need to optimize for getting something *usable* onto the user's screen as *quickly as possible*. This has an impact on what we must focus on to make a page seem fast: things such as prioritizing *above-the-fold* content and *time-to-first-byte;* even exploiting low-level transport-layer knowledge, such as *TCP packet size*, to achieve an interactive and responsive page render in the first 14 KB of data sent from the web server.

In general, following Google's **Response-Animation-Idle-Load** (**RAIL**) approach, you are doing well if you can achieve:

- Initial server response within **100 ms**
- Initial usable and responsive page content load within **1 s**
- Frame rate of **60 fps**

These numbers will translate into a site that loads fast and that feels responsive, without any lag. This is a site that users are more likely to stay on.

Waterfall charts

A performance waterfall chart depicts, on a timeline, how web page resources are downloaded and processed by the browser. It gives a clear visual representation of the sequence in which items are downloaded, how they are dependent, and where there are performance bottlenecks.

Waterfall charts are available in many of the performance testing tools that you might use to test your pages. They are indispensable in helping us achieve our performance goals.

WebPagetest.org

WebPagetest is one of the best online tools for testing web page performance. It's an open source project that generates waterfall charts and allows you to test on (a limited number of) real devices and browsers, and on a variety of network types and qualities, from various locations around the globe. It's free to use, and you can find it here: `webpagetest.org`.

WebPagetest also reports the number of requests by type and size, and gives a film-strip snapshot visualization of the render progress. It also allows you to replay a video of the page as it rendered during the test.

In the following image we can see a portion of the performance output for our news page:

Waterfall report for our AMP page in WebPagetest.org

PageSpeed Insights

PageSpeed Insights is an easy-to-use high-level web performance testing tool. It's a free service run by Google, available at `developers.google.com/speed/pagespeed/insights`.

It offers a quick-and-dirty heuristic analysis of your web pages, based on categories of performance best-practices that your site is scored against. It will also offer suggestions such as minifying text content and compressing images where appropriate.

While it will probably be able to demonstrate that your AMP pages perform better than your non-AMP pages, it doesn't offer the same degree of insight as some of the other tools, and it isn't good at handling the subtleties of performance, sometimes scoring fast AMP pages poorly.

For this reason, it's not recommended to rely solely on PageSpeed Insights to determine the performance of your web pages.

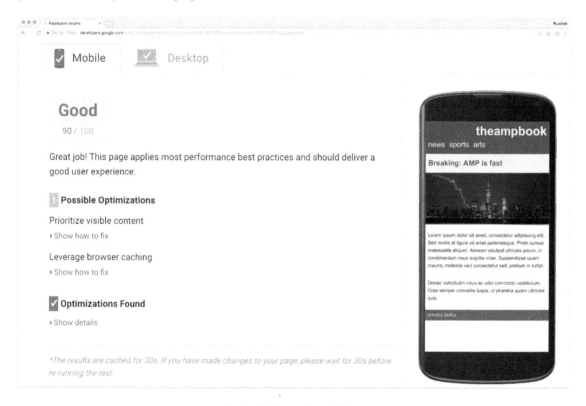

PageSpeed Insights report for our AMP page

Remote debugging with developer tools

The modern web browser is a wonderful piece of software. On top of everything else, it also provides web performance profiling, offering deep insights and performance data for your web pages. Not only that, but the developer tools of most modern desktop web browsers will allow you to hook up a mobile device to the machine via USB and inspect web page source code and profile performance. This is a super cool and indispensable feature for mobile web developers as it allows you to test and debug your web pages on real mobile devices, using real mobile networks and hardware.

While developer tools generally allow you to simulate mobile screen sizes and network speeds, *there is no substitute for testing on real mobile devices.*

To enable remote debugging in Chrome for Android, perform the following steps:

1. Enable USB debugging on the Android device. To do this:
    1. Go to **Settings** | **About Phone** and scroll until you see **Build number**.
    2. Tap **Build Number** seven times, until you see a message **You are now a developer**. A new item **Developer options** will now be available in your Settings menu.
    3. Go to **Settings** | **Developer options** and check USB debugging. You may need to confirm a pop-up message.
2. Connect the device to the desktop via USB.
3. In Chrome, on your desktop, open the developer tools and select **Menu** | **More Tools** | **Remote Devices** (on some versions of Chrome this might be **Menu** | **More Tools** | **Inspect Devices**).
4. On the desktop, you should now see a list of web pages that are open on the device. Choose the one that you want to inspect.

You can now inspect the page, and use Chrome's DevTools as if it was running on the desktop browser. In addition, you can also *screencast* your mobile device's screen to a panel within the desktop developer tools. This allows you to interact with the device directly from the desktop computer, without having to physically touch the device.

The following image shows a remote debugging session with Chrome, complete with a waterfall chart of the performance of our news page:

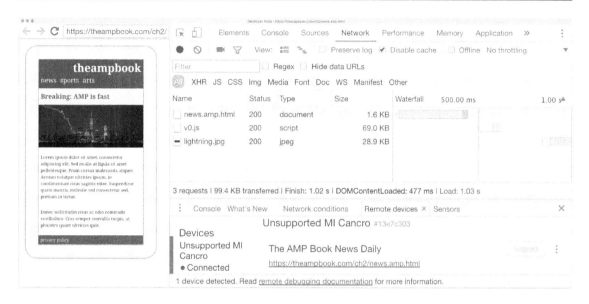

Remote debugging with Chrome's developer tools

For iOS devices, the Safari browser for macOS offers a similar remote debugging functionality.

For fun, you can compare the performance of each of the following pages:

- The original non-AMP page
- The AMP page served from the original server
- The AMP page served from AMP Cache

Unless your existing non-AMP page is particularly well crafted, we'd expect to see better performance as we advance through this list in any of the test tools.

Summary

In this chapter, we continued to learn the basics of AMP. By now you should be familiar with most of the concepts needed to get a simple AMP page up and running. In particular, in this chapter we walked through the process converting a non-AMP HTML page to AMP-HTML. This gave us the opportunity to introduce and explore some important topics, including AMP validation and web performance. During the validation process, we saw what happens when we include a forbidden HTML tag in an AMP page, and we then made use of our first AMP component: `amp-img`.

Now that we know the basics, in the following chapters, we'll start to see how we can build more enticing pages with more advanced layouts and features.

3
Making an Impression - Layout and Page Design in AMP

In this chapter, we will learn about layout and design techniques in AMP. We'll build on the news article example page from the previous chapter by adding typical article page features. We'll explore various presentation techniques, such as *related-content thumbnail lists*, and *pull-quotes*, and we'll see how to handle layout on larger screen sizes with responsive design. We'll look at how to include custom fonts and options for laying out text. We'll also expand our understanding of CSS in AMP pages by seeing how media queries can be used to deliver alternative styles and layouts at the page or the individual element level.

The following list summarizes what we'll learn:

- AMP layout and design, and the `layout` attribute
- Responsive images in AMP
- Art-directed images and image `srcset`
- CSS styling, media, and element queries
- Fonts and text layout

Laying out elements in AMP pages

In the last chapter we briefly saw how to fix validation errors with `amp-img` by adding `layout="responsive"` to the image element, but there wasn't much explanation about what was happening. When we added the `layout` attribute, we were tapping into AMP's powerful layout system.

The AMP-HTML layout system

AMP's layout system is key to reducing rendering and scrolling-jank. AMP uses a *static layout system* that relies on a set of attributes to define the layout and sizing of elements. These are `layout`, `width`, `height`, `sizes`, and `heights`. With these attributes, AMP is able to efficiently calculate the layout and size of each element even before anything is fetched from the network.

 AMP's layout system is built on web technologies, and to use it effectively, you'll need to have an understanding of CSS and HTML, and to be able to use them constructively to support your desired AMP layouts. We'll see this later in this chapter.

The layout attribute

The `layout` attribute in AMP gives the developer a very powerful, per-element tool for declaring how elements should be displayed on the page. It offers a convenient way to implement common layout patterns that would otherwise require complex CSS to build. This makes the layout attribute extremely useful, especially considering AMP's 50 KB CSS limitation.

The `layout` attribute can be applied to any AMP element (but not regular HTML elements), and can take the following values:

Value	Behavior
`container`	Element size is defined by its children, like an HTML `div`
`fill`	Element takes up all available space
`fixed`	Element has fixed `width` and `height`, and both must be specified
`fixed-height`	Element takes all available space, and the mandatory `height` is fixed

`flex-item`	All `flex-item` sibling elements take the available space of the parent when it is a flexible container (`display: flex`). `width` and `height` are not required
`nodisplay`	Element does not display, and takes up no space. `width` and `height` are not required
`responsive`	Element takes all available space, and resizes height to keep the aspect ratio given by mandatory `width` and `height` attributes

If no value is supplied for the `layout` attribute of a component, its layout will be inferred as follows:

If	Layout
`height` is present, and `width` is `auto` or absent	`fixed-height`
`width` and `height`, and `sizes` or `heights` are present	`responsive`
`width` and `height` are present	`fixed`
`width` and `height` are absent	`container`

Using responsive layout

Responsive design is built directly into AMP, and is one of the most useful layouts offered by the `layout` attribute. We saw how to use `amp-img` with the `responsive` layout in our news article example from the last chapter:

```
<amp-img
  src="img/feature.jpg"
  width="768"
  height="305"
  layout="responsive" >
</amp-img>
```

Note that even though we are using the `responsive` layout, we still need to specify the `width` and `height` attributes. Shouldn't it just grow and shrink to fit the viewport? There are two reasons why the width and height attributes are needed:

1. To calculate the *aspect ratio* of the image so that it is displayed correctly as it is resized.
2. To calculate the page layout before anything is downloaded; this is required by AMP's static layout system.

Our example from the last chapter was a nice first attempt at a news article page, but there's a problem with it. It's not optimized for larger screens. When viewed on a larger screen, the main feature image becomes blocky and pixelated.

Why does this matter--isn't AMP just for small screens? Doesn't the *M* in AMP stand for *Mobile*? Well, *no* and *yes* (respectively), but it's more nuanced than this. Even in a mobile format, there is a multitude of different device screen sizes that must be accommodated; our AMP pages should look good on all of them. And there is also the idea of **Canonical AMP pages**: an approach to web publishing where AMP is used exclusively to build a website, for desktop and mobile. In both theses cases, responsive design helps to deal with the wide variety of viewport sizes that must be handled.

Canonical AMP pages

Canonical AMP pages are standalone AMP pages. That is, they serve as both the desktop and the mobile web page. AMP has good media query support, as well as strong responsive layout features, and so AMP isn't *mobile-only*, rather it's mobile *first*: It is optimized for mobile, but can be expanded to other device types too. The canonical approach is being promoted by the AMP team, and reflects how much AMP has changed and grown beyond it's original purpose.

To support this, the AMP project runs a dedicated site, AMP Start (`ampstart.com`), that publishes a set of free-to-use-and-modify canonical AMP page templates, along with pre-built, reusable AMP UI components. These components include styled buttons, input types, annotated hero images, carousels, navigation elements, footers, and many other useful UI components:

One of the free templates available at ampstart.com

It's a good place to start if you're looking for prebuilt, ready-to-use templates and components that you can get up and running quickly. Of course, you're reading this book because you want to learn how to build AMP pages yourself, so we won't go into any more detail about AMP Start here.

With canonical AMP pages, you still need to provide a canonical link in the document `head`, but it will point to itself:

```
<link rel="canonical" href="https://theampbook.com/canonicalpage.html" />
```

Note that when building canonical web pages that are intended to be viewed on desktops as well as mobile devices, responsive design techniques become very useful in ensuring that the page scales well on larger screens. We'll see some of these techniques in action in the next few sections of this chapter.

Art-direction and responsive images

Let's get back to the issue with the responsive image in our article page example. The problem is that on wider viewports, the image becomes stretched and pixelated as it is scaled. This is because the intrinsic size of our original image is smaller than the viewport on larger screens.

To get around this, you might decide to use a larger image, so that no matter how big the screen is, the image will never be scaled up. The problem with this approach is that it's not good for performance. In most cases, the user will end up downloading a larger image than is needed. Since images are one of the biggest contributors to the page size, if you have a few images like these, they can add up to poor page-load times.

Luckily, there is an HTML5 feature that AMP supports that offers a way to fix this: the srcset attribute.

Using srcset to optimize image loading

With srcset, we can specify different images to use at different viewport widths. The browser will then choose the most appropriate image for the user's device by picking the smallest image that is as large as, or larger than, the viewport width.

 We'll use the news article page from the last chapter as the starting point for the examples in this chapter. This file can be found at /ch3/news-start.html. To follow along with the examples, you can add code to this file. Another file, /ch3/news.html, combines most of the examples into a single page.

Building on our news article example from the last chapter, let's replace the amp-img feature image with the following (full code at /ch3/feature.html):

```
<amp-img src="img/feature.jpg"
    srcset="img/feature-1200.jpg 1200w,
            img/feature-lrg.jpg 1080w,
            img/feature-med.jpg 768w,
            img/feature.jpg 320w"
    width="768"
    height="305"
    layout="responsive"
        alt="Feature image">
</amp-img>
```

The `srcset` attribute takes a comma-separated list of alternative images that can be used, as well as the width of each. For example, in the preceding code, `feature-lrg.jpg` is the filename, and `1080w` tells the browser that this image has a width of 1080 pixels.

Save this page on your web server and load it in your desktop browser (or visit `theampbook.com/ch3/feature.html`) and look at the **Network** tab of the developer tools:

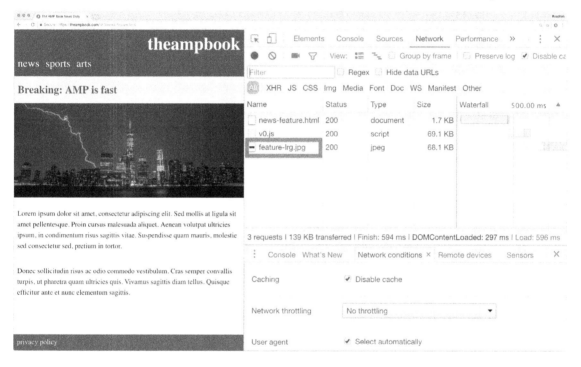

Developer tools showing srcset image download on the desktop browser (/ch3/feature.html)

Depending on the width of your browser viewport, you should see which image was actually downloaded. Was it the one you were expecting? As you resize the browser, you will see alternative images being fetched whenever there is a better match for the viewport size.

Note that we are still using `layout="responsive"` with our different `srcset` images. This means that no matter what image is chosen by the browser, AMP will still resize this image to fill the viewport so that all viewport sizes will have a similar experience.

If working locally, you can download the images required for the examples in this chapter at `/ch3/img/` (that is, `theampbook.com/ch3/img/` or `github.com/ruborg/amp/tree/master/ch3/img/`).

Using the heights and sizes attributes

The `heights` and `sizes` attributes allow us to further tweak the display of our responsive images. The `sizes` attribute lets us use a media query to define how wide an image should be displayed, depending on the size of the user's viewport. Take the following code, for example:

```
sizes="(min-width: 640px) 50vw, 100vw"
```

This means that for screen sizes of 640 pixels and wider (`min-width: 640px`), the image should take up 50 percent of the viewport width (`50vw`). For all other screen sizes--that is-- those less than 640 pixels, display the image at 100 percent of the viewport width: (`100vw`).

The `heights` attribute achieves a similar effect, but unlike `sizes`, it applies to the height of the image instead of the width, for example:

```
heights="(min-width:500px) 200px, 80%"
```

When the `heights` or `sizes` attribute is specified along with `width` and `height`, the `layout` defaults to `responsive`.

Adding a related articles section with thumbnail images

Our article page is still a fairly *bare-bones* experience at the moment. Let's try to improve it. A common design pattern is to include a related or recommended content section at the end of an article. Let's add this to the bottom of our page. It will consist of a list of three or four articles, with thumbnails and text. Building this will help to improve our understanding of AMP's layout system.

For the list of items, we'll use an unordered list `ul`. Each item in the list will have an HTML5 `figure` element, which in turn will have a thumbnail image, `amp-img`, and associated text `figcaption`.

We'll use `layout="fixed"` for the thumbnail images so that they will all be a fixed size; we'll explore other options shortly (full code at `/ch3/related-float.html`):

```
<figure class="related-thumb">
  <amp-img src="img/penguin.jpg" width="125" height="75" layout="fixed">
  </amp-img>
  <figcaption>
    If a penguin can find a soul mate, I'm sure I can too
    <span class="author">Rebekah Crane</span>
  </figcaption>
</figure>
```

We'll add a touch of styling for the caption and author text:

```
figcaption {
  font-family: Georgia;
  font-weight: bold;
}

.author {
  color: #bbb;
  display:block;
}
```

If you look at this in a browser, the text caption displays underneath the image. Ideally, we'd like this to be to the right of the thumbnail. We can achieve this with a little CSS. The *old school* way to achieve this might be to use the CSS `float` property like this:

```
.related-thumb amp-img {
  margin-right:5px;
  float:left;
}
```

Related content thumbnail using float: left to align the caption (/ch3/related-float.html)

Now the text flows around the image. However, since we are building a list of three or four items, if we use the `float` property like this, we'll need to clear the `float` before the next item or the list items will keep floating to the side of the previous one and it will be a mess. Perhaps there's a better way to achieve this layout.

Using CSS3 flexbox for layout in AMP

AMP is a modern framework, and has been built with modern priorities such as performance at its core. It makes use of modern web technologies, and this includes support for CSS3 and the **Flexible Box Model** (**flexbox**). Flexbox is often regarded as an improvement over the **Box Model** as it doesn't use floats.

Let's see if there's a better way to achieve our desired layout with flexbox. First, remove the `float:left` style from the `.related-thumb amp-img` selector that we added in the last section. Then apply the following styles to the `figure` items, using `.related-thumb` to target them (full code at `/ch3/related-flex.html`):

```
.related-thumb {
  display:flex;
  align-items: center;
}
```

The AMP-HTML markup for our list should look like this (first two items shown):

```
<ul class="related-items">
  <li>
    <figure class="related-thumb">
      <amp-img src="img/penguin.jpg" width="125" height="75"
layout="fixed">
      </amp-img>
      <figcaption>
        If a penguin can find a soul mate, I'm sure I can too
        <span class="author">Rebekah Crane</span>
      </figcaption>
    </figure>
  </li>

  <li>
    <figure class="related-thumb">
      <amp-img  src="img/cat.jpg" width="125" height="75" layout="fixed">
      </amp-img>
      <figcaption>
        What greater gift than the love of a cat
        <span class="author">Charles Dickens</span>
      </figcaption>
```

```
      </figure>
    </li>
    ...
  </ul>
```

Applying `flex` to the `figure` element means its children will expand to fill the available space. Note the use of `layout="fixed"` on the `amp-img` tags here. While we don't mind the headline stretching or shrinking to fit into the available space, we want all the images to remain the same size. (Technically though, according to the table we saw earlier, since we have already specified `width` and `height`, `layout="fixed"` will be inferred if the attribute is absent; we've left it in here to be explicit.)

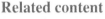

Related content thumbnail images displaying incorrectly on narrow viewports

Nearly there! It looks good on wider screens, but not so great on narrow ones, as shown in the preceding image. We also need to impose a minimum width on our images, otherwise a longer headline can affect the width of the associated thumbnail image, resulting in a nonuniform layout:

```
.related-thumb amp-img {
  min-width: 125px;
  margin-right:5px;
}
```

This results in a correctly aligned list on small screens, as shown in the following image:

Related content

 If a penguin can find a soul mate, I'm sure I can too
Rebekah Crane

 What greater gift than the love of a cat
Charles Dickens

 A snow-white swan with a scary tattoo holding a chain saw
Jim Benton

 Charley is a mind-reading dog
John Steinbeck

Related content thumbnails correctly aligned on small screens (/ch3/related-flex.html)

Scaling up for larger screens

This is a nice, simple solution, and it achieves what we wanted: a vertical display of related content thumbnails and titles. But it could be better. On wider screens, it would be nice if:

- The list could be displayed horizontally
- The images could grow in size to fit with the available space

Let's see how to achieve these goals.

Using flex and media queries for horizontal layout

To achieve the first goal, we can apply the following properties to the list container:

```
.related-items {
  display:flex;
  flex-wrap: wrap;
  list-style: none;
}
```

This nearly gets us there. However, it's a little messy: there is no consistency in item width, and depending on the screen width, the list will end up being both horizontal and vertical (as shown in the following image), when we wanted it to be *either* horizontal or vertical:

Related content

 If a penguin can find a soul mate, I'm sure I can too Rebekah Crane

 What greater gift than the love of a cat Charles Dickens

 A snow-white swan with a scary tattoo holding a chain saw Jim Benton

 Charley is a mind-reading dog John Steinbeck

Related content thumbnails with a flexible container: incorrect alignment

We can fix this with a media query. Let's say we have four items. When displayed horizontally, we'll want each to take up 25 percent of the available space. We'll use a width of 50rem as our breakpoint:

```
@media (min-width:50rem) {
  figure {
    margin:40px;
  }

  .related-thumb {
    flex-basis:25%;
    flex-wrap:wrap;
  }

  .related-thumb amp-img, .related-thumb figcaption{
    flex-basis:100%
  }

  .related-items li {
    width:25%;
  }
}
```

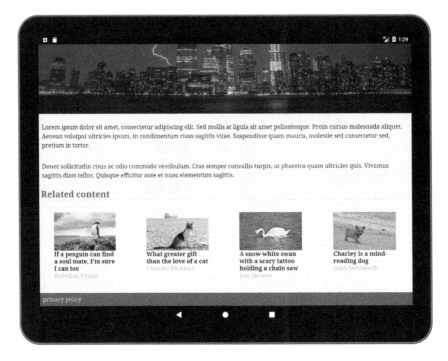

Horizontal thumbnail layout on larger screen (tablet device in landscape orientation)

This will give us a 4x1 horizontal list of items on wider screens and a 1x4 vertical list on small screens.

We can push this even further. On mid-sized screens, let's go for a 2x2 grid. To achieve this, we'll add another media query that matches screens between our default and our large screen media queries (full code at /ch3/related-flex-media.html):

```
@media (min-width:35rem) and (max-width:50rem) {
    ...
    .related-items li {
    width:50%;
    }
}
```

Using responsive images and srcset to deliver high quality images on all screen sizes

To achieve the second goal, we can use `layout="responsive"` again, so that the thumbnails will scale for larger screens. The HTML for each item in the list now looks like this:

```
<li>
  <figure class="related-thumb">
    <amp-img src="img/penguin.jpg" width="125" height="75"
layout="responsive"></amp-img>
    <figcaption>
      If a penguin can find a soul mate, I'm sure I can too
      <span class="author">Rebekah Crane</span>
    </figcaption>
  </figure>
</li>
```

Thumbnails in 2x2 grid and with layout="responsive" scaling up on a larger screen (tablet device in portrait orientation)

There is a problem with this solution, however. It's the same problem that we had earlier when our main feature image was scaled up on large screens: it became pixelated. The same thing will happen with our thumbnails. Thankfully, we can apply the same solution as before using `srcset`:

```
<amp-img src="penguin.jpg"
         srcset="img/penguin-sm.jpg 125w,
                 img/penguin.jpg 640w"
         width="125"
         height="75"
         layout="responsive"
</amp-img>
```

Now, on larger screens, the browser will automatically use the higher resolution image.

Using element media queries to display art-directed images

There is yet another improvement we can make to our thumbnail images (this will be the last one for now). Right now, we have different resolutions for each of our images, specified by the `srcset` attribute, and the browser will choose the most appropriate one based on the viewport size. One issue with this is that it can be harder to see detail in the smaller images as they are scaled down. For example, an image might contain text that is legible at higher resolution, but not at lower resolution. In these cases, it can make sense to edit the image, to crop it, or zoom into some particular detail, and provide a new image that is more visually suitable at lower resolution.

We saw earlier how CSS `@media` queries can be used in AMP pages in much the same way as you would use them in a standard HTML page. When the viewport changes orientation or is resized, the media queries are re-evaluated. AMP extends the functionality of media queries beyond what is possible with regular CSS by allowing media queries to target *individual elements* with the `media` attribute.

We can use this to provide cropped versions of our images to display on small screens. This is a bit like using the HTML5 `picture` element to choose between different images, except that the `media` attribute can be applied to *any* AMP element, not just `amp-img` (full code at `/ch3/news-related.html`):

```
<amp-img media="(min-width: 35.01rem)"
         src="img/penguin.jpg"
         width="125"
         height="75"
         layout="responsive"
         srcset="img/penguin-sm.jpg 125w,
                 img/penguin.jpg 640w">
</amp-img>
<amp-img media="(max-width: 35rem)"
         src="img/penguin-crop.jpg"
         width="125"
         height="75"
         layout="responsive">
</amp-img>
```

In AMP, an element's media query is evaluated, and if it matches the current viewport, then the element is displayed, otherwise the element is hidden. In this code, we use two mutually exclusive media queries. So, for viewports greater than `35rem`, the first `amp-img` element will be displayed and the browser will choose an image from one of the images provided in `srcset`. For viewports `35rem` and below, the first `amp-img` will be hidden and the second one will be displayed, and, for the previous code sample, the cropped version of our penguin image will be used.

Note that to implement art-directed images like this on your own website, you'll need to edit and crop your images with an image editor application, such as GIMP, Photoshop, or an online image manipulation service.

 It's often worth running your images through a dedicated image optimizer or compression application to reduce file size. ImageOptim (`imageoptim.com`) is a nice drag-and-drop application that can significantly reduce the byte-size of your images.

The result is shown in the following image, where the cropped versions of our thumbnails are displayed on a small screen:

Thumbnails using an art-directed cropped versions on a small screen, implemented with element media query (/ch3/news-related.html)

Note that if you look at the full source for this example, you'll see that we've built up this code statically, and we've repeated the same code four times, once for each thumbnail item. In a real environment, you might use a server script to generate this AMP-HTML code in a loop. We'll also see how we can build lists like this dynamically directly in AMP pages in `Chapter 7`, *Dynamic Content and Data-Driven Interaction*.

Another point to note here is that, while AMP has built-in support for the different layout styles of its components, it's not a silver bullet for all your layout needs. As with traditional HTML web pages, you will need to spend time planning your page layout, and you'll need the CSS knowledge and skills to implement it.

Using flex-item layout

We've already seen practical examples of AMP's `fixed` and `responsive` layouts. Another useful layout is `flex-item`. Flex items take up all available space in a `display: flex` parent. There are many layout possibilities, so we'll just give a quick overview of some of them, and later in the chapter we'll see how to apply the `flex-item` layout to text and images in our article page example.

Horizontal flex items

Flex items can be horizontal. In the following CSS, we have given the parent a fixed size, exactly three times as wide as it is high:

```
.flex-container-row {
    display: flex;
    flex-direction: row;
    width: 450px;
    height: 150px;
}
```

The following markup shows increasing numbers of flex items within the flex parent:

```
<div class="flex-container-row">
  <!-- 1 flex item -->
  <amp-img src="img/placeholder.png" layout="flex-item"></amp-img>
</div>

<div class="flex-container-row">
  <!-- 2 flex items -->
  <amp-img src="img/placeholder.png" layout="flex-item"></amp-img>
  <amp-img src="img/placeholder.png" layout="flex-item"></amp-img>
</div>
...

<div class="flex-container-row">
  <!-- 7 flex items -->
  <amp-img src="img/placeholder.png" layout="flex-item"></amp-img>
  <amp-img src="img/placeholder.png" layout="flex-item"></amp-img>
  ...
  <amp-img src="img/placeholder.png" layout="flex-item"></amp-img>
</div>
```

The following image shows the results of having a number of flex items, ranging from one to seven, in the container. Note how the flex items are stretched depending on how many there are. The only time they aren't stretched is when there are three, because we are using square placeholder images, and the container's width is three times its height:

Horizontal flex items being stretched or squashed to fit a container. From top: 1 item, 2 items, 3 items, 5 items, 7 items

Vertical flex items

Flex items can also be arranged vertically in columns. This time, we flip the width and height dimensions of the parent so that it is three times as high as it is wide:

```
.flex-container-col {
    display: flex;
    flex-direction: col;
    width: 150px;
    height: 450px;
}
...

<div class="flex-container-col">
  <!-- 1 flex item -->
```

```
    <amp-img src="img/placeholder.png" layout="flex-item"></amp-img>
</div>

<div class="flex-container-col">
  <!-- 2 flex items -->
  <amp-img src="img/placeholder.png" layout="flex-item"></amp-img>
  <amp-img src="img/placeholder.png" layout="flex-item"></amp-img>
</div>
...

<div class="flex-container-col">
  <!-- 7 flex items -->
  <amp-img src="img/placeholder.png" layout="flex-item"></amp-img>
  <amp-img src="img/placeholder.png" layout="flex-item"></amp-img>
  ...
</div>
```

Vertical flex items being distorted depending on how many there are

Again, note how the flex items are distorted in the preceding examples. This is fine for containers, but it might not be what you're after when it comes to images.

Full width flex item container

If you want the parent container to stretch to the full width of the page, you can omit a width and height value for the parent, but you will need to provide a height for the flex-item children:

```
.flex-container-row {
    display: flex;
    flex-direction: row;
}
```

```
...

<div class="flex-container-row">
  <amp-img src="img/placeholder.png" layout="flex-item" height="200">
  </amp-img>
  <amp-img src="img/placeholder.png" layout="flex-item" height="100">
  </amp-img>
</div>
```

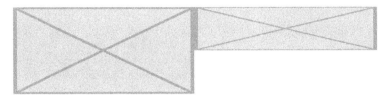

Full width flex parent with fixed height flex item children

Flex items with specific proportions

We can also specify specific proportions for each of the items in our flex layout. The following code shows how you could split the available space 25-50-25 between three flex items:

```
.flex-50 {
  flex-basis: 50%;
}

.flex-25 {
  flex-basis: 25%;
}
...

<div class="flex-container-row">
  <amp-img class="flex-25" src="img/placeholder.png" layout="flex-item">
  </amp-img>
  <amp-img class="flex-50" src="img/placeholder.png" layout="flex-item">
  </amp-img>
  <amp-img class="flex-25" src="img/placeholder.png" layout="flex-item">
  </amp-img>
</div>
```

Flex items filling a flex container proportionally

Mixing flex and non-flex items

We can also have flex and non-flex items together in the same flex parent. Non-flex items must declare their `width` and `height` attributes explicitly, and the remaining space will be divided between the flex items:

```
<div class="flex-container-row">
  <amp-img src="img/placeholder.png" width="250" height="150"
layout="fixed"></amp-img>
  <amp-img src="img/placeholder.png" height="100" layout="flex-item">
</amp-img>
  <amp-img src="img/placeholder.png" layout="flex-item"></amp-img>
  <amp-img src="img/placeholder.png" layout="flex-item"&gt;</amp-img>
</div>
```

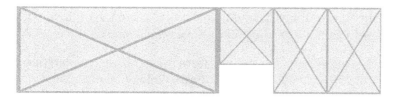

Mixed flex and non flex items filling a flex container

 Note that we are demonstrating these layouts with uniform, square images so that their distortion will show how different layouts will affect components. It is unlikely that you will ever want actual images to distort like this, but it will be useful to know what to expect when applying these layouts to other components, such as `amp-fit-text` and `amp-carousel`, that we'll see later.

That's probably enough about flex layouts for now. We'll see how to use this last flex layout later in the chapter.

Using placeholders and fallbacks to improve user experience

To deliver the best user experience, placeholder and fallback elements should be used when appropriate. Placeholders are displayed *in place* of an element until that element is ready to be rendered, while fallbacks are displayed *instead* of an element when the element is not supported in a browser.

Placeholders

An element with the `placeholder` attribute acts as a placeholder for its parent. Placeholders are displayed immediately for an element, before the element has been downloaded or initialized. When the actual element is ready, the placeholder is hidden, and the element content is displayed.

Thus, placeholders can be used to stand in place of a *slower-to-load* element. You might use this, for instance, to display a fast-loading, low-resolution image in place of a video or high-resolution image. The latter is the same trick that sites such as Medium (`medium.com`) and Facebook use to deliver a quick page-loading experience. They show a small, low-resolution image that has been blown up to the size of the actual banner image. The user gets to see the proper page layout almost immediately, with a blurred version of the main feature image. This is swapped out when the high-resolution version is ready.

Let's implement this for our article's main feature image. First, prepare the small placeholder version of the image. Open the original image, in our case `/ch3/img/feature.jpg`, in an image editor application or online service, and resize it to 40 pixels wide. Save the image as `feature-tiny.jpg`.

After running it through an optimizer, your placeholder image should be down to around 200-300 B in size. This will load quickly even on slow networks.

Now we need to write the AMP-HTML. To set an element as a placeholder, we just need to add the `placeholder` attribute. So, to add a placeholder for our feature image, we could use this code (`/ch3/placeholder.html`):

```
<amp-img src = "img/feature.jpg"
    srcset = "img/feature-1200.jpg 1200w,
              img/feature-lrg.jpg 1080w,
              img/feature-med.jpg 768w,
              img/feature.jpg 320w"
    width = "768"
```

```
        height = "305"
        layout = "responsive"
        noloading>
    <amp-img placeholder
            src = "img/feature-tiny.jpg"
          width = "768"
         height = "305"
         layout = "responsive">
    </amp-img>
  </amp-img>
```

Yes, we're using an `amp-img` placeholder for an `amp-img`! In general, though, you might be more likely to use placeholders for videos or other large elements.

We've also added a `noloading` attribute to the feature image element. AMP displays a *loading* indicator by default for components like `amp-img`. Adding the `noloading` attribute hides this indicator. The idea here is that since we are using a placeholder image anyway, we don't really need the loading indicator, so we disable it.

We can confirm the placeholder is working for poor connections in the developer tools:

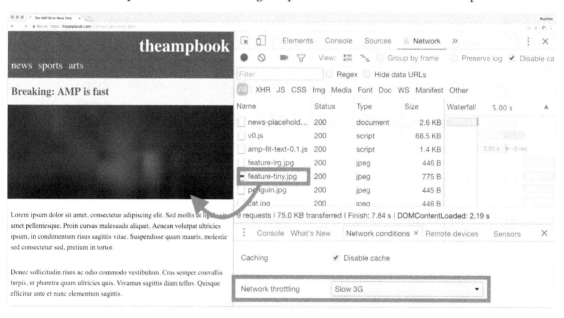

Demonstrating the use of a placeholder image on a (simulated) slow network (/ch3/placeholder.html)

We can simulate a slow connection in Chrome's DevTools as shown in the previous image (or indeed you can set your own mobile device to use 2G). You should see that the placeholder image, `feature-tiny.jpg`, is loaded and displayed very quickly, and is eventually replaced with the full-resolution image.

Fallbacks

The `fallback` attribute is used to indicate that an element should be used instead of a parent element when the parent is not supported. We'll be covering the `amp-video` component in more detail later, but as an example, you could add a fallback message for browsers that don't support HTML5 video like this:

```
<amp-video width=640 height=380 src="cats.mp4">
  <div fallback>
    <p>HTML5 video not supported</p>
  </div>
</amp-video>
```

Using custom CSS in AMP pages

We have seen that CSS is a key part of layout and design in AMP, as it is in HTML. In fact, AMP components come with built-in, default styles that are defined in a CSS file, `amp.css`, that's automatically included by the AMP library. For custom CSS styling in your AMP pages, there are restrictions on what you can do. You should already know that:

- All styles must be defined in the `<head>` of the document; no in-line styles
- A maximum of 50 KB of CSS is permitted
- External stylesheets can't be used

There are also some further restrictions you should be aware of:

Style	Restriction	Description
`!important` qualifier	Not allowed	Allows AMP to enforce its styling rules
Class and tag names that start with `-amp-` and `i-amp-`	Not allowed	User stylesheets cannot define or reference CSS selectors for these classes and tags
`behavior`, `-moz-binding`	Not allowed	Security restriction

`filter`	Not allowed	Performance restriction
`transition`	Restricted	Only GPU-accelerated properties allowed: `opacity`, `transform`, `-vendorPrefix-transform`
`@keyframes {...}`	Restricted	Only GPU-accelerated properties allowed: `opacity`, `transform`, `-vendorPrefix-transform`

Adding custom fonts to AMP pages

One important aspect of web page design that we haven't looked at yet is the use of custom fonts. Not only is the choice of font important to the reading experience, but fonts can help differentiate a web page and give it its own identity. The fonts you choose for your web pages will be largely dictated by your personal preference and the theme of your website, so we won't make any font recommendations here. Rather, we'll demonstrate how you can get your preferred fonts to display, and leave the choice up to you.

There is already a range of web-safe fonts available on most systems. These include:

- Arial/Helvetica
- Courier/Courier New
- Georgia
- Times/Times New Roman
- Trebuchet MS
- Verdana

For many web pages, this will be enough to provide a decent reading experience, so you don't necessarily need to include any other fonts. Custom fonts are desirable in many cases, however, so let's see how to add them to AMP pages.

AMP doesn't permit the inclusion of external stylesheets in your markup, so the use of `<link rel="stylesheet" ... >` is generally banned, except for fonts. Custom fonts can be loaded in two ways:

1. Using `<link rel="stylesheet"...>`:

   ```
   <link
   href="https://fonts.googleapis.com/css?family=UnifrakturCook:700"
   rel="stylesheet">
   ```

   Note that in this approach you may only include fonts from the following whitelisted providers:

   - Typography.com: `https://cloud.typography.com`
   - Fonts.com: `https://fast.fonts.net`
   - Google Fonts: `https://fonts.googleapis.com`
   - Font Awesome: `https://maxcdn.bootstrapcdn.com`

2. Using `@font-face` in your `<style amp-custom>` CSS, for example:

   ```
   <style amp-custom>
     @font-face {
       font-family: "Ubuntu";
       src: url("http://example.com/fonts/ubuntu.woff")
       format('woff');
     }
     body {
       font-family: "Ubuntu", serif;
     }
   </style>
   ```

 Note that fonts included with `@font-face` must include the URL scheme `http` or `https`.

Google has a very nice font picker at `https://fonts.google.com/`. You can use it to choose a font and it will give you the code you need to include in your page, ensuring that your page will still validate.

Using custom fonts to improve page design

Now that we know how to add custom fonts, let's apply some to our content. We'll use a sans serif font, *PT Sans*, for our navigation links, and a serif font, *Droid Serif*, for our main paragraph text (both chosen from Google Fonts). First, we'll add the include-link that Google Fonts generated when we chose the fonts; this gets added to the `head` of the page (`/ch3/fonts.html`):

```
<link href="https://fonts.googleapis.com/css?family=Droid+Serif|PT+Sans"
rel="stylesheet">
```

Now we just have to apply these to the relevant elements of our page. For the navigation links, use the following:

```
.primary-nav li {
  font-family: "PT Sans", sans-serif;
}
```

And we'll apply Droid Serif to all other text:

```
body {
  font-family: "Droid Serif", serif;
}
```

Finally, let's stick with *Georgia* for our logo and `h1` texts. Note that we don't need to include Georgia explicitly, as it's available on most systems, but we can provide a fallback in any case:

```
.logo, h1 {
  font-family:Georgia, "Times New Roman", serif;
}
```

This resulting page should look something like the following image:

Article page showing custom web fonts, and some text effects we'll learn about shortly (/ch3/fonts.html)

You may have seen the `amp-font` component already, and you might be wondering what it's for. You don't need `amp-font` to include custom fonts, but you can use it to define timeouts and fallback for when custom fonts fail to load.

Text layout with CSS and HTML

So we know how to customize the font. What about text layout? CSS can be applied to text in AMP, just like normal HTML. AMP also provides some additional text layout features.

Pull-quotes are quite common in news article content. It's a technique that's used to emphasize an important part of the text. One way to achieve this is by using a simple HTML `blockquote` tag (`/ch3/pullquotes.html`):

```
<blockquote class="pull-quote">
   The whale is a mammiferous animal without hind feet
</blockquote>
```

Then we'll add a left border to the quote by adding the following CSS:

```
.pull-quote {
  border:none;
  border-left:6px solid #999;
  font-size:1.5rem;
  padding-left:1rem;
}
```

When viewed in a browser, you should see something like this:

Suspendisse quam mauris, molestie sed consectetur sed, pretium in tortor.

> # The whale is a mammiferous animal without hind feet

Donec sollicitudin risus ac odio commodo vestibulum. Cras semper convallis turpis, ut

Pull-quote using <blockquote> element (/ch3/pullquotes.html)

This is nice, but we can do better. Let's add a stylized quotation mark as a visual effect to really make the pull-quote stand out. We can achieve this with CSS, using the `before` pseudo-selector:

```
.pull-quote::before {
  content: '\00201C';
  font-size: 8rem;
  font-family: Georgia, serif;
  color: #ff8c00;
  position: absolute;
  left: -0.5rem;
  line-height: 7rem;
  padding-left: 1rem;
}
```

This CSS will output the value of the `content` property--in this case, it's `\00201c`, which is the unicode value for a double quotation symbol--before any element with class `pull-quote`. The remainder of the CSS just positions and styles the quote symbol.

The result is a nice, professional-looking pull-quote, as shown in the following image (`/ch3/pullquotes.html`):

quam mauris, molestie sed consectetur sed, pretium in tortor.

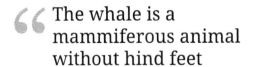

The whale is a mammiferous animal without hind feet

Donec sollicitudin risus ac odio commodo vestibulum. Cras semper convallis turpis, ut

Pull-quote with <blockquote> element and styling

Text layout with <amp-fit-text>

We could also achieve this with AMP's `amp-fit-text` component. This component allows us to specify a fixed width and height, and minimum and maximum font sizes, and `amp-fit-text` will scale the font to fit the text within these constraints. Let's change our pull-quote example to use `amp-fit-text` instead of `blockquote`.

Since `amp-fit-text` is an extended component, it must be explicitly loaded in the `head` of the page like this:

```
<script async custom-element="amp-fit-text"
src="https://cdn.ampproject.org/v0/amp-fit-text-0.1.js"></script>
```

Next, add this code somewhere within the main content in the body of the page:

```
<amp-fit-text width="400"
              height="75"
              layout="responsive"
              min-font-size="24"
              max-font-size="48">
   The whale is a mammiferous animal without hind feet
</amp-fit-text>
```

The min-font-size and max-font-size attributes ensure that the pull-quote will be neither too small on small screens, nor too large on large screens.

This sort of works, but we've lost some of the nice styling. Once again, we can spruce it up visually with a stylized quotation mark. This time, let's take this opportunity to demonstrate SVG support in AMP.

Adding SVG graphics to AMP pages

The **Scalable Vector Graphics** (**SVG**) format is an efficient, vector-based graphics format that is supported in AMP. Since it's vector-based, this means that it scales to any resolution, which makes it a perfect fit for responsive web design where graphics must often be scaled to fit different screen sizes:

Raster (bitmap) versus SVG (vector) images (source: wikipedia)

This time, we'll update our pull-quote example by using an SVG image for the quotation mark instead of the CSS pseudo-selector solution we saw before. We can add SVG in line in AMP-HTML pages.

Creating SVG graphics is beyond the scope of this book, but many applications, such as Potrace (`potrace.sourceforge.net`) and Adobe Illustrator, support SVG. The following SVG markup was created in Illustrator by simply exporting a text quotation mark as SVG. We'll add this to our page:

```
<svg version="1.1" id="Layer_1" xmlns="http://www.w3.org/2000/svg"
xmlns:xlink="http://www.w3.org/1999/xlink" x="0px" y="0px"
   viewBox="0 0 113.7 99.4" enable-background="new 0 0 113.7 99.4"
xml:space="preserve">
  <g>
    <path d="M52.6, 69.3c0, 4.3-1.7, 8-5.2, 11.3c-3.5, 3.2-7.5, 4.8-12.3,
4.8c-7.4, 0-13.1-2.4-17-7.3c-4-4.9-5.9-11.7-5.9-20.3c0-8, 3.4-16.2,
10.2-24.3c6.8-8.2, 15-14.4, 24.7-18.6l4.4, 7.1c-7.6, 3.7-13.6, 8-17.9,
12.9c-4.3, 4.9-6.8, 10.8-7.5, 17.8h5.7c4.2, 0, 7.6,0.5, 10.2, 1.4c2.6, 0.9,
4.7, 2.2, 6.4, 3.9c1.5, 1.6, 2.6, 3.4, 3.3, 5.3C52.3, 65.3, 52.6, 67.3,
52.6, 69.3z M102.2, 69.3c0, 4.3-1.7,8-5.2, 11.3c-3.5,3.2-7.5,
4.8-12.3,4.8c-7.4, 0-13.1-2.4-17-7.3c-4-4.9-5.9-11.7-5.9-20.3c0-8,
3.4-16.2, 10.2-24.3c6.8-8.2, 15-14.4, 24.7-18.6l4.4, 7.1c-7.6, 3.7-13.6,
8-17.9, 12.9c-4.3, 4.9-6.8, 10.8-7.5, 17.8h5.7c4.2, 0, 7.6, 0.5, 10.2,
1.4c2.6, 0.9, 4.7, 2.2, 6.4, 3.9c1.5, 1.6, 2.6, 3.4, 3.3, 5.3C101.9, 65.3,
102.2, 67.3,102.2, 69.3z"/>
  </g>
</svg>
```

This time, to style it, we'll make use of AMP's `flex-item` layout that we saw earlier. We'll put the SVG image and the `amp-fit-text` component into a flex parent container, and we'll set the layout of the `amp-fit-text` component to be `flex-item`:

```
<div class="pull-parent">
  <svg class="pull-quote">
  ...
  </svg>

  <amp-fit-text class="pull-quote-text"
                width="400"
                height="75"
                layout="flex-item"
                max-font-size="42">
    The whale is a mammiferous animal without hind feet
  </amp-fit-text>
</div>
```

Now add a small bit of CSS to the `<style>` tag in the document `head` to set the parent as a flex element:

```
.pull-parent {
  display: flex;
}
```

Now we have a nice, professional-looking pull-quote that we can use in our article pages:

quam mauris, molestie sed consectetur sed,
pretium in tortor.

66 The whale is a mammiferous animal without hind feet

Donec sollicitudin risus ac odio commodo
vestibulum. Cras semper convallis turpis, ut

Pull-quote implemented with <amp-fit-text> and SVG

Note that `amp-fit-text` will try to size the text within the specified parameters, but it will truncate the text where this is not possible.

For example, the following code would produce truncated text because a relatively large `min-font-size` has been specified. When this happens, ellipses are automatically added in WebKit and Blink based browsers:

```
<amp-fit-text width="400"
              height="75"
              min-font-size="30"
              max-font-size="42">
    The whale is a mammiferous animal without hind feet
</amp-fit-text>
```

We have used `amp-fit-text` for a simple pull-quote here, but it could also be used for things such as image captions, article teasers, and so on. In fact, a further improvement to the related content thumbnail listing example we saw earlier would be to use `amp-fit-text` to ensure that the caption text was not too long. This is left as an exercise for the reader.

Summary

In this chapter, we learned about layout and presentation in AMP. We improved our article page with the help of various AMP layout techniques, SVG graphics, image art-direction, and CSS styling. This added flair and improved the appeal of the page. While building this we learned about the AMP layout system, the `layout` attribute, the use of custom fonts, and some new custom components.

We also saw how to use responsive images, and how to build responsive canonical AMP pages. We saw how to implement the blurred placeholder image technique that are used by sites such as Medium and Facebook. And we saw how to use SVG in AMP pages, and how to implement text that will fit into any container.

The layout and style techniques we introduced are static with respect to user interaction: Users can consume the content, but they can't interact with it. We'll see in the next chapter how we can improve on this and engage the audience further by introducing interactive layout and components.

4
Engaging Users with Interactive AMP Components

This chapter looks at how to deliver better user experiences with the interactive components available in AMP. Our example article page is beginning to look nice and enticing, but so far there has been no way for visitors to interact with it. Building on our example, we'll learn how to add more interactive UI components that will both help to improve the user experience and improve how the site design looks.

All the techniques in this chapter have two things in common that help to enhance the user experience:

- They require some kind of interaction or trigger from the user
- They are designed to make the most of the limited screen space available on mobile devices

Specifically, we'll be looking at the following topics:

- Creating collapsible content sections with `<amp-accordion>`
- Building navigation menus with `<amp-sidebar>` and `<amp-carousel>`
- Building tabbed content with `<amp-selector>`
- How to generate dismissable pop-up user notifications with `amp-user-notification`
- The Action and Event model in AMP

Building collapsible content with <amp-accordion>

Collapsible content can help provide a great user experience on mobile devices, where screen space is restricted. An *accordion* UI component is a list of content sections, each of which can be in an expanded or collapsed state. You've probably seen accordions on the web before and maybe you've designed a web page that uses them. They're widely used on the web, with many different use cases, such as collapsing web page comment sections or for providing an expandable overview of article categories, in a news site, for example. We'll implement this latter use case shortly.

AMP comes with an extended component for building accordions: `amp-accordion`. Let's see how it works.

 The examples in this chapter will build on the news article page from the previous chapter. The starting point can be found at `/ch4/news-start.html` and you can follow along with the examples by building on the code in this file.

First, as usual, you need to include the extended component in the `head` of your document:

```
<script async custom-element="amp-accordion"
src="https://cdn.ampproject.org/v0/amp-accordion-0.1.js"></script>
```

Next, we'll add some content sections. AMP uses the HTML5 `section` tag for this, with the following conditions:

- Each `section` must be a direct child of `amp-accordion`
- Each `section` must have exactly two children:
  - The first child must be a header tag: one of h1, h2, ..., h6, or `header`
  - The second child can be any valid AMP-HTML tag, that is, an AMP component or an HTML tag, even another `amp-accordion`:

We'll start with the following code (`/ch4/accordion.html`):

```
<amp-accordion>
  <section>
    <h3>Item 1</h3>
    <div>The section content</div>
  </section>
  <section>
    <h3>Item 2</h3>
    <amp-img src="img/penguin.jpg" layout="fixed" width="125"
```

```
        height="75"></amp-img>
    </section>
    ...
  </amp-accordion>
```

This should result in an accordion like the one shown in the following image:

Item 1
The section content
Item 2

Item 3

AMP accordion with items 1 and 2 expanded, item 3 collapsed (/ch4/accordion.html)

So, that seems straightforward. Out of the box, we get a simple, functional accordion, but it's going to need some styling before we can show it to the world.

First, let's develop the content a bit more. So far, we've worked on an article page for a website. Let's say we wanted to show a list of categories with some top stories in each category. We can build this list and make each section expandable with amp-accordion.

Building an expandable top stories category list

Let's build out the AMP-HTML first. There will be a section for each of our main categories. The category name will be the header in each section, and we'll then add some top stories as li list items as the content for each section. We can reuse the thumbnail and text layout we developed for the related content examples in the last chapter. The AMP-HTML code will look like this:

```
<amp-accordion>
  <section>
    <h3>news</h3>
      <ul>
        <li>News story 1 content</li>
        <li>News story 2 content</li>
        ...
      </ul>
  </section>
  <section>
    <h3>sports</h3>
```

```
      <ul>
        <li>Sports story 1 content</li>
        <li>Sports story 2 content</li>
        ...
      </ul>
  </section>
  ...
</amp-accordion>
```

Recall from the last chapter our *related content* items that included an image and caption. Let's reuse that now. So, each `section` of the `amp-accordion` will look something like this:

```
<section>
  <h3 class="category-title">news</h3>
    <ul>
      <li>
        <figure class="related-thumb">
          <amp-img media = "(min-width: 35.01rem)"
                   src = "img/penguin.jpg"
                   ...
          </amp-img>
          ...
          <figcaption>News story 1 content</figcaption>
        </figure>
      </li>
      ...
```

The markup is too long to show here, but you can see the full code for this example at `/ch4/accordion-2.html`.

Styling <amp-accordion>

We can style the header and section of the accordion with CSS. Let's keep it simple with a grey, top border as divider between sections and no background color:

```
.category-title {
  font-family: Georgia, 'Times New Roman', serif;
  font-size: 1.5rem;
  color: #005689;
  background: none;
  border:0;
  border-top: 1px solid #ddd;
  padding:0.25rem;
}
```

This gives us a nice list of *top stories* expandable by category:

Top stories accordion, expandable by category (/ch4/accordion-2.html)

Improving the accordion with an expanded state indicator

An interesting thing to note is that if any section of an accordion is expanded, AMP will apply the attribute `expanded` to that section. We can use this to improve the UX of the accordion. Now we can target an accordion section in CSS based on its expanded state, like this:

- **Expanded**: `amp-accordion` **`section[expanded]`** `{...}`
- **Collapsed**: `amp-accordion` **`section:not([expanded])`** `{...}` (or simply `amp-accordion section {...}` if we add the expanded styles after the collapsed styles)

So, we could add rudimentary expanded/collapsed indicators with CSS pseudo elements like this:

```
amp-accordion section[expanded] h3::before {
  content: '+';
}

amp-accordion section:not([expanded]) h3::before {
  content: '-';
}
```

It's pretty basic, but it works. Let's improve this by moving the open/close button to the right-hand side of the section header, and we'll use a *chevron* character as the button (rotated in CSS):

```
amp-accordion section[expanded] h3::after {
  content: '❮';
  position: absolute;
  right: 0.5rem;
  color: #005689;
  transform: rotate(90deg);
}

amp-accordion section:not([expanded]) h3::after {
  content: '❯';  /* Unicode: U+276F */
 position: absolute;
 right: 0.5rem;
 color: #005689;
 transform: rotate(90deg);
}
```

Now our top stories accordion looks pretty good--we could use this in a real website:

Top stories accordion, with expanded state indicators; rudimentary version (left) and final version (/ch4/accordion-3.html)

By default, `amp-accordion` will *remember* the expanded/collapsed state of each section across sessions. Use the attribute `disable-session-states` if you want an accordion to *not* remember its state across sessions.

It's accordions all the way down!

Our example accordion content is made up of basic HTML and `amp-image` elements so far. A few paragraphs back, it was suggested that an `amp-accordion` component could be nested within another `amp-accordion`. Let's see how that might work.

We need to have a header tag as the first child of an `amp-accordion` element, and then we'll use another `amp-accordion` as the second child:

```
<amp-accordion>
  <section>
    <h3>Section 1</h3>
    <amp-accordion> <!-- Section 1 content -->
      <section>
        <h3>Section 1.1 header</h3>
        <div>Section 1.1 content</div>
      </section>
      <section>
        <h3>Section 1.2</h3>
        <div>Section 1.2 content</div>
      </section>
    </amp-accordion>
  </section>
</amp-accordion>
```

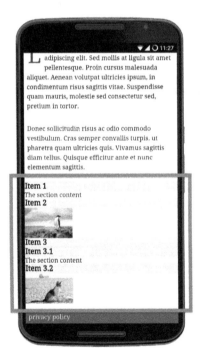

Hierarchical AMP accordion: different levels are hard to distinguish with default styling (/ch4/accordion.html)

An immediate problem with this is that it's very hard to see the hierarchy. We could address this by applying different color or indentation styles to distinguish different levels. We'll see an example of this later.

Building navigation menus

Navigation is a key component of all but the simplest websites. So far, we haven't given it much attention, apart from a few horizontal links in our example page. In AMP, there are a few options for building navigation menus.

Horizontal navigation menus

Our example currently has only a few navigation items, but as we add more we can see a problem with the design: we'll quickly run out of horizontal space. We could just let the links wrap down to the next line, but maybe we can do better. Let's look at a few quick fixes we can apply to improve the situation.

Scrollable horizontal navigation

We can make a very simple improvement simply by applying CSS `whitespace: nowrap`, and `overflow-x: scroll` styles to our horizontal navigation bar. This will allow the menu items to extend beyond the edge of the page. The HTML for our links will look like this (`/ch4/nav-div.html`):

```
<div class="primary-nav">
  <ul>
    <li><a href="#">news</a></li>
    <li><a href="#">sports</a></li>
    <li><a href="#">arts</a></li>
    ...
  </ul>
</div>
```

And the CSS looks like this:

```
.primary-nav {white-space: nowrap;overflow-x: scroll;}
```

We also style the navigation links:

```
.primary-nav a {
  font-family: 'PT Sans', sans-serif;
  color:#fff;
  font-size: 1.5rem;
}
```

So far, so good! However, the list can look truncated if a menu item runs off screen mid-item. It's even worse if the menu runs off screen *between* items; the user won't realize there are more options off screen. We can apply a visual cue--a gradient fade-out toward the edge--to indicate that there's more. To achieve this, we'll apply the gradient to the after pseudo element of the navigation div:

```
.fade::after {
  content:'';
  width:20%;
  height:1.5rem;
  position:absolute;
  right:0;
  bottom:0;
  background:linear-gradient(to right, rgba(0,86,137,0) 1%,rgba(0,86,137,1)
100%);
  pointer-events: none;
}
```

Note the use of pointer-events: none here. Without it, links underneath the pseudo element wouldn't be clickable:

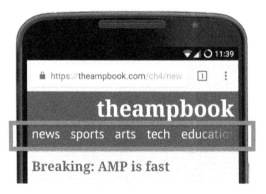

Simple horizontal scrollable navigation menu, with fade to the right (/ch4/nav-div.html)

This works, but there's another problem that's harder to fix: users without touchscreens won't be able to scroll to the off-screen items.

Building a navigation menu with <amp-carousel>

AMP has a component that can help here: `amp-carousel`. This component is mostly used with images and galleries, as we'll see in the next chapter, but it can also be used to build a scrollable horizontal navigation bar.

First, we need to import the script. Add the following to the document `head`:

```
<script async custom-element="amp-carousel"
src="https://cdn.ampproject.org/v0/amp-carousel-0.1.js"></script>
```

Basic `amp-carousel` usage looks like this:

```
<amp-carousel height="1.8rem" layout="fixed-height" type="carousel">
   ...
</amp-carousel>
```

The main thing to note here is the `type` attribute which can take one of the following values:

- `type="carousel"`: This is the default and it displays as a horizontal scrollable list. We'll use this for our navigation menu.
- `type="slides"`: Only one item (slide) is displayed at a time. We'll see this in the next chapter.

Let's now add the navigation items to the carousel, replacing the previous navigation menu (`/ch4/nav-carousel.html`):

```
<amp-carousel height="1.8rem" layout="fixed-height"
              type="carousel" controls class="primary-nav">
    <span><a href="#">news</a></span>
    <span><a href="#">sports</a></span>
    <span><a href="#">arts</a></span>
    ...
</amp-carousel>
```

We'll style the navigation items as they were before we added them to the carousel:

```
.primary-nav a {
  font-family: 'PT Sans', sans-serif;
  color: #fff;
  font-size: 1.5rem;
  text-decoration:none;
  padding-right: 0.5rem;
}
```

We're nearly there! Our navigation bar supports touch scrolling, but importantly it now also automatically renders *previous* and *next* buttons that are useful for advancing through the carousel (shown in the next figure). This solves the issue we had with the pure HTML navigation bar on non-touchscreen devices.

We just need to style the buttons now. We can remove the default styling with this CSS:

```
.amp-carousel-button {
  background:0;
}

.amp-carousel-button-next {
  right:0;
}
```

Now we can add our own more suitable *arrow* icon, again using the `after` pseudo element (code for right arrow shown as follows, left is similar):

```
.amp-carousel-button-next::after {
  content: ')';
  right:0;
  text-align: right;
  background:linear-gradient(to right, rgba(0,86,137,0) 0%,rgba(0,86,137,1)
50%);
  color: #fff;
  position: absolute;
  bottom:0;
  font-size: 2rem;
  line-height: 2rem;
  font-weight: bold;
  width:20px;
}
```

And we're done! This works, and it looks good:

Horizontal nav menu with <amp-carousel>, showing default buttons on left, and styled buttons on right (/ch4/nav-carousel.html)

Adding the attribute `controls` to `amp-carousel` will prevent the previous and next buttons from fading when inactive, so that they'll be visible at all times.

Sometimes though, a horizontal navigation bar is not enough. A common UI pattern is to display navigation items, sometimes with sub-items, within a sidebar menu. Let's see how to do this in AMP.

Adding side navigation with <amp-sidebar>

Sidebar or *off-screen* navigation is well suited to small screen devices. Generally, a navigation menu is hidden off to one side of the screen. The menu is revealed by clicking a button, and often it slides in from the side.

Sidebar navigation is supported out-of-the-box in AMP via the `amp-sidebar` component. This is an extended component, so it must be explicitly included with the following code:

```
<script async custom-element="amp-sidebar"
src="https://cdn.ampproject.org/v0/amp-sidebar-0.1.js"></script>
```

Let's add a sidebar menu to our article example page. There are a few things to note about `amp-sidebar` before we use it:

- It must be a direct child of the `body` tag
- It must use the `nodisplay` layout: `layout="nodisplay"`
- The sidebar items **can** include any AMP-permitted HTML elements

- The sidebar items **can't** include any AMP element, **except** `amp-accordion`, `amp-img`, `amp-fit-text`, `amp-list`, `amp-live-list`, and `amp-social-share`
- There can only be one `amp-sidebar` in any AMP page.

So, let's give it a shot. Since we are building a list of links, we'll use `li` elements for each of the sidebar navigation items. Add the following to the example page, right after the `<body>` tag:

```
<amp-sidebar id="sidenav" layout="nodisplay" side="left">
  <ul>
    <li>Nav item 1</li>
    <li>Nav item 2</li>
    <li>Nav item 3</li>
  </ul>
</amp-sidebar>
```

Note that we've added the following attributes:

- `id="sidenav"`: We need an `id` so that we can trigger the menu; we'll see how to do this shortly
- `layout="nodisplay"`: As noted earlier, this is required
- `side="left"`: To attach the sidebar to the left side of the page

 Use the attribute `side="left"` if you want the sidebar to slide in from the left, and `side="right"` if you want it to slide in from the right.

If you open this in the browser, you won't see much! So where's the sidebar? We won't be able to see it until it's triggered to open somehow. So, we're going to need a mechanism to trigger it.

Triggering the sidebar

We can use any element to trigger the sidebar menu, such as a *hamburger* menu image, or a plain old button. Let's start with a simple HTML button, and we can spruce it up as we go.

Add the following markup to the page after the closing `</amp-sidebar>` tag:

```
<button on="tap:sidenav.open">Menu</button>
```

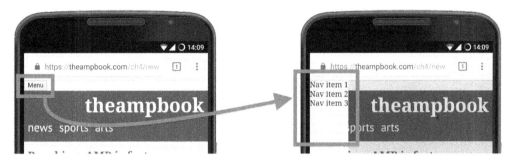

First attempt at sidebar nav with amp-sidebar (/ch4/sidebar.html): tapping the button (left) triggers the sidebar (right)

This gives us a button that we can click to open the sidebar menu. Mission accomplished? Not quite! It looks pretty awful: it's unstyled, and the button is poorly positioned, pushing the rest of the page content down. It's going to need a bit of tidying up.

But before we do that, we've introduced something new and strange--something that sort of looks like JavaScript--in the `on="tap:sidenav.open"` attribute. But we know it can't be JavaScript, because user scripts are forbidden in AMP. This attribute can be broken down as follows:

- `tap` represents an **event**
- `sidenav` represents a **target** (notice that it matches the `id` of our sidebar)
- `open` represents an **action**

We seem to have stumbled across the AMP **Action and Event model**. We'll take a look at this in more detail shortly. First, let's finish implementing the sidebar.

Styling the sidebar with CSS

We noted earlier that there can only be one `amp-sidebar` per page, so we could target it simply with `amp-sidebar` as selector. We also gave our sidebar an `id` of `sidenav`, so we can also use this to target it.

We'll match the background color to the header color of our example page, set its width, and give it a nice drop shadow effect:

```
#sidenav {
  background-color: #005689;
  padding: 0.5rem;
  width: 200px;
  box-shadow: 0.2rem 0 1rem rgba(0,0,0,0.5);
}
```

Next, we can style the sidebar items. We used `<li>` elements for each item, so they're easy to target:

```
#sidenav li {
  font-family: 'PT Sans', sans-serif;
  font-size: 1.5rem;
  line-height: 2.625rem;
  list-style: none;
  border-bottom: 1px solid #10679b;
}
```

And finally, we'll set the style of the sidebar link text to match the primary navigation links of our page:

```
#sidenav a {
  color: #fff;
  text-decoration:none;
}
```

The full code so far can be found at `/ch4/sidebar-2.html`. We'll look at improving the button next.

Adding an SVG hamburger menu button

Let's replace the ugly menu button with a nicer hamburger button that fits in with our design. We can use an inline SVG image for this:

```
<svg class="sidenav-btn" on="tap:sidenav.open" role="button" tabindex="0"
width="30px" height="30px" xmlns="http://www.w3.org/2000/svg"
viewBox="0 0 30.5 24.5">
  <g fill="none" stroke="#fff" stroke-linecap="round"
stroke-miterlimit="10" stroke-width="2.5px">
    <line x1="1.25" y1="1.25" x2="29.25" y2="1.25"></line>
    <line x1="1.25" y1="12.25" x2="29.25" y2="12.25"></line>
    <line x1="1.25" y1="23.25" x2="29.25" y2="23.25"></line>
```

```
    </g>
  </svg>
```

 Note the `on="tap:sidenav.open"` attribute: it's the action event model again, we'll get to this shortly. Whenever this element is tapped, AMP will look for an element with ID `sidenav` and apply the action `open`.

We'll position the menu button on the left side of the header bar. To do this, we'll wrap the site title/logo and the menu button in a flex container like this:

```
<div class="header-top">
  <svg class="sidenav-btn" on="tap:sidenav.open" ...>
  ...
  </svg>
  <div class="logo">theampbook</div>
</div>
```

We style them with this CSS:

```
.header-top {
  display: flex;
}

.sidenav-btn {
  padding-top:0.5rem;
}

.logo {
  width:100%;
}
```

We have another problem. Since we have configured the menu to slide in from the left with `side="left"`, when the menu slides out, it will obscure our new button. This isn't too much of an issue, because tapping anywhere outside the menu will close it, but for good UX, we should add a close button anyway. Again, we can use an SVG image for this. We'll add this code just inside the `<amp-sidebar ...>` tag:

```
<svg class="sidenav-close" xmlns="http://www.w3.org/2000/svg" width="21"
height="21" on="tap:sidenav.close" role="button" tabindex="0"
viewBox="0 0 21.97 21.97">
  <title>Close sidebar</title>
  <path fill="none" stroke="#fff" stroke-width="2.5" stroke-miterlimit="10"
d="M1.25 20.72L20.72 1.25m-19.47 0l19.47 19.47" stroke-linecap="round"/>
</svg>
```

Note the `on="tap:sidenav.close"`. This time, AMP will apply the `close` action whenever the element is tapped.

We just need a slight modification to the sidenav CSS, to position the close button to the right, and align the menu items to the left:

```
#sidenav {
  ...
  text-align: right;
}

#sidenav li
{
  ...
  text-align: left;
}
```

The result is shown in the following image (`/ch4/sidebar-3.html`):

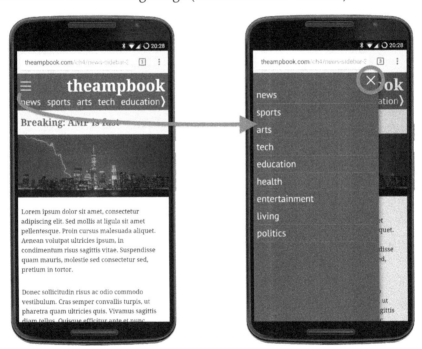

SVG hamburger menu icon (left) that triggers amp-sidebar menu with SVG close button (right)

A note on accessibility

When building your own sidebar menus, you may come across validation errors like these:

- **The attribute 'role' in tag 'li' is missing or incorrect, but required by attribute 'on'**
- **The attribute 'tabindex' in tag 'li' is missing or incorrect, but required by attribute 'on'**

What do they mean? The AMP validator checks that pages follow accessibility guidelines where appropriate. So when we add the `on="tap"` action to the `li` element, we are making it clickable and interactive. Hence, we must add `role="button"` to indicate it's clickable, and `tabindex` to make it focusable. You'll see this in various code examples throughout the book. (Of course, you should be doing these things anyway, not just because the validator is forcing you to!)

Hierarchical navigation menus with <amp-sidebar> and <amp-accordion>

Earlier, we saw how to use `amp-accordion`. Let's combine this with `amp-sidebar` to make a hierarchical sidebar menu. This would be useful for any site with a hierarchical information architecture, or with a content structure made of categories or tags, or with a multi-tiered sitemap, to give a few examples.

Recall that our sidebar items were simply `li` list items. We'll get our hierarchical menu to work like this:

- Any childless item (that is, has no sub-items) will remain as `<li><a href="#">item</a></li>`.
- Any item with children will be represented with an `amp-accordion` element within the `li` element. The menu item text for these items will now be the accordion section header, and the sub-items will be another unordered list `ul`.

So the structure will look like this:

```
<ul>
  <li class="sidebar-parent-container">
    <amp-accordion disable-session-states>
      <section>
        <h3>news</h3>
        <ul>  <!-- children -->
```

```
      <li><a href="#">news</a></li>
      <li><a href="#">europe</a></li>
      ...
    </ul>
  </section>
  <section>
    <h3>sports</h3>
    <ul>  <!-- children -->
      <li><a href="#">sports</a></li>
      <li><a href="#">football</a></li>
      ...
    </ul>
  </section>
  </amp-accordion>
 </li>
<li><a href="#">arts</a></li>
<li><a href="#">tech</a></li>
```

We noted earlier that it was difficult to distinguish between parents and their sub-items, but we can fix this with prudent use of color and indentation.

We'll fade the background color with this CSS:

```
#sidenav li.sidebar-parent-container section {
  background-color:rgba(255, 255, 255, 0.1);
}
```

And we indent as appropriate with the following styles. Child `li` items essentially get padded twice, providing the necessary indentation:

```
#sidenav li.sidebar-parent-container ul, li:not(.sidebar-parent-container)
{
  padding-left:0.5rem;
}
```

One final thing we need to do is add the expand/collapse indicators we built earlier. It's more or less the same code as earlier:

```
amp-accordion section h3::after {
  font-family: 'PT Sans', sans-serif;
  position: absolute;
  right: 17px;
  font-size: 22px;
  transform: rotate(90deg);
}

amp-accordion section[expanded] h3::after {
  content: '‹';
```

```
}
amp-accordion section:not([expanded]) h3::after {
  content: ')';
}
```

Sidebar navigation with <amp-sidebar> and <anp-accordion> (/ch4/sidebar-4.html)

The finished product is nice, professional-looking, and easy to use. We could definitely ship this!

Scaling up

While hamburger menus (menus that are triggered with a button with an icon that looks like a hamburger) are extremely popular, they have been criticized by UX experts because they give no hint about what actions are possible. You have to activate the menu before even knowing what you might click next. Another issue, although mitigated somewhat due to the ubiquity of the hamburger menu, is that some users mightn't even recognize that the hamburger icon represents a menu at all.

For some sites, the hamburger-activated sidebar menu will be enough. For others, there are various techniques we can use to make the most of the available space, such as the following:

- Maintain a horizontal navigation bar of important primary links near the header of the page, and use the sidebar for secondary links. If there are too many primary links, consider adding horizontal scrolling; we saw how to do this earlier.
- Use media queries to show or hide the primary navigation and hamburger sidebar as appropriate, depending on the screen size.

Implementing tabbed content with <amp-selector>

Another widely used and intuitive UI pattern is *tabbed content*. Tabs provide different views within a context. There are many use cases for tabs. In e-commerce, they can be used to provide information about different aspects of a product, such as the *product overview, product specifications,* and *product reviews.* Many popular news sites use tabs to display lists of *Most read* and *Top stories* article lists that you can switch between. Let's add this to our news article example page: we'll have **Related content** in one tab, and **Most read** in another.

While tabbed content is not supported out of the box with a dedicated component, it *can* be implemented in AMP with the use of the amp-selector custom element. This is a component that displays a list of options that the user can choose from.

Include it with the following:

```
<script async custom-element="amp-selector"
src="https://cdn.ampproject.org/v0/amp-selector-0.1.js"></script>
```

There are two attributes that we can use on children of amp-selector that help us to implement tabs:

- option: Adding this attribute allows us to set a child element as being *selectable.*
- selected: This attribute specifies the currently selected element. When a new element is selected, AMP will apply the selected attribute to this element and remove it from the *de*selected element.

This is all we need to implement tabs. To build it, we'll do the following:

- Use `amp-selector` as the container for the tab selector buttons, and the tab content panels
- Use a `div` for each of our two tab selector buttons
    - Add the `option` attribute to each of the tab selector `div`s, making them selectable. AMP will then add the `selected` attribute to the selected `div`.
- Use a `div` for each of our two tab content panels
    - Each tab panel `div` will be placed adjacent to its tab selector `div`, so that it can be easily targeted by CSS when the `selected` attribute is applied to its associated tab selection button
    - The tab panel will be displayed or hidden depending on whether its sibling has the `selected` attribute or not

Sounds difficult? It's not really! First, the `amp-selector` container code. We'll add a CSS class `tab-container` that we'll use to target the tab panel with shortly:

```
<amp-selector layout="container" class="tab-container" role="tablist">
  ...
</amp-selector>
```

Next, let's add the tabs:

```
<div class="tab-selector" role="tab" option="related-content" selected>
  <h2>Related articles</h2>
</div>
<div class="tab-content" role="tabpanel">
  Related articles content...
</div>
<div class="tab-selector" role="tab" option="most-read">
  <h2>Most read</h2>
</div>
<div class="tab-content"role="tabpanel">
  Most read content...
</div>
```

Notice that we've included the `option` attribute so now the tab selector `div`s will be selectable. The values `related-content` and `most-read` are not important for this example; we just need for the `option` attribute to be present. Note also that we've already applied the `selected` attribute to the **Related content** tab--this tab will now be visible by default.

The rest is CSS. Set the `amp-selector` to be a flex container:

```
.tab-container {
  display: flex;
  flex-wrap: wrap;
}
```

Hide the tab content by default:

```
.tab-content {
  display: none;
  width: 100%;
  order: 1;
}
```

We also set the `order` property to `1`, so that it's greater than the default `order` of the tab-selectors, so that the tab-selectors will be displayed above the content `div`s.

And then, when the sibling selector tab of a tab content `div` is selected, then show the content:

```
.tab-selector[selected]+.tab-content {
  display: block;
}
```

We style the selected and unselected tabs differently, so that we can see which one is selected:

```
.tab-selector {
  list-style: none;
  flex-grow: 1;
  cursor: pointer;
  background-color: #ddd;
}

.tab-selector[selected] {
  outline: none;
  background: #fff;
  border-top: 1px solid #ddd;
}
```

Related articles   Most read
Most read content...

First attempt at tabs with amp-selector

If you check this out in your browser now (/ch4/tabs.html), you'll see that this gives us our basic tabs. So far, so good! Now we need to get our article lists into the tabs. We already have a list of articles in the **Related content** markup that we developed in the last chapter (and that we used earlier in this chapter--we're getting good mileage out of this code!). All we need to do is take the related content code, and copy it into the content tab panel <div class="tab-content"></div>.

The **Most read** tab will have more or less the same code, just with different text and images:

```
<div class="tab-selector" role="tab" option="related-content" selected>
 <h2>Related content</h2>
</div>
<div class="tab-content" role="tabpanel">
  <ul class="related-items">
    <li>
     <figure class="related-thumb">
        <amp-img media = "(min-width: 35.01rem)"
                  src = "img/penguin.jpg"
        ...
        </amp-img>
        <figcaption>...</figcaption>
      </figure>
    </li>
    ...
</div>
```

We've omitted most of the content here for brevity: we've only included one related content item, and we've condensed that too.

Now we just need to make some styling adjustments to the tabs so that they fit in with the rest of the page, and that's it: a very nice **Related content** and **Most read** set of tabs, that will work on small and large screens:

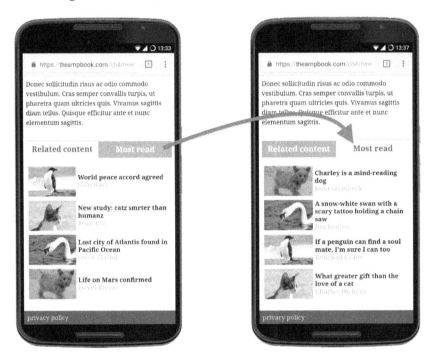

Tabbed content with amp-selector, final version (/ch4/tabs-2.html)

Displaying user notifications

AMP has a useful built-in component, `amp-user-notification`, for displaying pop-up, dismissable notifications. A common use for this component is to display a *cookie warning* (a requirement for sites that use cookies in the EU). By default, the notification is displayed at the bottom of the screen. It's not limited to displaying cookie warnings of course; it could show a notification about new content, a special offer, a newsletter sign-up, or number of credits or unread articles, to name just a few. Let's see how it works.

The first thing to note is that we need *two* scripts to use `amp-user-notification`:

`amp-user-notification`:

```
<script async custom-element="amp-user-notification"
```

```
        src="https://cdn.ampproject.org/v0/amp-user-notification-0.1.js"></script>
```

amp-analytics:

```
   <script async custom-element="amp-analytics"
   src="https://cdn.ampproject.org/v0/amp-analytics-0.1.js"></script>
```

We could display a simple cookie notice like this:

```
<amp-user-notification layout="nodisplay" id="cookie-notification">
   This site uses cookies to track your every move
   <button on="tap:cookie-notification.dismiss">I accept</button>
</amp-user-notification>
```

The look and positioning of the notification can be styled with CSS:

```
amp-user-notification {
   color: #fff;
   padding: 0.5rem;
   background-color: #7faac4;
}
```

The result is shown in the following image:

Cookie notification with <amp-user-notification> (/ch4/notification.html)

This would get annoying for the user if it was displayed on every page even after dismissal. So how does AMP know when to show the message? There are two ways: with *local storage* and with *server endpoints*.

By default, AMP will use local storage to store the dismissal status of a notification for a user, which is great; it means our cookie example is done! If the user has dismissed the notification, AMP will check the local storage, and won't show it again. Things get interesting, however, with *server endpoints*.

Using server endpoints to store the dismissal state of user notifications

AMP also allows us to specify two optional URL endpoints to use with `amp-user-notification`. The first is specified in the attribute `data-show-if-href`, and the second in the attribute `data-dismiss-href`:

- `data-show-if-href`: This can be used to determine whether the notification should be shown. A request is made to the URL when the notification is first loaded. If the server sends a JSON response of `{"showNotification": true}` then the notification is shown.
- `data-dismiss-href`: A request is made to the second URL on dismissal of the notification. This can be used to store that this user has dismissed the notification.

 If there are multiple notifications they are queued and displayed in sequence; the next one shown after the previous one has been dismissed.

The Action and Event model in AMP

Earlier, we had our first encounter with events and actions in AMP. This is like a constrained version of the JavaScript event model. You can attach event listeners and define handlers for events on AMP page elements using the `on` attribute.

Attaching event handlers with the on attribute

An event handler can be attached to any element, HTML or AMP-HTML, with the `on` attribute, using the following syntax:

```
on="event:target[.action]"
```

When AMP encounters this markup on an element, it listens for event `event` on the element. When it fires, it searches for an element with ID `target`, and applies action `action`. The action component is optional. When absent, the default action for `target` will be fired, if it has one.

We've seen this a few times already. For example, when we defined buttons to open and close our `amp-sidebar` menu, we used: `<svg ... on="tap:sidenav.open" ... >` and `<svg ... on="tap:sidenav.close" ... >`. So, when there was a tap on our SVG open or close images, AMP applied the appropriate action, `open` or `close`, to the element with ID `sidenav`, which was the sidebar.

In fact, since `open` is the default action for `amp-sidebar`, we could have just used `<svg ... on="tap:sidenav" ... >` for the open button.

Events and actions

So far, the only event we've seen is `tap`, and the only actions we've seen are `open`, `close`, and `dismiss`. You might be curious about what others are available. While `tap` applies to all elements, most events in AMP are specific to particular elements. For example, forms have `submit` , `submit-success`, and `submit-error` events, and `input` elements have a `change` event , while `amp-selector` has a `select` event, to name a few. There are many more; for a full list of AMP events and actions, see `Appendix B`, *Actions and Events.*

Handling multiple events on a single element

What about multiple events? No problem, AMP's got you covered! You can attach further event handlers simply by appending them to the `on` attribute, separating each extra event with a semicolon:

```
on="event:target[.action][;event2:target2[.action2]...]"
```

This opens up all kinds of possibilities. For example, you could conditionally show elements based on a form success or failure submission event:

```
on="submit-success:message1.show;submit-error:message2.show"
```

Triggering multiple actions for a single event

Multiple actions can be triggered for a single event by separating each action with a comma:

```
on="tap:target1.action1[,target2[.action2]...]"
```

So, for example, you could close a menu and open a lightbox with a single tap:

```
on="tap:sidenav.close,lightbox.open"
```

Using actions on any HTML element

We mentioned earlier that a `tap` listener can be applied to any HTML or AMP-HTML element. Equally, there are some actions that can be applied to any element. These are `hide`, `show`, and `toggleVisibility`. Thus, you could build a basic modal dialog with something like this:

```
<div id="confirm">Are you sure you want to continue?</div>
<a on="tap:confirm.hide">Cancel</a> <a href="confirm-page.html">Confirm</a>
```

Or you could toggle a settings panel with code like this:

```
<div id="settings">Your account settings...</div>
<button on="tap:settings.toggleVisibility">Settings</button>
```

The `show` action will only work on elements that were previously hidden with `hide` or `toggleVisibility` actions, or with the `hidden` attribute. It won't work if CSS `display:none` or AMP `layout=nodisplay` was used.

While this event-action model makes possible some very useful interactions, it's a bit limited. Later, we'll see an even more powerful interaction model in AMP, `amp-bind`, which gives the developer a basic coding layer on top of AMP--it's JavaScript, but not as we know it!

Summary

Things are really getting exciting now! We've explored some interactive AMP components that have helped to improve the user experience and breathe life into our web pages. We've seen how to build solid navigation menus, how to make the most of limited screen space with expandable content, and how we can listen for events and trigger associated actions that open up many possibilities for user interaction.

This trend will continue into the next chapter when our web pages will come truly alive as we explore how to add rich media components such as audio and video. We'll also move beyond simple article pages and start to think about how we can start to apply AMP to e-commerce pages.

5

Building Rich Media Pages in AMP

In this chapter, we'll explore how we can add rich media into our web pages with AMP. We'll move beyond article pages and start looking at e-commerce. We'll be focusing mostly on visual media with image galleries and videos (and audio for good measure), and we'll see how we can build compelling e-commerce product pages. We'll also be exploring social media support in AMP, and we'll see how Instagram, Twitter, and Facebook posts can be integrated.

The main topics we'll cover are:

- Interactive product image galleries with `amp-carousel`
- Audio and video in AMP: `amp-video`, `amp-youtube`, and `amp-audio`
- Full page video overlays with `amp-lightbox`
- Social media in AMP
- Tabbed product content

Showcasing products with <amp-carousel>

When it comes to e-commerce, `amp-carousel` really shines. We saw `amp-carousel` briefly in the last chapter, where we used it to build a horizontal navigation menu. This time, we'll make use of it to showcase products. For our examples, we'll have a products listing page, and a product detail page. Each product will have a name, a description, a price, and several images.

In our product listing page, we'll show just a thumbnail image, the product name, and the price. eBay was an AMP early-adopter, and we can look to its AMP implementation for inspiration. It contains several carousels promoting different categories of products; we'll build something similar. We can also take UX design cues from other e-commerce retailers, such as Amazon and AliExpress. Our product listing page will contain carousel lists of similar products. We'll then add a product page, and we'll see how various AMP media components can be used to present the product.

 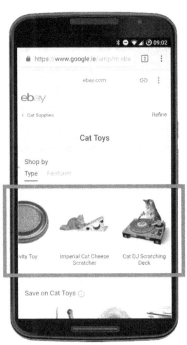

E-commerce pages: AliExpress with highlighted hero carousel (left), and eBay with highlighted product carousel (right)

For our e-commerce pages, we'll start off with a new page template which will make use of some of the components that we've previously worked with, such as sidebar and primary navigation menus.

Building a carousel of products

Let's begin our e-commerce product listing page with a carousel of products--we'll use t-shirts for our products. Clicking on any item on the carousel will load up the product details page for that item.

The starting point for the examples in this chapter is
`/ch5/product-start.html`. You can follow along with the examples by
building on the code in this file.

Before using `amp-carousel`, it must be included with:

```
<script async custom-element="amp-carousel"
src="https://cdn.ampproject.org/v0/amp-carousel-0.1.js"></script>
```

Each immediate child of the `<amp-carousel>` tag is treated as an item of the carousel. Let's
start with the thumbnail images. A first attempt we'll add the following to the body of our
page (`/ch5/product-listing.html`):

```
<amp-carousel id="product-carousel" width="auto" height="160"
layout="fixed-height" type="carousel" controls>
  <amp-img src="img/tshirt-0-f-red-160.png"  width="160" height="160">
  </amp-img>
  <amp-img src="img/tshirt-10-f-black-160.png" width="160" height="160">
  </amp-img>
  <amp-img src="img/tshirt-5-f-blue-160.png" width="160" height="160">
  </amp-img>
  <amp-img src="img/tshirt-6-f-green-160.png" width="160" height="160">
  </amp-img>
</amp-carousel>
```

In this code we used the following attributes:

- `height="160"` and `layout="fixed-height"`: This controls the height of the
  carousel precisely
- `type="carousel"`: This specifies a standard film-strip carousel, with previous
  and next navigation buttons; we'll see `type="slides"` later
- `controls`: This ensures the navigation buttons are always visible; sometimes you
  might not want this

 When the `layout` attribute is absent, and we've included `width` and
`height` attributes, `layout` is inferred as `fixed`

This gives us our basic carousel with thumbnail images. We still need to display more
information, such as the product name and price. We also want each item to link into the
product page. So let's replace each `amp-img` item in the previous code with the following:

```
<a href="product.html">
```

```
    <amp-img src="img/tshirt-0-f-red-160.png" width="160" height="160">
    </amp-img>
    <div class="item-name">T-Shirt: Super Pouvoir</div>
    <div class="item-price">€9.99</div>
</a>
```

We can apply some simple styling to the product links:

```
.product-carousel a {
  text-decoration: none;
  text-align: center;
  color: #555;
  font-size: 0.9rem;
  font-family: "PT Sans", sans serif;
}

.item-price {
  font-size: 1.2rem;
  font-weight: bold;
}
```

Already this looks similar to the product carousel that eBay uses on its site:

Product carousel, with product image, name, and price (/ch5/product-listing.html)

Hero promotion with <amp-carousel> slides

Before we start the product details page, let's pimp up the product listing page a bit more. A common design pattern is to promote special offers and product categories in a sliding hero carousel at the top of the page. Let's add this. This time we'll add the attribute `type="slides"` to the `amp-carousel` element, and have it automatically advancing through some main categories and offers, with nice, large hero images.

We'll start off with this markup for the carousel element, using responsive layout (`layout="responsive"`) so that it will fill the viewport:

```
<amp-carousel id="hero-images"
  width="1024"
  height="480"
  layout="responsive"
  type="slides">
  ...
</amp-carousel>
```

Autoplaying <amp-carousel> slides

On carousels with `type="slides"`, we can add the attribute `autoplay` to cycle through the slides automatically. The time between slide transitions can be adjusted by adding the attribute `delay`--for example, `delay="2000"` will give a two second delay, so the carousel markup will look like this:

```
<amp-carousel id="hero-images"
            width="1024" height="480"
            layout="responsive"
            type="slides"
            autoplay
            delay="2000">
  ...
</amp-carousel>
```

Since this is a hero carousel, each slide of which is going to be an offer or promotion, we want each item to be clickable and to lead to the associated offer page, so each slide item will be contained within an `a` tag:

```
<a href="product-page.htm">
  <amp-img src="img/tshirt-banner-1024.jpg" layout="responsive"
width="1280" height="600"></amp-img>
</a>
```

Note that we're using `layout="responsive"` here, so it doesn't matter that the height of the image is greater than the height of the carousel; the dimensions will be used to calculate the aspect-ratio of the image. The full carousel code so far, for three hero banner images, looks like this (`/ch5/hero-carousel.html`):

```
<amp-carousel id="hero-images" width="1024" height="480"
layout="responsive" type="slides" autoplay>
  <a href="#">
    <amp-img src="img/tshirt-banner-1280.jpg" width="640" height="300"
      layout="responsive" alt="Tshirt banner"></amp-img>
  </a>
  <a href="#">
    <amp-img src="img/trousers-banner-1280.jpg" width="640" height="300"
      layout="responsive" alt="Trousers banner"></amp-img>
  </a>
  <a href="#">
    <amp-img src="img/tshirt-offer-1280.jpg" width="640" height="300"
      layout="responsive" alt="Tshirt offer"></amp-img>
  </a>
</amp-carousel>
```

Adding call-to-action text to carousel images

It's often useful to include some promotional, or **call-to-action** (**CTA**), text with each slide of a hero slide carousel. Recall that only direct children of `amp-carousel` are carousel items, so any child tags of a carousel item are associated with that item. In our carousel code so far, each `a` tag is a carousel item, so we could add the caption like this:

```
<a href="#">
  <amp-img src="img/tshirt-banner-1280.jpg" width="640" height="300"
layout="responsive"></amp-img>
  <div class="caption">T-SHIRT SALE 50% OFF</div>
</a>
```

But we can do better. This is a perfect chance to use the `amp-fit-text` component we saw in `Chapter 3`, *Making an Impression: Layout and Page Design in AMP*. Recall that `amp-fit-text` will automatically grow or shrink text to fit into its container:

```
<a href="#">
  <amp-img src="img/tshirt-banner-1280.jpg" width="640" height="300"
layout="responsive"></amp-img>
  <div class="call-to-action">
    <amp-fit-text width="320"
                  height="50"
                  layout="responsive"
```

```
            min-font-size="14px"
            max-font-size="48px">
  T-SHIRT SALE 50% OFF
  </amp-fit-text>
  </div>
</a>
```

We need a little CSS to position and style the text (`/ch5/hero-captions.html`):

```
#hero-images .call-to-action {
  text-align: center;
  position: absolute;
  bottom: 0;
  left: 0;
  right: 0;
  padding: 0.5rem 1.2rem;
  background: rgba(240, 240, 240, 0.6);
  color: #333;
  font-family: 'PT Sans', sans-serif;
}
```

Product listing page, showing the hero carousel, without captions (left) and with captions (right)

It's probably clear by now that we can have multiple carousels per page: In the product listing page we just built, we included three. Next, let's work on the product details page.

Building a product image gallery

Assuming that the user has clicked through to a product, let's see how we can present it in an appealing way. We'll start with a gallery of product images, only one of which will be visible at a time, with thumbnail previews that can be used to browse the images. This will work as you'd expect any product image viewer to work: Clicking a thumbnail will display the large version of the thumbnail, replacing the currently displayed image.

There are a few different ways to build this in AMP. The approach we're going to take here will combine techniques we've seen previously, with some new functionality. We'll combine the Action and Event model we learned about in the last chapter, with a slide carousel, and the amp-selector component.

Product image gallery with thumbnail previews

Let's start with the basic gallery. We'll use amp-carousel to house the main product images, and we'll separately use a list of amp-imgs for our thumbnails. First, the carousel:

```
<amp-carousel id="product-carousel" width="600" height="600"
layout="responsive" type="slides">
  <amp-img src="img/tshirt-0-f-red-640.png" width="300" height="300"
layout="responsive"></amp-img>
  <amp-img src="img/tshirt-0-f-black-640.png" width="300" height="300"
layout="responsive"></amp-img>
  <amp-img src="img/tshirt-0-f-blue-640.png" width="300" height="300"
layout="responsive" ></amp-img>
  <amp-img src="img/tshirt-0-f-green-640.png" width="300" height="300"
layout="responsive"></amp-img>
</amp-carousel>
```

This time, note the use of:

- type="slides": We only want a single product image to be displayed at a time
- id="product-carousel": We're going to need to target a carousel by id shortly
- layout="responsive": The product images will grow or shrink to fit the viewport

Next, the thumbnail preview images. We'll just use smaller versions of the main product images:

```
<amp-img src="img/tshirt-0-f-red-120.png" width="60" height="60">
</amp-img>
<amp-img src="img/tshirt-0-f-black-120.png" width="60" height="60">
</amp-img>
<amp-img src="img/tshirt-0-f-blue-120.png" width="60" height="60">
</amp-img>
<amp-img src="img/tshirt-0-f-green-120.png" width="60" height="60">
</amp-img>
```

Work in progress: product image carousel image preview thumbnails (/ch5/product-carousel.html)

So, now we have a carousel, and a list of thumbnails. How do we link them, so that clicking a thumbnail will display the associated image in the carousel? The answer lies with the AMP Action and Event model, and an `amp-carousel` action method we haven't seen before: `goToSlide()`.

Jumping to a specific image with goToSlide()

The `goToSlide()` method allows us to advance a carousel to a specific slide. It takes the index of the slide that should be displayed, starting at `0`. So, with our product carousel, we can attach a `tap` event like this to each of the product thumbnails:

```
on="tap:product-carousel.goToSlide(index=3)"
```

This translates roughly as: "When this element is tapped, find the element with `id` equal to `product-carousel`, and display slide `3`."

The markup for each of the thumbnails will now look something like this:

```
<amp-img on="tap:product-carousel.goToSlide(index=0)"
         role="button" tabindex=""
         src="img/tshirt-0-f-red-120.png"
         width="60" height="60">
</amp-img>
```

Highlighting the selected thumbnail

The product image gallery we have is nice. It could be nicer, however, if there was a visual indicator to highlight the selected thumbnail. From the last chapter, we know that `amp-selector` will add a `selected` attribute to the selected option, so this could help. We could add a border or glow to the selected thumbnail in CSS based on this attribute, and this would serve to indicate which thumbnail was selected.

So, let's put the `amp-img` thumbnails inside an `amp-selector` tag (`/ch5/product-carousel-selector.html`):

```
<amp-selector class="carousel-thumbs" layout="container">
  <amp-img on="tap:product-carousel.goToSlide(index=0)"
           src="img/tshirt-0-f-red-120.png" width="60" height="60"
           option="1" selected role="button" tabindex="">
  </amp-img>
  <amp-img on="tap:product-carousel.goToSlide(index=1)"
           src="img/tshirt-0-f-black-120.png" width="60" height="60"
           option="2" role="button" tabindex="">
  </amp-img>
  ...
</amp-selector>
```

Note that we add the `option` attribute to each thumbnail, as required by `amp-selector`, and we set the first as default, selected with the `selected` attribute.

With a little CSS, we can now highlight the selected thumbnail:

```
.carousel-thumbs amp-img[selected] {
  border:2px solid red;
  box-shadow: 0 0 2px #f00;
}

amp-selector [option][selected] {
  outline:0;
}
```

In some browsers, there is a blue flash to highlight the tap when selecting a thumbnail. This is undesirable in this case, and it can be hidden with the following non-standard CSS:

```
amp-selector {
  -webkit-tap-highlight-color: rgba(255, 255, 255, 0);
}
```

Reducing code with <amp-selector>

Now that we're using `amp-selector`, we can improve on the code we wrote earlier to change the slide. The `amp-selector` component exposes a `select` event which is fired whenever an option is chosen by the user. We can determine which option was selected with `event.targetOption`. So instead of adding the `on="tap:product-carousel.goToSlide(index=0)"` event handler to every `amp-img` option as we did earlier, we can instead use the `select` event of the `amp-selector` element like this:

```
<amp-selector class="carousel-thumbs" layout="container"
    on="select:product-carousel.goToSlide(index=event.targetOption)">
```

Each `amp-img` thumbnail will now look like the following, with the `on="tap..."` event removed:

```
<amp-img src="img/tshirt-0-f-red-120.png"
         width="60" height="60"
         option="1"
         role="button" tabindex="">
</amp-img>
```

This simplifies the carousel code: it's more flexible, easier to read, and easier to maintain. The thumbnail highlight is shown in the following image:

Product carousel (type="slide"), with thumbnails highlighted using <amp-selector> (/ch5/product-carousel-selector.html)

There's still a small issue with this: If we use the carousel navigation buttons, or swipe the images on a touchscreens, then the thumbnail highlight does not change. There are a few ways to deal with this:

- Hide the carousel buttons altogether; arguably they're not needed here anyway:

```
.amp-carousel-button {
  display: none;
}
```

- Wrap the `amp-selector` around the carousel (as well as the thumbnails), so that when the carousel buttons are tapped, the selected thumbnail becomes deselected. With this approach, no thumbnail will be highlighted when the navigation buttons are used, but this is an improvement over the wrong thumbnail being highlighted.

- There is a third method, using `amp-bind`, that would solve the issue. We'll see `amp-bind` in Chapter 8, *Programming in AMP - amp-bind* and we'll stick with the first solution in our product page for now.

Adding video to AMP pages

Why stop at images? Video is used widely in all kinds of sites, including e-commerce and news pages. Let's add a promotional video to our product page. There are different ways to do this depending on whether the video is self-hosted or provided by a third-party video service, such as YouTube.

Hosting your own videos with <amp-video>

The first way to embed video in AMP is to use `amp-video`. This is an AMP replacement for the HTML5 `video` tag. You should use this if you want to host the video yourself.

First, as usual, you need to import the component:

```
<script async custom-element="amp-video"
src="https://cdn.ampproject.org/v0/amp-video-0.1.js"></script>
```

Then you can use it like this:

```
<amp-video width="640" height="480"
          src="https://theampbook.com/ch5/video/videoclip.mp4"
          poster="video-snaphsot.jpg" controls>
  <div fallback>
    <p>Your browser doesn't support HTML5 video</p>
  </div>
  <source type="video/mp4" src="videoclip.mp4">
  <source type="video/webm" src="videoclip.webm">
</amp-video>
```

 Including multiple sources is an HTML5 feature, which allows the browser to choose a video format that it supports or prefers.

Note the use of the following attributes:

- `poster="video-snaphsot.jpg"`: This will be displayed while the video is loading and before the play button is hit
- `controls`: As with `amp-carousel`, this determines whether or not the controls will always be visible
- `autoplay`: As with `amp-carousel`, this determines whether the video will play automatically when visible

Autoplay videos are muted by default, and will be unmuted when the user taps the video.

Embedding hosted videos

The second way to include videos in your pages is to embed videos from a hosted video service. This is a popular way to deliver promotional video content on the web since it means you do not have to worry about hosting bandwidth yourself. Many different services are supported. For example:

- **YouTube**:

```
<amp-youtube data-videoid="AR5N2bXv0V8" width="560" height="315"
layout="responsive"></amp-youtube>
```

- **Vimeo**:

```
<amp-vimeo data-videoid="217051213" width="1280" height="720"
layout="responsive"></amp-vimeo>
```

Many other hosted video platforms are also supported, including Hulu, Vine, Brightcove, and Dailymotion, to name a few (you can see the full list in Appendix A, *AMP Components*). The format for each component is pretty similar across each of the services, each requiring the ID for the video.

We'll use YouTube in our example page. First we include the YouTube component:

```
<script async custom-element="amp-youtube"
src="https://cdn.ampproject.org/v0/amp-youtube-0.1.js"></script>
```

Then we just need to provide the AMP-HTML markup to display the video:

```
<amp-youtube data-videoid="AR5N2bXv0V8"
             width="560" height="315"
             layout="responsive">
</amp-youtube>
```

 You should use the actual video width and height with the `amp-youtube` component, even when using `layout="responsive"`, so that the video will retain the correct aspect ratio. You can get the width and height from the YouTube video page, under the **Sharing | Embed** tab.

The result is shown in the next image (`/ch5/video.html`):

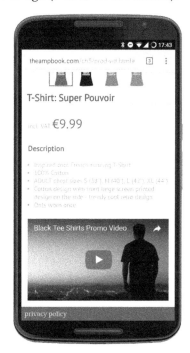

Product page with embedded YouTube video

We've also added a product description and price to the product page in the last example. Since this was built using basic HTML and CSS, and nothing AMP-specific, we won't go into the details here, but you can see how it was built in the example source.

Note that whatever the video source, self hosted or third party, the video data will be lazy-loaded as needed. And, once again, we can use the `autoplay` and `controls` attributes as before.

Adding audio to AMP pages

While we're at it, let's see how to embed an audio clip into an AMP page. It's much the same as for video: There are AMP components for self-hosted audio clips, and for third-party hosted audio with SoundCloud.

Embedding self-hosted audio with <amp-audio>

Just as `amp-video` is a replacement for the HTML5 `video` tag, `amp-audio` is a replacement for the HTML5 `audio` tag. Import it with:

```
<script async custom-element="amp-audio"
src="https://cdn.ampproject.org/v0/amp-audio-0.1.js"></script>
```

You can use it with code like this:

```
<amp-audio width="640" height="100"
src="https://theampbook.com/ch5/audio/audioclip.mp4" autoplay controls
muted loop>
  <div fallback>
    <p>Your browser doesn't support HTML5 audio</p>
  </div>
  <source type="audio/mpeg" src="audioclip.mp3">
  <source type="audio/ogg" src="audioclip.ogg">
</amp-audio>
```

Again, note the use of the attribute `autoplay`, as well as the attributes `muted`, which sets the audio clip as muted by default, and `loop`, which will loop the clip when it reaches the end.

Embedding third-party hosted audio

Third-party audio embeds are supported via `amp-soundcloud`. Import it with:

```
<script async custom-element="amp-soundcloud"
src="https://cdn.ampproject.org/v0/amp-soundcloud-0.1.js"></script>
```

Its basic usage looks like this:

```
<amp-soundcloud height="300px"
                layout="fixed-height"
                data-trackid="195265654"
                data-visual="true">
</amp-soundcloud>
```

Adding this to the product page looks like this (`/ch5/audio.html`):

Embedded SoundCloud audio clip, classic mode (left) and visual mode, with height 350px (right)

Note the use of the following attributes:

- `layout="fixed-height"`: This is the only permitted layout
- `data-visual="true"`: This optional attribute renders the clip in full-width *visual* mode

The official documentation for `amp-soundcloud` recommends that visual mode uses a height of `300px`, `450px`, or `600px` to match the SoundCloud embed code, so that the clip will resize correctly.

Showcasing your products with \<amp-lightbox\>

The *lightbox* is a common UI component that's used for displaying content, such as images and videos. It's usually rendered as a full-screen overlay with a dark background, often with controls to navigate sets of images and to close the lightbox.

Let's get back to our product example page. We'll demonstrate `amp-lightbox` by adding a lightboxed video. When the user clicks a button, the video will be opened up within a full screen lightbox, and will start playing immediately.

First, we need to include the `amp-lightbox` component:

```
<script async custom-element="amp-lightbox"
src="https://cdn.ampproject.org/v0/amp-lightbox-0.1.js"></script>
```

(Don't forget to include the YouTube component that we saw earlier). We'll start by creating the lightbox that will hold the video, and a button that can be used to launch the video lightbox (full code at `/ch5/video-lightbox.html`):

```
<button class="btn-video" on="tap:vid-lightbox">Launch video</button>
<amp-lightbox id="vid-lightbox" layout="nodisplay">
  ...
</amp-lightbox>
```

`amp-lightbox` **must always have** `layout="nodisplay"`.

Note that we've attached the `tap` event to the default action of the element with an `id` of `vid-lightbox`. Now we'll add the video itself:

```
<amp-lightbox id="vid-lightbox" layout="nodisplay">
  <amp-youtube width="560"
               height="315"
               layout="responsive"
               data-videoid="AR5N2bXv0V8">
  </amp-youtube>
</amp-lightbox>
```

We're also going to need a way to close the lightbox. We can use the same SVG graphic we used to close the sidebar menu in the last chapter. We'll place this image and the video inside a flex container so that the close button is at the top-right of the video:

```
<div class="flex-container">
  <div class="flex-row">
    <svg class="btn-close" xmlns="http://www.w3.org/2000/svg" width="21"
height="21" on="tap:vid-lightbox.close" role="button" tabindex="0"
viewBox="0 0 21.97 21.97">
      <path fill="none" stroke="#fff" stroke-width="2.5"
stroke-miterlimit="10" d="M1.25 20.72L20.72 1.25m-19.47 0l19.47 19.47"
stroke-linecap="round" />
    </svg>
    <amp-youtube width="560"
                 height="315"
                 layout="responsive"
                 data-videoid="AR5N2bXv0V8">
    </amp-youtube>
  </div>
</div>
```

Then we can add a dark, faded background to the lightbox:

```
amp-lightbox {
  background: rgba(0,0,0,0.8);
}
```

We position the items using flexbox:

```
.flex-container {
  display: flex;
  align-items: center;
  width: 100%;
  height: 100%;
}
.flex-row {
  flex:auto;
```

```
    text-align: right;
}
```

Finally, we'll style the close button (full code at `/ch5/video-lightbox.html`):

```
.btn-close {
  cursor: pointer;
  padding: 0.5rem;
}
```

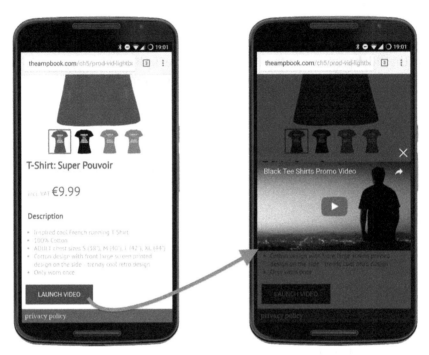

Product page with lightboxed video. The button on the left is tapped to launch the YouTube video in a lightbox (right)

Lightboxing product images

Earlier, we saw how to build a product image gallery that used `amp-carousel` under the hood: Clicking a thumbnail displayed the associated product image. We could extend this further so that if the main product image is clicked, then it is opened in a lightbox.

To achieve this, we can use `amp-image-lightbox`. This is a specialized lightbox component that will display any image that activates it with via the `on` event, without having to include the image element directly within the `amp-image-lightbox` element.

Let's add it to our page (`/ch5/product-lightbox.html`):

```
<script async custom-element="amp-image-lightbox"
src="https://cdn.ampproject.org/v0/amp-image-lightbox-0.1.js"></script>
```

We need to use a responsive layout with `amp-image-lightbox`, and we also need to give it an `id` that we can target with the `on` event handler:

```
<amp-image-lightbox id="image-lightbox" layout="nodisplay">
</amp-image-lightbox>
```

Now we just have to target it with `on="tap:image-lightbox"`, attached to the product image within the carousel:

```
<amp-img src="img/tshirt-0-f-red-640.png"
        width="300" height="300" layout="responsive"
        on="tap:image-lightbox" role="button" tabindex="">
</amp-img>
```

And that's it!

Well, almost. As we noted at the start of the book, AMP is still a new technology. It's ready for production--over two billion live AMP pages will testify to that--but there are kinks occasionally. There's currently a bug (`github.com/ampproject/amphtml/issues/9288`) with `amp-image-lightbox` that causes a lightboxed image within a carousel to ignore its responsive layout and stretch. We can add a CSS workaround to fix this, using the `object-fit` property like this:

```
.image-lightbox img {object-contain: fit}
```

This should work in most cases, but if it doesn't, a slightly more involved workaround is to use flex containers for the carousel images.

First, wrap each image in the carousel within a flex container like this:

```
<div class="flex-container">
    <amp-img src="img/tshirt-0-f-red-640.png"
             width="300" height="300" layout="responsive"
             on="tap:image-lightbox" role="button" tabindex="0">
    </amp-img>
</div>
```

Then add a small bit of CSS to position the image:

```
.flex-container {
   max-width: 400px;
   max-height: 400px;
}

amp-image-lightbox .flex-container {
   display: flex;
   align-items: center;
}
```

One of these approaches should work so that your lightboxed image retains its aspect-ratio.

Closing the lightbox

The lightbox can be closed by clicking or tapping outside the image, or hitting *ESC* on a keyboard, but once again, we can provide a better UX by adding a dedicated close button. We can add it directly to the lightbox element as follows, using our trusty SVG close button again:

```
<amp-image-lightbox id="image-lightbox" layout="nodisplay">
  <svg class="btn-close" xmlns="http://www.w3.org/2000/svg" width="21"
height="21" on="tap:image-lightbox.close" role="button" tabindex="0"
viewBox="0 0 21.97 21.97">
    <path fill="none" stroke="#fff" stroke-width="2.5" stroke-
miterlimit="10" d="M1.25 20.72L20.72 1.25m-19.47 0l19.47 19.47" stroke-
linecap="round" />
  </svg>
</amp-image-lightbox>
```

We can style it like this:

```
amp-image-lightbox {text-align: right}
.btn-close {padding:1rem;}
```

A lightboxed product image, displayed using <amp-image-lightbox> (/ch5/product-lightbox.html)

Note that there is one thing missing from this example that would improve the UX: being able to swipe through to the next image in the carsousel without leaving the lightbox. This behavior could be achieved with `amp-bind`, a programming layer for AMP that we'll explore in Chapter 8.

 In this example we used `amp-image-lightbox`, which is a specialized version of `amp-lightbox`. You can display an image with `amp-lightbox` too, but you would need two `amp-img` elements in your page instead of one--one for the non-lightboxed image, and one for the lightbox content--essentially duplicating your code.

Using social media in AMP pages

We saw earlier how to embed video content in our AMP pages. We can also embed video content (as well as non-video content) hosted on popular social media platforms, such as Facebook, Twitter, and Instagram too.

Facebook

Import the `amp-facebook` component with:

```
<script async custom-element="amp-facebook"
src="https://cdn.ampproject.org/v0/amp-facebook-0.1.js"></script>
```

Then embed a Facebook post with the following code, copying the URL from the Facebook post page. In the case of videos, you can find the width and height of the video from the **Options | Embed** dialog accessed from the Facebook video post.

```
<amp-facebook width="560"
              height="315"
              layout="responsive"
              data-embed-as="video"
              data-href=
"https://facebook.com/FirstMediaBlossom/videos/10154760841464586">
</amp-facebook>
```

Note the `data-embed-as` attribute. When a Facebook video post is embedded with this `data-embed-as="video"` value, then *only* the video player is embedded, and not the surrounding text, if there is any. If this attribute is absent, then it defaults to the value `post`, and the whole post is embedded, including any text.

When using `data-embed-as="post"` make sure to leave enough space for Facebook to lay out the post, as even with `layout="responsive"` it won't be resized to fit into a small container.

Examples, `/ch5/facebook-video.html`, and `/ch5/facebook-post.html`, are shown in the following image. Note that `layout="responsive"` does not work as expected when embedded as a post, and the embed is cut off due to lack of space in the desktop view on the right:

Embedded Facebook post, with data-embed-as="video" (left) and data-embed-as="post" (right)

Which approach is more suitable for you will depend on your application. For a product page, it's probably better to embed it just as a video where possible.

Twitter

The `amp-twitter` component is imported with:

```
<script async custom-element="amp-twitter"
src="https://cdn.ampproject.org/v0/amp-twitter-0.1.js"></script>
```

A tweet can be embedded with this code, using the ID from the URL of the tweet in the `data-tweetid` attribute:

```
<amp-twitter width="640"
             height="480"
             layout="responsive"
             data-tweetid="865110380518965248">
</amp-twitter>
```

Instagram

The `amp-instagram` component is imported with:

```
<script async custom-element="amp-instagram"
src="https://cdn.ampproject.org/v0/amp-instagram-0.1.js"></script>
```

An Instagram post can be embedded with:

```
<amp-instagram data-shortcode="BUO3zdK190s" width="200" height="200"
layout="responsive" data-captioned>
</amp-instagram>
```

Note the use of the `data-captioned` attribute; this adds the Instagram post caption to the embed.

You can find an example with both a Twitter post and an Instagram post at `/ch5/twitter-instagram.html`.

Promoting products with social media

The value of social media sharing buttons is questionable--recent research suggests that only 0.2 percent of visitors will use these buttons (`moovweb.com/anyone-use-social-sharing-buttons-mobile`)--but they are still popular with publishers nonetheless. Some implementations are are notoriously bad for increasing page weight. The AMP implementation is, like everything in AMP, implemented efficiently.

We can add sharing buttons to our product page with the `amp-social-share` component (`/ch5/product-social.html`).

Import the component with:

```
<script async custom-element="amp-social-share"
src="https://cdn.ampproject.org/v0/amp-social-share-0.1.js"></script>
```

Once the script is imported, you can use one of the following right out of the box:

```
<amp-social-share type="email"></amp-social-share>
<amp-social-share type="facebook" data-param-
app_id="123456789101112"></amp-social-share>
<amp-social-share type="twitter"></amp-social-share>
<amp-social-share type="linkedin"></amp-social-share>
<amp-social-share type="pinterest"></amp-social-share>
<amp-social-share type="tumblr"></amp-social-share>
<amp-social-share type="gplus"></amp-social-share>
<amp-social-share type="whatsapp"></amp-social-share>
```

Each one of these will import a share button for the service referenced in the `type` attribute, with an inline SVG image icon. The default size is `60x44` pixels. You can override the sizes and even provide custom icons. Change the size with `width` and `height` attributes like this:

```
<amp-social-share type="twitter" width="32" height="32"></amp-social-share>
```

To change the icon, just target the button via CSS, and set the background image:

```
amp-social-share[type="facebook"] {
  background-image: url(IMAGE_URL);
}
```

Setting default share text

By default, the `amp-social-share` component will pull out the site URL from the `rel=canonical` link. In many cases, you can also configure the shared URL and message, depending on the social media service, by setting values for `data-param-*` attributes. The most common are `data-param-url`, which generally defaults to the canonical page URL, and `data-param-text`, which defaults to the current page title.

For example, you could configure the Twitter share to link to a specific product page, and to include the text **Check out this awesome t-shirt**, with the following code:

```
<amp-social-share type="twitter"
    data-param-url="https://theampbook.com/ch5/product.html"
    data-param-text="Check out this awesome tshirt. Only worn once!">
</amp-social-share>
```

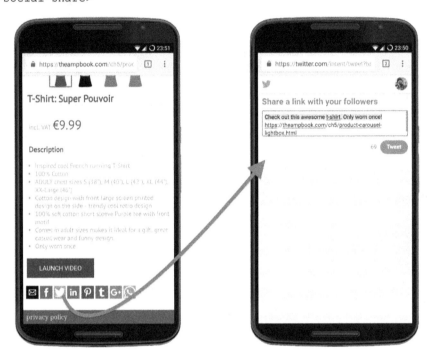

Social sharing buttons, with custom text for Twitter (/ch5/product-social.html)

Most of the main social networks will work without any configuration. Facebook is an exception, however, and requires an attribute `data-param-app_id`. For this, to work you need to create an application on the Facebook platform (`developers.facebook.com/docs/apps/register`), and copy the `app_id` into this attribute.

Improving product SEO with metadata

In `Chapter 1`, *Ride the Lightning with AMP* we learned a little bit about metadata and the AMP search results carousel. Now that we've changed our focus to e-commerce, there is some metadata geared towards e-commerce that you should include to maximize your search visibility. These include the `brand` and `offers` schema.org types. To get the best SEO results, you can provide metadata to help search engines to better index your product pages:

```
<script type="application/ld+json">
{
    "@context": "http://schema.org/",
    "@type": "Product",
    "name": "T Shirt: Super Pouvoir",
    "image": "",
    "description": "Lorem ipsum",
    "mpn": "123456",
    "brand": {
        "@type": "Clothing",
        "name": "FunisherRunning"
    },
    "offers": {
        "@type": "Offer",
        "priceCurrency": "EUR",
        "price": "9.99",
        "priceValidUntil": "2021-01-01",
        "itemCondition": "http://schema.org/NewCondition",
        "availability": "http://schema.org/InStock",
        "seller": {
            "@type": "Retail",
            "name": "TheAmpBook"
        }
    }
}
</script>
```

This can be included in either the `head` or `body` of your AMP page.

 Apart from including AMP components scripts, this is the only other time that the `<script>` tag is allowed in AMP pages, and it must contain the attribute `type="application/ld+json"`.

Using tabs in product pages

We can bring together some of the things we've learned in this and previous chapters, to build a more complete product page. Depending on the type of product, it's often useful to present product information as a set of tabs. We can use the same approach to building tabs as we use in the last chapter. This time, the tabs will be **Description**, and **Delivery**.

We won't dive too deep into the code here, since we covered it in the last chapter. All that's really needed is to put the description and delivery content into tab containers, and add the tab selector buttons, as we did last time:

```
<amp-selector role="tablist" layout="container" class="tab-container">
  <div role="tab" class="tab-selector" selected option="1">
    Description
  </div>
  <div role="tabpanel" class="tab-content">
  ... Description content ...
  </div>
  <div role="tab" class="tab-selector" option="2">
    Delivery
  </div>
  <div role="tabpanel" class="tab-content">
  ... Delivery content ...
  </div>
</amp-selector>
```

The rest is based on CSS similar to what we had in the last chapter. The result is a decent product page, that works well on desktop and small screen devices alike (`/ch5/product.html`):

Product page with tabs, on mobile (left) and tablet (right)

Summary

In this chapter, we've seen how to make use of rich media in AMP pages. We changed focus from articles to e-commerce pages, and we built two pages--a product listing page, and a product details page--to demonstrate how AMP supports useful design and interaction components, such as image carousels and slide galleries, as well as lightboxes, videos, and social media links.

While this gets us started with e-commerce, there are still some important features missing: in particular, *search*, and *payments*. In the next chapter, we'll be covering forms, and we'll see how a product search could be integrated into an AMP product page. Then, in `Chapter 9`, *When AMP is Not Enough: Enter the Iframe*, we'll see how to integrate payments to complete the e-commerce prototype.

6
Making Contact - Forms in AMP

In this chapter, we're going to improve our prototype by adding some e-commerce essentials. Forms will be central to everything we build next. While we saw some interactive UI elements in the previous chapters, forms really open up a whole new level of interaction by providing the ability to generate user requests, and to submit and collect user input.

It will be necessary to learn a few other things along the way, including form validation and `amp-mustache` templates. We'll also need to set up some server-side code, to handle submissions and state. This is not strictly AMP, so we'll keep this to a minimum.

In particular, in this chapter, we'll see how AMP's form support can be used to enhance the user experience by exploring the following features:

- Sign-up forms
- XHR/AJAX form submissions
- Form validation
- Product search forms
- Shopping carts

Using forms in AMP

Before we start building forms, let's get the basics out of the way. The first thing to know is that whenever *any* form is used in an AMP page, then the `amp-form` extension script *must* also be included:

```
<script async custom-element="amp-form"
src="https://cdn.ampproject.org/v0/amp-form-0.1.js"></script>
```

Submitting forms in AMP

Forms in AMP can be submitted as full page GET requests, or as XHR (or AJAX) GET or POST requests:

- If you use `method="GET"` in your form, you must then define a submission endpoint in either the `action` or `action-xhr` attribute
- If you use `method="POST"` then you must only use `action-xhr` for your submission endpoint
- Endpoints must be served on an HTTPS URL, and must not link to the AMP cache CDN
- Finally, you must also include the `target` attribute, and it can have a value of either `_blank` (opens in new window) or `_top` (opens in current window)

The following inputs are not permitted: `<input type=button>`, `<input type=file>`, `<input type=image>`, and `<input type=password>`.

A simple newsletter sign-up form

Time to get our hands dirty. Let's start off small with a newsletter sign-up form. With just a single input text field for an email address, and a **submit** button, this is going to be one of the simplest forms you can build! We'll eventually add this form to the sidebar of the product page we developed in the previous chapter.

The starting point for the examples in this chapter is `/ch6/form-start.html`. You can follow along with the examples by building on the code in this file.

First, let's set this up as a GET form, and afterwards, we'll change it to a POST submission to see what we need to do differently (`/ch6/signup.html`):

```
<form method="get" action="/ch6/signup.php" target="_top">
  <input type="email" name="email" id="email" required>
  <input type="submit" value="Sign me up!">
</form>
```

We're using a PHP server to handle the form submission here due to its wide availability and ease of use. You can use any server technology you want.

When we submit the form using a GET request, the server will simply retrieve the value of the email field, and if it's a valid email address, then we'll display a success message.

The following PHP code is used to grab and validate the email address (`/ch6/signup.php`):

```
$email = isset($_REQUEST["email"])?$_REQUEST["email"]:"";
$email = filter_var($email, FILTER_SANITIZE_EMAIL);
if (filter_var($email, FILTER_VALIDATE_EMAIL)) {
  // Show thank you message
} else {
  // Show fail message
}
```

This is a simple solution that does what we need it to do. There is a drawback, however. Recall that we can't use an AMP Cache URL as the endpoint. This means that we are potentially not getting maximum benefit from AMP, because when the form is submitted, the user is directed back to the origin server, for an entire page load.

Submitting the form via a POST XHR request could help us here; let's see how.

Submitting XHR AJAX forms in AMP

This time, we'll rewrite our form to use the POST method instead of GET, and `action-xhr` with our new endpoint instead of `action` (`/ch6/signup-xhr.html`):

```
<form method="post" action-xhr="/ch6/signup-xhr.php" target="_top">
  <input type="email" name="email" id="email" required>
  <input type="submit" value="Sign me up!">
</form>
```

For XHR requests, AMP expects a JSON response with the following:

- `Content-Type` header should be `Content-Type: application/json`
- A 2xx HTTP status response code for successful submissions
- Any other status code for error responses

The form endpoint specified in action-xhr must start with https:// or // and must be served from either an HTTPS URL or from localhost.

Handling XHR responses with <amp-mustache>

Now we come to a neat trick in AMP. We can use amp-mustache templates to parse the form response and automatically populate and display a success or error message as appropriate.

amp-mustache is an AMP implementation of the *Mustache* template syntax. You can find out more about mustache.js at github.com/janl/mustache.js.

To set this up, we need to do the following:

1. Add submit-success and submit-error attributes to any direct child elements of the form element.
2. Add a <template type="amp-mustache">...</template> element to display the success or error templates.

So our form will look like this:

```
<form method="post" action-xhr="/ch6/signup-xhr.php" target="_top">
  ...
  <div submit-success>
    <template type="amp-mustache">
      ...
    </template>
  </div>
  <div submit-error>
    <template type="amp-mustache">
      ...
    </template>
  </div>
</form>
```

Once we have a JSON response from the server, amp-mustache can automatically pull out JSON variables from the response. We'll set up the server endpoint to respond like this for successful submissions:

```
{
```

```
        "email": "ruadhan@theampbook.com"
    }
```

And like this for an error submission:

```
    {
        "email": "ruadhan@theampbook.com",
        "message":  "The email address is already subscribed."
    }
```

Applying `amp-mustache` to these JSON responses, we can now use `{{email}}` and `{{message}}` syntax to retrieve the values of `email` and `message` respectively. Back to the form--let's add success and error messages:

```
<div submit-success>
  <template type="amp-mustache">
    Congrats {{email}} is now signed up!
  </template>
</div>
<div submit-error>
  <template type="amp-mustache">
    There was a problem with {{email}}: {{message}}
  </template>
</div>
```

And of course, don't forget to include the `amp-mustache` script:

```
<script async custom-template="amp-mustache"
src="https://cdn.ampproject.org/v0/amp-mustache-0.1.js"></script>
```

Creating the server in PHP

We won't dwell on the PHP server code as it's not strictly AMP. The code we use here is the following (`/ch6/signup-xhr.php`):

```
header('Content-Type: application/json');
header('Access-Control-Allow-Credentials: true');
header('Access-Control-Allow-Origin:
https://theampbook-com.cdn.ampproject.org');
header('Access-Control-Expose-Headers: AMP-Access-Control-Allow-Source-
Origin');
header('AMP-Access-Control-Allow-Source-Origin: https://theampbook.com');

$email = isset($_REQUEST["email"])?$_REQUEST["email"]:"";

// Handle malformed email address
if(!filter_var($email, FILTER_VALIDATE_EMAIL)) {
```

```
    header("HTTP/1.0 400 Error");
    $content = '{"email":"'.$email .'", "message":"The email address is not
valid"}';
}

// Pretend it's already subscribed
else if($email=="subscribed@example.com") {
    header("HTTP/1.0 409 Conflict");
    $content = '{"email":"'.$email .'", "message":"The email address is
already subscribed"}';
}

else {
    // It's ok
    header("HTTP/1.0 200 Ok");
    $content = '{"email":"'.$email .'"}';
}

echo $content;
```

This code performs the following actions:

- If the email is not valid, it returns a 400 error HTTP code and an error message
- If the email is equal to subscribed@example.com, then it returns a 409 error HTTP code and an **email already subscribed** error message
- Otherwise, it returns an HTTP 200 code and success message

Note that we have included a few other headers:

- Access-Control-Allow-Credentials: true: Required by AMP Cache
- Access-Control-Allow-Origin: https://theampbook-com.cdn.ampproject.org: Required by AMP Cache, and should match your **cache domain URL**
- Access-Control-Expose-Headers: AMP-Access-Control-Allow-Source-Origin: Allows the response to include the next header
- AMP-Access-Control-Allow-Source-Origin: https://theampbook.com: Required by AMP, and should match your **source domain URL**

 This is an example of a Cross-Origin Resource Sharing (CORS) request in AMP. CORS is required because AMP pages can be served from the AMP Cache. If these headers are not included, then the CORS request from the AMP Cache will fail. Read more about CORS in AMP at github.com/ampproject/amphtml/blob/master/spec/amp-cors-requests.md

Hiding the form on success

AMP has another small trick up its sleeve that we can exploit to improve the form submission UX. On successful submissions, AMP applies the class `amp-form-submit-success` to the `form` element. Thus, we can use CSS to hide the form fields when we don't need them any more:

Sign-up form: form is hidden on successful submission (/ch6/signup-xhr.html)

Custom form validation

AMP has built-in validation strategies that you can tap into by adding the `custom-validation-reporting` attribute to the `form` element, with one of these values:

- `show-first-on-submit`: Displays only the first validation error when a form is submitted
- `show-all-on-submit`: Displays validation errors for all invalid inputs after the form is submitted
- `as-you-go`: Shows validation errors for an invalid input field after the user has interacted with that field, but before the form has been submitted

Let's add this to our form element (`/ch6/signup-validation.html`):

```
<form method="post" action-xhr="/ch6/signup-xhr.php" target="_top"
    custom-validation-reporting="as-you-go">
    ...
</form>
```

We can also define custom validation messages for different kinds of validation errors. This works by associating a particular error with a particular input field. Take, for instance, for our email field:

```
<input type="email" name="email" id="email" required>
```

We could add the following custom validation messages to this field:

```
<span visible-when-invalid="valueMissing"
      validation-for="email">Provide your email yo!</span>
<span visible-when-invalid="typeMismatch"
      validation-for="email">Email not valid yo!</span>
```

Note that the `validation-for` attribute should match the name of the field. In addition to `valueMissing`, we can apply other validations such as `patternMismatch`, and `typeMismatch`. AMP will handle the displaying of these messages as appropriate.

Finally, just to show that we can, let's also move the form into the sidebar menu of our e-commerce page. This is a simple copy and paste into the correct place in the sidebar, along with some CSS styling, so we won't go into it here, but you can see the code in `/ch6/signup-sidebar.html`. The result, with custom validation, is shown as follows:

Sign-up form embedded in amp-sidebar, showing *as-you-go* validation errors (/ch6/signup-sidebar.html)

UX improvement - visual feedback on submission

When an XHR form is submitted in AMP, other than disabling the **submit** button, there is no default indication that something is happening. If the endpoint is slow to respond then the user won't know what's happening. We can improve this.

When a form is submitted, AMP adds the class `amp-form-submitting` to the `form` element. We can use this to tweak the UI and display a *loading* indicator when this class is present.

First, let's add the indicator markup. You can use any kind of *loader* or *spinner* you want here, but keep in mind the CSS animation restrictions we mentioned in `Chapter 1`, *Ride the Lightning with AMP*. We're using a `div` element here, added just after the **submit** button:

```
<input type="submit" value="Sign me up!">
<div class="loader"></div>
```

We can style the loader div using the `:before` pseudo element. Using the `border-radius` property, we can create a circular spinner:

```
.loader::before {
  content: '';
  display: inline-block;
  width:1rem;
  height:1rem;
  vertical-align: middle;
  border-radius: 50%;
  border: 2px solid #ccc;
  border-top-color: #333;
  animation: loader .8s linear infinite;
}
```

And then we add a `keyframes` animation:

```
@keyframes loader {
    to {transform: rotate(360deg);}
  }
```

Finally, we make use of the `amp-form-submitting` class to hide or show the loading indicator and **submit** button when appropriate:

```
form .loader {
  display: none;
}
form.amp-form-submitting .loader {
  display: inline-block;
}
```

```
form.amp-form-submitting [type="submit"] {
  display: none;
}
```

Newsletter signup with animated SVG icon

The code for this example is in /ch6/signup-spinner.html. Note that an artificial three-second delay was added to the server code (/ch6/signup-xhr-delay.php) to demonstrate the spinner.

Building a product search form

In the previous chapter, we talked about some features that we could add to enhance our e-commerce product page experience. One of these was a product search box. Let's look at this next.

Of course, to search for products in all but the simplest cases will require integration with an inventory system or database. While that aspect is outside the scope of this book, we can put all the other pieces in place.

We'll try to build something similar to Amazon's search box:

Amazon's page header with search box shown on a narrow viewport

Let's start with an XHR form like we saw earlier (full code at /ch6/product-search.html):

```
<form method="post" action-xhr="/ch6/product-search-xhr.php">
  ...
</form>
```

After that, we'll add a search input text field and a **submit** button inside the form element:

```
<input name="keywords" type="search" placeholder="Search" required>
<input type="submit" value="">
```

Styling the search form

We can use CSS to style the input elements to get the effect we want. First, the keyword field:

```
input[type="search"] {
  border-top-left-radius: 4px;
  border-bottom-left-radius: 4px;
  padding:0 0.5rem;
  font-size: 1.4rem;
  width: 100%;
}
```

Note the border-top-left-radius and border-bottom-left-radius properties; these give us rounded corners! Next, the **submit** button. We're going to add an SVG magnifying glass search icon as the background image:

```
input[type="submit"] {
  width:2.5rem;
  background-repeat: no-repeat;
  background-image: url('img/search-icon.svg');
  background-size: 1.4rem 1.4rem;
  background-position: 50% 50%;
  border-top-right-radius: 4px;
  border-bottom-right-radius: 4px;
  margin-left:-4px;
  background-color: #febd69;
}
```

The main things to note here are the following:

- The background image: `background-image: url('img/search-icon.svg')`
- The background color: `background-color: #febd69`
- The right-hand side rounded corners (`border-top-right-radius: 4px;`), to match the left-hand side rounded corners of the text field input

The rest of the CSS here is just concerned with tweaking the layout. So far, this gives us a nice styled form, similar to Amazon's:

Page header with search box implementation on small viewport

The Chrome browser adds a yellow background when autocomplete is enabled on input fields. This can clash with your design, so we use this CSS hack to disable it: `input:-webkit-autofill { -webkit-box-shadow: 0 0 0px 1000px white inset;}`.

The server response - a JSON list of products

Now we need to build the server endpoint. This will simply match the search keywords against our products. A real e-commerce site might have a sophisticated search that performs partial matching and relevance ranking of a database of products, but once again, this is out of scope here. In this prototype, only one search term will return data: `tshirt`.

When the user searches for `tshirt`, we'll return a JSON payload with a list of products in an array, like this:

```
{
  "keywords": "tshirt",
  "results": [
    {
      "name": "T-shirt: Super Pouvoir",
      "price": "€9.99",
      "description": "Super cool super power t-shirt",
      "image": "img/tshirt-0-f-red-120.png"
```

```
    },
    {
      "name": "T-shirt: La Biere",
      "price": "€10.99",
      "description": "Beer t-shirt",
      "image": "img/tshirt-10-f-black-120.png"
    },
    ...
  ]
}
```

We saw earlier how we can handle XHR responses with the `submit-success` attribute and `amp-mustache` templates. We'll apply that here. This time, we can use `{{name}}`, `{{price}}`, `{{description}}`, and `{{image}}`. But how do we iterate over the list?

 Many e-commerce search solutions provide *autocompletion* on the search input. We'll see how to implement autocomplete in `Chapter 8`, *Programming in AMP - amp-bind*.

Iterating over JSON data with <amp-mustache>

Another nice feature of `amp-mustache` is its ability to iterate over arrays. The JSON payload from the server endpoint contains an array of products that matched the search keywords. Once we know the name or key of the JSON object array--`results` in this case-- we can use the following mustache syntax to get at the data:

```
{{#results}}
  ...
{{/results}}
```

With this, we could use the following template to simply output the data returned by the server:

```
<div submit-success>
  <template type="amp-mustache">
    {{#results}}
      <div>{{name}}, {{price}}, {{description}}, {{image}}</div>
    {{/results}}
  </template>
</div>
```

Let's improve this. Since we have a relative URL to each product's thumbnail image, we can display the thumbnail along with the title, description, and price. This sounds a little like the article thumbnail, title, and author layout we used in Chapter 3, *Making an Impression - Layout and Page Design in AMP*, so let's reuse that. Recall that each article thumbnail item had code like this:

```
<figure class="related-thumb">
  <amp-img src="img/image.jpg" width="125" height="75" layout="responsive">
  </amp-img>
  <figcaption>
    Description
    <span class="author">Author</span>
  </figcaption>
</figure>
```

Let's rework this for our products. We'll use the same basic layout, but tweak the styling:

```
<ul class="related-items">
  {{#results}}
    <li>
      <figure class="related-thumb">
        <amp-img src="{{image}}" width="60" height="60"
layout="responsive">
        </amp-img>
        <figcaption>
          <span class="title">{{name}}</span>
          <span class="price">{{price}}</span>
          <span class="description">{{description}}</span>
        </figcaption>
      </figure>
    </li>
  {{/results}}
</ul>
```

Note how we have plugged the {{image}} JSON property into the amp-img element in the template; this will display the thumbnail image for each product.

Also note that in this example, we have used just a single image source for each thumbnail, but you could easily apply the same responsive image approach using image srcset and media queries that we used in Chapter 3 to display more detailed images for larger viewports.

 We won't include the CSS layout styling here, for space reasons. It's very similar to the CSS used in Chapter 3 and you can see the full code at /ch6/product-search.html.

By combining this code with the `amp-mustache` template, we are able to build a responsive product search results list without too much trouble, shown in the following image:

Product search results with responsive layout on various devices with different resolutions (/ch6/product-search.html)

Showing the search status

We can make use of the `amp-form-submitting` class that AMP adds to the form element to give the user more feedback about what is happening during the search. First we'll create two `div` elements, one to be displayed before the search, and one to be displayed while the search is being performed:

```
<div class="main-content before-search">
  <h2>Product search</h2>
  <p>No results yet</p>
</div>

<div class="main-content searching">
  <h2>Product search</h2>
  <p>Searching...</p>
</div>
```

Now it's just a matter of applying CSS styles based on the `amp-form-submitting` class to show and hide these containers as appropriate:

```
form.amp-form-submitting .before-search {
  display: none;
}

form .searching {
  display: none;
}

form.amp-form-submitting .searching {
  display: block;
}

form.amp-form-submit-success .before-search, form.amp-form-submit-success
.searching {
  display: none;
}
```

Animating the search icon

In our email sign-up form, we added an animation spinner effect. Let's add a similar effect here. This time, we'll animate the icon on the search button to give the user some instant feedback that something is happening. First, add the loader element after the **submit** button:

```
<input name="keywords" type="search" placeholder="Search" required>
<input type="submit" value="">
<div class="loader"></div>
```

The CSS is very similar to what we used earlier, making use of the exact same `@keyframes` animation as before (omitted here):

```
.loader:before {
  content: '';
  width: 2.5rem;
  background-repeat: no-repeat;
  background-image: url('img/search-icon.svg');
  background-size: 1.4rem 1.4rem;
  background-position: 50% 50%;
  animation: loader .8s linear infinite;
  height: 2.5rem;
  display: inline;
  position: absolute;
  margin-left:-2.5rem;
```

```
}
```

Again, AMP will add the `amp-form-submitting` class to the form element when the form is submitted. We use slightly different CSS this time because we don't want to hide the whole form; we'll just hide the **submit** button icon and show the spinner instead:

```
form.amp-form-submitting .loader {
  display: inline;
}
form .loader {
  display: none;
}
form.amp-form-submitting [type="submit"] {
  background-image: none;
}
```

This results in a really nice animated spinner while the search is being performed.

A caveat with the submit-success approach

There is a drawback with this setup. Earlier, we mentioned that the `submit-success` attribute--which is key to displaying the search form response--can only be used on direct child elements of the `form` element. This makes it trickier to design the page markup if the form inputs are not right beside the results, as is the case in our page (the form is in the header, but the results are displayed in the body of the page). So, in the final markup for this example, we had to do the following:

1. Place the `form` tag outside the `header` tag.
2. Remove the `main` content tag, so that the `submit-success div` remained as a direct child of the `form` element.
3. Add a `main-content` style to the `submit-success` (and every other content container) `div` so that it had the correct margins.

The markup structure ended up like this:

```
<form ... >
  <header>
  ...
  </header>
  <!-- <main> -->
  ...
  <div class="main-content submit-success">
    ...
  </div>
```

```
    ...
    <!-- </main> -->
</form>
```

You can work around it, but it's just something to be aware of. In Chapter 8, *Programming in AMP: amp-bind*, we'll see another technique that uses amp-bind and amp-list--two components we haven't seen yet--to give more flexibility in search forms should you need it.

Implementing a shopping cart in AMP

What e-commerce site would be complete without a shopping cart? Let's see how we can add one to our e-commerce prototype. We'll start out with a very simple implementation, and we'll build on it in the next chapter. First, we'll add an **add-to-cart** button and form to the product page (/ch6/product-cart.html):

```
<form method="post" action-xhr="/ch6/add-to-cart.php" target="_top">
  <input type="hidden" name="price" value="9.99">
  <input type="hidden" name="product_id" value="tshirt-1">
  <input type="hidden" name="product_name" value="T-Shirt: Super Pouvoir">
  <input class="btn" type="submit" value="Add to cart">
</form>
```

For now, we'll include price and product_id as hidden fields in our form (in a real application with a proper backend, you might only need to pass the product_id).

When the button is clicked, the form will submit to the server endpoint, and the item will be added to the cart. But how will the server know which cart to add the item to? We'll need some way to track which user's cart we are dealing with. This brings us to another neat trick that AMP has up its sleeve: **variable substitution**.

Variable substitution in AMP

AMP provides a mechanism whereby you can include special variables that will be replaced with actual values at runtime. There's a long list of such variables that can provide information about the client, such as SCREEN_WIDTH and SCREEN_HEIGHT, or about performance, such as PAGE_LOAD_TIME and SERVER_RESPONSE_TIME, among others. There are also miscellaneous variables such as RANDOM, which will be replaced with a random number, and QUERY_PARAM, which can be used to access query string parameters.

You can find out more about the available variables in the AMP specification (`github.com/ampproject/amphtml/blob/master/spec/amp-var-substitutions.md`).

One variable we are interested in here is `CLIENT_ID`. When the AMP runtime encounters `CLIENT_ID` in a page, it will generate and substitute a unique ID for this user. This is useful because it gives us a way to identify the user on subsequent visits, whether the user comes via the AMP cache or via the origin domain. And if we can identify the user, then we can implement our shopping cart, since we now have a way to associate a cart with a user.

Using CLIENT_ID to identify a shopping cart

To get the `CLIENT_ID` to the server, we can just add it as a hidden field in our form like this:

```
<input name="client_id"
       type="hidden"
       value="CLIENT_ID(cart)"
       data-amp-replace="CLIENT_ID">
```

The main things to note here are the following:

- `CLIENT_ID(cart)`: The `CLIENT_ID` variable behaves like a function, and we have to pass in an argument as the namespace for the variable. We used `cart` here.
- `data-amp-replace`: This attribute is required for certain variables, including `CLIENT_ID`. Without it, AMP won't perform the required substitution.

If you inspect the DOM in developer tools as you submit the form, you should see that a value has been substituted, and the hidden field will look something like this:

```
<input name="client_id" value="amp-kpuFhUICiKITER7UoMVPOX7rtd0WE-
qHbctOcMBoj_fi3gMXaBN2vNcWlxyasgdh" data-amp-replace="CLIENT_ID"
class="user-valid valid" type="hidden">
```

Note that for this to work, the `amp-analytics` script must be included in the page:

```
<script async custom-element="amp-analytics"
src="https://cdn.ampproject.org/v0/amp-analytics-0.1.js"></script>
```

Building the shopping cart server

Now let's look at the server. When an item is added to the cart, we need to keep track of the total price, as well as the product ID, product name, and price for each product. Once again, the details of how to build an e-commerce backend don't really belong in a book about AMP, so we'll just describe it briefly here (and you can see the code at /ch6/add-to-cart.php, and /ch6/CartFileStorage.php).

On the server, we'll use a simple file-based system to store the carts. Each cart will be identified by the CLIENT_ID. When the add-to-cart form is submitted to the server, the server should do the following:

1. Retrieve the cart from file storage by matching CLIENT_ID.
2. Add the new item to the cart, update the total cost, and save the cart to persistent storage.
3. Send a JSON response with the cart data (items and price).

Then, back on the client, we can parse the JSON response and show that the operation was successful with a summary of the cart. The JSON response from the server will look like this:

```
{
  "cart_total_price": "19.98",
  "cart_items": [
    {
      "product_id": "tshirt-1",
      "product_name": "T-Shirt: Super Pouvoir",
      "image": "img/tshirt-0-f-red-120.png",
      "price": "9.99",
      "quantity": "1"
    },
    {
      "product_id": "tshirt-2",
      "product_name": "T-Shirt: La Biere",
      "image": "img/tshirt-10-f-black-120.png",
      "price": "7.99",
      "quantity": "1"
    },
    ...
  ]
}
```

This is a similar structure to the search response JSON we had earlier, so we can probably use a similar `amp-mustache` template to parse the cart data.

Handling the shopping cart server response

We could use `submit-success` and `amp-mustache` to display an appropriate confirmation or error message as we did earlier. This time, however, we'll show a summary of the cart on successful form submission. We can implement this as a `div` container fixed to the bottom of the viewport.

The basic setup is the same as before. We add the `submit-success` attribute to a container `div`, and we include the mustache template inside this `div`, using `{{cart_total_price}}` to grab the total cart price from the JSON data:

```
<div submit-success class="overlay">
  <template type="amp-mustache">
    <div class="cart-price">Sub-total: €{{cart_total_price}}</div>
    <div id="cart">
      {{#cart_items}}
        ...
      {{/cart_items}}
    </div>
  </template>
</div>
```

Note that we have included `id="cart"` on the `div` parent of the `{{#cart_items}}` mustache tag; we'll be using this later.

We also use `class="overlay"` to style the cart summary using `position: fixed`:

```
.overlay {
  position: fixed;
  bottom: 0;
  left:0;
  background-color: rgba(0,0,0,0.85);
  width: 100%;
  z-index: 9999;
}
```

Next, we use the `{{#}}`...`{{/}}` mustache syntax to iterate over the cart items in the JSON response like this:

```
{{#cart_items}}
<div class="product">
  <span class="cart-thumb">
```

```
      <amp-img src="{{image}}" width="36" height="36" layout="fixed">
      </amp-img>
    </span>
    <div class="cart-item-details">
      <span class="product-name">{{product_name}}</span>
      <div class="cart-item-price">{{quantity}} &times; €{{price}}</div>
    </div>
  </div>
</div>
{{/cart_items}}
```

Using `{{product_name}}`, `{{quantity}}`, and `{{price}}`, we can display all the relevant details for each product in the cart. We can show a small thumbnail too with `<amp-img src="{{image}}" ...>` as a nice visual effect:

Adding an item to the cart with amp-form and submit-success, and displaying the cart contents (/ch6/product-cart.html)

Dismissing the cart summary

We probably don't want the cart summary to take up too much of the screen space unnecessarily, so we should add a way to hide it. Rather than just dismissing it altogether, let's give the user a way to minimize and maximize it. In Chapter 4, *Engaging users with interactive AMP components*, we saw how to show or hide arbitrary HTML elements with the Action and Event model. We can apply the same approach here to give the user a way to show or hide the cart summary.

We'll add show and hide buttons just inside the submit-success container. These will be just like the ones we used to expand and collapse the amp-accordion, also in Chapter 4. We'll also attach some actions to the tap event of the <div class="cart-price" ... > container--this will act like a *tappable* header:

```
<div submit-success class="overlay">
  <span id="btn-hide"></span>
  <span id="btn-show" hidden></span>
  <div class="cart-price"
       on="tap:cart.toggleVisibility,btn-hide.toggleVisibility,
btn-show.toggleVisibility">
    Sub-total: €{{cart_total_price}}
  </div>
</div>
```

The on event handling might look tricky, but it's just three actions that hide or show the cart and buttons as appropriate. When the header is tapped, we do the following:

1. Toggle the cart's visibility: tap:cart.toggleVisibility.
2. Toggle the visibility of the **hide** and **show** buttons: btn-hide.toggleVisibility and btn-show.toggleVisibility.

Note that we also add the `hidden` attribute to the **show** button to ensure it's hidden by default:

Show/hide cart implementation

Redirecting after form submission

Another option after a successful form submission is to redirect the user to a confirmation or success page by adding the `AMP-Redirect-To` header to the server response. This means we could redirect the user to a dedicated cart page after submitting the add-to-cart form. However, once the user is on the cart page, we still need to figure out how to get the cart data from the server without having the user submit a form; again, we'll see how to achieve this in the next chapter.

Summary

We've seen some interesting things in this chapter. We've seen how forms work in AMP and how they can be used to improve the e-commerce experience by adding features such as product search and cart functionality. We're still missing an important part of the puzzle: *checkout* functionality. We'll come back to this in `Chapter 9`, *When AMP is not enough - Enter the iFrame*.

In the meantime, there are other limits to what we have done here. For example, when we add an item to the shopping cart, we might like to display an **Added to cart** message *as well as* update the cart summary. But with `submit-success`, we are limited to just a single container that we can update. Or what if we wanted to show a cart summary on every product page? What we've built so far requires that the user submits a form before we get the data back from the server. In the next chapter, we'll see how we can dynamically load content automatically or based on user interaction, with `amp-list` and `amp-live-list`, so that we can show the cart on every page and remove items from the cart.

7
Dynamic Content and Data-Driven Interaction

In the last chapter, we saw how we could send and receive data to and from a server endpoint using forms. A drawback was that we couldn't fetch any data without user interaction--the user had to submit a form before any data was retrieved. While that model has its uses, it's not suitable for all situations. We couldn't, for example, show the contents of a shopping cart when the user arrived on a page--we'd have to wait for the user to interact with the page first.

In this chapter, we'll see a solution to this issue, so that we can dynamically fetch server data on page load, *or* when triggered by user interaction, using `amp-list`. We'll also explore other use cases for dynamic content and data in AMP pages.

Specifically, we'll cover the following topics:

- Fetching data dynamically with `amp-list`
- Removing items from a shopping cart
- Automatically refreshing dynamic content with `amp-live-list`
- Implementing a live-updating Twitter search
- Implementing a live-updating sports leaderboard

Dynamic content - fetching JSON data on page load

There are many uses cases for being able to retrieve content dynamically. For example, we might want to display a cart summary like we saw in the last chapter. Or on a product page, we might want to pull in a list of related products. On an article page, we might want to pull in a list of comments. AMP provides a very useful tool to help achieve these goals: `amp-list`.

The <amp-list> component

The `amp-list` component can be used to fetch JSON content dynamically from a server endpoint. It's included with the following script:

```
<script async custom-element="amp-list"
src="https://cdn.ampproject.org/v0/amp-list-0.1.js"></script>
```

The server response is expected to contain an array property, with default name `items`:

```
{
  "items": [...]
}
```

Since we're dealing with JSON here, you're probably thinking that we can use `amp-mustache` again, like we did in the last chapter, and you'd be right! So, if we had `name`, `price`, `quantity`, and `image` JSON properties, a simple `amp-list` (and its `mustache` template) could look like this:

```
<amp-list src="https://theampbook.com/ch7/data.json" width="200"
height="400" layout="responsive">
  <template type="amp-mustache">
    {{name}}, {{price}}, {{quantity}}, {{image}}
  </template>
</amp-list>
```

When using `amp-list`, however, the `amp-mustache` template will, by default, look for an array called `items` in the JSON data, and render it. If your JSON has a name other than `items` for the array property, you can specify this by adding the `items` attribute to the `<amp-list>` element, and setting it to the new name:

```
<amp-list src="..." items="my_items" ... >
```

This `amp-list` will now look for an array property called `my_items` instead. If the array is nested, you can specify it by `parent.my_items`.

We can also specify a template by `id`, instead of nesting it as a child element of `amp-list`. In this case, we'd use something like the following, where the template code can be anywhere else in the AMP document body:

```
<amp-list src="..." template="my_template">
  ...
</amp-list>
...
<template type="amp-mustache" id="my_template">
  ...
</template
```

That's the basics out of the way; let's see `amp-list` in action!

Fetching a list of related products with <amp-list>

As its name suggests, `amp-list` is good for processing lists. Let's go back to our product page and add a list of *related products* to the bottom. This is a good fit for `amp-list` because it means we can deliver dynamic content in our AMP pages, even when served via the AMP Cache.

> Additionally, you could personalize `amp-list` content by appending the `CLIENT_ID` parameter that we saw in the last chapter to the `amp-list` URL. This would allow you to differentiate between users and send them different content as needed.

To start with, we'll set up the server to respond with a JSON array of related products like this (full JSON listing at `/ch7/related-products.json`):

```
{
  "items":[
    {
      "product_id":"tshirt-2",
      "name":"T-Shirt: La Bierre",
      "price":"9.99",
      "image":"img/tshirt-10-f-black-320.png",
      "url":"..."
    },
    ...
```

```
    ]
  }
```

This should look familiar--it's similar to the JSON data returned by the server endpoint in our search prototype in the last chapter. This means we should be able to reuse the same markup that we used in the last chapter to display our related items. This should save us some time. (We really are getting great mileage out of this chunk of code!)

 The starting point for the examples in this chapter is /ch7/product-start.html, unless noted otherwise. You can follow along with the examples by adding code to this file.

In the previous chapter, we used {{#results}}...{{/results}} mustache syntax to iterate over our product search results. With amp-list, we don't necessarily need to do this, since amp-list looks out for a JSON property called items by default. So, using the template from the last chapter, we should be able to display the JSON data with something like this:

```
<amp-list src="/ch7/related-products.json.php">
  <template type="mustache">
    <figure class="related-thumb">
      <amp-img src="{{image}}" width="60" height="60"
layout="responsive"></amp-img>
      <figcaption>
        <span class="title">{{name}}</span>
        <span class="price">{{price}}</span>
        <span class="description">{{description}}</span>
      </figcaption>
    </figure>
  </template>
</amp-list>
```

 Note that amp-list makes a CORS request, so the appropriate CORS headers must be set in the response, as outlined in the last chapter, or the request will fail. In this example we use related-products.json.php so that we can set the correct headers via PHP.

This code should work fine; we'd still need to style it, but it should work as expected. However, the observant reader might notice that in the previous chapter, each item in the search results template used an <li> tag, and the whole list was inside a <ul> tag like this:

```
<template type="amp-mustache">
  <ul class="related-items">
    {{#results}}
      <li>
```

```
                <figure class="related-thumb"> ...</figure>
            </li>
        {{/results}}
    </ul>
    ...
</template>
```

So why didn't we reuse this template? It's to do with the markup that `amp-list` generates for the list.

Using list tags <ul> and <li> with <amp-list>

While `amp-list` is a powerful component, there's a small drawback to using it out-of-the-box: you can't control the list container markup. By default, `amp-list` will wrap the whole list with a `div` container like this:

```
<div role="list">
...
</div>
```

Then, for each item in the list, it will apply the content of your template, adding `role="list-item"`. This will be fine in many circumstances. But if you really want to use `<ul>` or `<ol>` and `<li>` lists, then you're stuck. You could add `<li>` to your template, but there's no way to give the list an `<ol>` or `<ul>` parent.

There is a workaround, however. We can modify the server JSON response so that now `items` will be a single element array, and its only element will be another array which contains the list of items, let's call it `results` (full JSON at `/ch7/related-products-results.json`):

```
{
  "items":[
    {
      "results":[
        {
          "product_id":"tshirt-1",
          "name":"T-Shirt: La Bierre",
          "price":"€9.99",
          "description":"French running T-Shirt, with beer graphic",
          "image":"img/tshirt-10-f-black-320.png",
          "url":"..."
        },
        ...
      ]
    }
```

```
    ]
  }
```

Then, `amp-list` will render the single item array using the template, and in the template, we can manually add mustache tags to iterate over the `results` property. Now we can reuse the template from the last chapter (`/ch7/related-products.html`):

```html
<ul class="related-items">
  {{#results}}
  <li>
    <a href="{{url}}">
      <figure class="related-thumb">
        <amp-img src="{{image}}" width="60" height="60"
layout="responsive"></amp-img>
        <figcaption>
          <span class="title">{{name}}</span>
          <span class="price">{{price}}</span>
          <span class="description">{{description}}</span>
        </figcaption>
      </figure>
    </a>
  </li>
  {{/results}}
</ul>
```

Related products implementation, showing responsive layouts on different viewport sizes (/ch7/related-products.html)

Don't forget the CSS styles from the last chapter too, or the layout won't work!

So, in using `amp-list`, we have a trade-off between using its out-of-the-box functionality and being stuck with its markup, or, with a little bit more work to render the JSON data, having full control of the markup and being able to use HTML list tags (`<ul>`, `<ol>`, and `<li>`) to display our list. In our prototype, we went with the latter so that we could reuse the markup and styles that we developed in earlier chapters in the book.

A note on <amp-list> container size

The size of an `amp-list` must be specified in advance. This might cause an issue when you don't know how much JSON data will be returned from a server endpoint. The AMP documentation recommends to give enough space for at least one item. AMP will then try to assign more space as needed. If the `amp-list` is near the bottom of the page, then it will usually be able to assign more space.

You can also include an `overflow` element that will be displayed in the event that AMP can't assign more space automatically with markup like this:

```
<div overflow role="button" aria-label="Show more" class="list-overflow">
  Show more
</div>
```

Fetching the shopping cart on page load

We just saw how to use `amp-list` to pull in a list of related products on a web page. Now let's try something a bit different. In the last chapter, we implemented a basic shopping cart: when an item was added to the cart, we displayed a summary of the cart contents after receiving a response from the server backend. A problem with this approach was that we couldn't show the cart summary on page load; we had to wait for the user to add an item and submit a form first. So if the user navigated to another page, for example, the cart summary would no longer be visible. We can fix this with `amp-list`.

We'll set it up so that on page load, `amp-list` will fetch the shopping cart, using the `CLIENT_ID` variable substitution we saw in the last chapter to identify the user.

First, we'll set up a server endpoint to return the same JSON data that represents the cart as before. Well, almost the same; we've added a new property, `cart_total_items`, that we'll display in the summary, and we've wrapped the entire JSON payload in a single-item array called `cart`:

```
{
  "cart": [
    {
      "cart_total_price":19.98,
      "cart_total_items":2,
      "cart_items":[
        {
          "product_id":"tshirt-1",
          "product_name":"T-Shirt: Super Pouvoir",
          "price":"9.99",
          "quantity":2,
          "image":"img/tshirt-0-f-red-120.png"
        },
        ...
      ]
    }
  ]
}
```

To build the `amp-list`, we need to point it at the endpoint, `/ch7/cart.php`, that returns this JSON data:

```
<amp-list src="/ch7/cart.php?client_id=CLIENT_ID(cart)"
    height="1" width="auto" layout="fixed-height"
    items="cart" template="cart_summary_template">
</amp-list>
```

There are a few things to note here:

- We've appended `client_id=CLIENT_ID(cart)` just as we did in the last chapter, to make sure that we get the correct cart for the user.
- Since we have included `items="cart"`, amp-list will look for a property called `cart` in the JSON data, instead of the default `items` property.
- We've given a `height` of 1 to the `amp-list`. This is because we'll display the cart summary as a fixed position `div` at the bottom of the viewport with CSS, as in the last chapter.
- We also specify the template to use as `template_cart_summary`, rather than nesting it inside the `amp-list` element. This is important because it allows us to decouple the template from the `amp-list`.

Showing the cart contents with `<amp-mustache>`

Now that we have an `amp-list` to fetch the JSON data that represents the cart contents, we need to write the mustache template next. In the last chapter we used an `amp-mustache` template in the `amp-form submit-success` container to handle the response from the server when we added an item to the cart. It would be great if we could use this template again.

Since we built the cart server endpoint to return JSON data similar to when adding a product, that is, the cart contents, then we should be able to re-use the add-to-cart template. So, how can we share the template between the `amp-list` and the `amp-form`?

Sharing a mustache template between `<amp-list>` and `<amp-form>`

Conveniently, we already have the solution. In the `amp-list` we just built, we included the attribute `template="cart_summary_template"`. Now we can place a mustache template with `id="cart_summary_template"` anywhere in the page, and `amp-list` will populate this template with the JSON data it retrieves. Since we already have a template in the `amp-form submit-success` container, and this template works with similar JSON data, if we set the ID of this template to match the `amp-list` template ID, that is, `cart_summary_template`, then the `amp-list` should be able use it.

Note that we're faced with the same issue as earlier in this chapter: if we use the default `amp-list` behavior then it will look for the `items` array and output it. This would be fine for many applications, but here we also need to get the `cart_total_price` and `cart_total_items` properties from the JSON data and display those too.

This is why we modified the server response earlier so that the JSON data was returned as a single item array. The `amp-list` will fetch the JSON array and parse the single item (this time called `cart`). Recall from earlier, the `cart` JSON array looks like this:

```
{
 "cart": [
  {
   "cart_total_price":19.98,
   "cart_total_items":2,
   "cart_items":[...]
  }
 ]
}
```

So, `amp-list` will pass the contents of `cart` to the mustache template, where we can access the data with the curly-braces syntax, `{{cart_total_items}}` and `{{cart_total_price}}`, and we can iterate over the items with `{{#cart_items}}`...`{{/cart_items}}` like we did before:

```
<template type="amp-mustache" id="cart_summary_template">
    <div class="overlay" id="cart_summary">
        <span id="btn-hide" ></span> <span id="btn-show" hidden></span>
        <span class="item-count">{{cart_total_items}} items</span>
        Sub-total: €{{cart_total_price}}
        <div id="cart">
            {{#cart_items}}
                <div class="product">
                    <span class="cart-thumb">
                        <amp-img src="{{image}}" width="36" height="36"
layout="fixed"></amp-img>
                    </span>
                    <div class="cart-item-details">
                        <span class="product-name">{{product_name}}</span>
                        <div class="cart-item-price">{{quantity}} &times;
€{{price}}</div>
                    </div>
                </div>
            {{/cart_items}}
        </div>
    </div>
</template>
```

There is one *quirk* we need to address, now that the template is being shared between `amp-list` and `amp-form`. When an item is added and the form is submitted, we have to explicitly hide the cart summary, or the `submit-success` template won't show the updated cart. We can achieve this with the `submit` event of `amp-form`:

```
<form method="post" action-xhr="/ch7/add-to-cart.php" target="_top"
      on="submit:cart_summary.hide">
```

We'll also need to include both the `amp-list` and the `amp-mustache` components, of course:

```
<script async custom-element="amp-list"
src="https://cdn.ampproject.org/v0/amp-list-0.1.js"></script>
<script async custom-template="amp-mustache"
src="https://cdn.ampproject.org/v0/amp-mustache-0.1.js"></script>
```

The full code for this example is at /ch7/product-cart.html, and is illustrated in the following image:

Shopping cart shown on page load with amp-list (left), and then updated via submit-success template after adding an item (right)

In this figure, on the left, we can see the amp-list cart summary that was fetched and displayed on page load; there are already two products in the cart. Then, on the right, an item has been added with the **ADD TO CART** button, and the template is updated via the submit-success container, resulting in a seamless cart summary for the user.

Removing items from the cart

Adding items to the cart is all well and good, but we'll need a way to remove items too. To achieve this we'll exploit the fact that amp-list fetches the cart contents when our product page loads. If we can append the product ID of an item to be removed from the cart to the amp-list URL, then the server can remove the item, and then return the cart contents as normal.

Let's set up a **Remove item** link next to each item in the cart. Each link will contain the product_id for its product. It could look something like the following, using amp-mustache to output the product_id as part of the href link:

```
<a href="?del={{product_id}}">Remove item</a>
```

So that we can style it better, the actual code we'll use is this:

```
<div class="cart-del"><a href="?del={{product_id}}">&times;</a></div>
```

When this link is clicked, the page will reload, but with ?del=some_product_id appended to the URL, like this:

```
https://theampbook.com/ch7/product.html?del=tshirt-1
```

Next, when the page reloads, we want to grab the product_id from the del parameter in the page URL, and append it to the amp-list URL.

Retrieving URL parameters with AMP's variable substitution

To obtain the product_id, we'll make use of AMP's variable substitution functionality again (we saw this in Chapter 6, *Making Contact Forms in AMP*). This time, we use QUERY_PARAM(del). When the AMP runtime encounters this, it will substitute in the value of the del parameter from the URL, which happens to be the product_id that we want to remove from the cart.

Then we'll want to get this value to the server. To do this, we'll append it to the amp-list URL like this:

```
<amp-list
src="/ch7/cart.php?client_id=CLIENT_ID(cart)&del=QUERY_PARAM(del)" ...>
```

All the work needed on the AMP side is done, so now we need to set up the server. If the `del` parameter is detected by the server, then any item in the cart with matching `product_id` will be removed, and the updated cart data will be returned.

If the `del` parameter is not present, then the server will simply return the cart data without modification, as normal. We won't go into the server code here, but it needs to return JSON in the same format as earlier. You can see the server prototype code at `/ch7/cart.php`.

The result (`/ch7/product.html`) is shown in the following image, which illustrates an item being removed from the cart:

Removing an item from the shopping cart by appending product_id to amp-list URL (/ch7/product.html)

Note that the server is also recalculating the price and the number of items in the cart whenever an item is removed.

Our cart is getting better: we can now add *and* remove items. If there is a criticism of the remove functionality, it would be that we have to perform a full page reload for it to work. This is perfectly fine; if you check out Amazon or eBay, this is what they do. But just because they do it doesn't mean we can't do it better! In the next chapter, we'll see how to do this as an XHR request, without requiring a whole page reload.

Live content updates with <amp-live-list>

Another component for updating content dynamically is amp-live-list. Despite its similar name, it functions quite differently to amp-list. The main differences are as follows:

- amp-live-list polls the source URL for new content at defined intervals, while amp-list performs a single fetch from a specified server endpoint
- amp-live-list works with AMP-HTML pages, while amp-list deals with JSON data

Target use cases for amp-live-list include live blogs, breaking-news feeds, or any kind of live data that updates at intervals, such as sports scoreboards.

Note that amp-live-list will request updates from the URL it was visited on. So if the page is served via the AMP Cache, then amp-live-list will request updates from the AMP Cache URL. In practice, this can mean slower updates than if being updated from the original URL, depending on how frequently the AMP Cache refreshes from your original page, and that depends at least in part on the caching headers your server sends.

Using <amp-live-list>

The amp-live-list component is included with the following script:

```
<script async custom-element="amp-live-list"
src="https://cdn.ampproject.org/v0/amp-live-list-0.1.js"></script>
```

The basic usage of `amp-live-list` is like this:

```
<amp-live-list id="my-amp-live-list" data-poll-interval="15000" data-max-
items-per-page="20">
  <button update on="tap:my-amp-live-list.update">Load more!</button>
  <div id="items">
    <div id="item-0">...</div>
    <div id="item-1">...</div>
    ...
  </div>
</amp-live-list>
```

The `amp-live-list` element must include the following:

- **An ID:** Multiple `amp-live-lists` can appear in a page, so they need to be individually identifiable
- **A child element with attribute** `update`**:** When there is new data, this element will be displayed so that the user can tap it to update the data (the actual button with the `on="tap..."` event can be a descendant of this element; the action doesn't have to be attached to the element with the `update` attribute)
- **A child element with id** `items`**:** The children of this element will be the items in the list

The following attributes are optional:

- `data-poll-interval`**:** Sets the polling frequency in milliseconds. The highest frequency (that is, the smallest value allowed) is 15 seconds (15,000 ms).
- `data-max-items-per-page`**:** Sets the max items per page. When this number is reached, the oldest items will be removed.

Each item within the `items` container (`<div id="items" ...>`) can have the following attributes:

- `id` (*required*): Each item needs to be individually identifiable.
- `data-sort-time` (*required*): This is used to insert items into the DOM. Items with a higher numeric value are considered newer and inserted before/above items with lower `data-sort-time`.
- `data-update-time` (*optional*): If this attribute is present on an item, and if it's greater than the last updated time, then the content of the item will be updated with the new data.

When the AMP runtime discovers new content (any direct child of `div#items` with a new `id`), it will display the update button, and the new content will be filtered and inserted into the DOM of the page as appropriate.

Items can also be updated or replaced in place, *without* requiring a user to press a button to perform the update. This is achieved by adding the `data-update-time` attribute.

Lastly, any particular item can be removed altogether by adding the appropriately named attribute `data-tombstone`. If `amp-live-list` sees that the server has added this attribute to an item, it will remove that item from the page.

 The starting point for the remaining examples in this chapter is `/ch7/amp-live-list-start.html`. To follow along with the examples you can add code to this file.

A simple <amp-live-list> example

Let's start with a simple example with the following code (full code at `/ch7/amp-live-list-example.html`):

```
<amp-live-list id="my-live-list" data-poll-interval="20000" data-max-items-per-page="10">
  <button update on="tap:my-live-list.update">
    Show latest updates!
  </button>
  <div items>
    <div id="item-1" data-sort-time="1">Item #1</div>
    <div id="item-2" data-sort-time="2">Item #2</div>
    <!-- <div id="item-3" data-sort-time="3">Item #3</div> -->
    <!-- <div id="item-4" data-sort-time="1">Item #4</div> -->
    <!-- <div id="item-4" data-sort-time="1"
                        data-update-time="6">Item #4 update!</div> -->
    <!-- <div id="item-1" data-sort-time="1" data-tombstone>Item #1</div> -->
  </div>
</amp-live-list>
```

Here, we have two items with simple integer timestamps, and four commented items. To give you a feel for how `amp-live-list` works, we'll simulate updates on the server by manually uncommenting items between `amp-live-list` polls.

You don't need to use milliseconds for your timestamps with `amp-live-list`; any sequence of numbers will work so long as more recent items have a higher number. Here, we used integers between `1` and `6`.

On initial page load, the markup will be rendered as it is ordered in the previous markup, that is, `item-1` and `item-2` will not be reordered even though `item-1` has a higher (more recent) timestamp.

Now uncomment `item-3` and save--but **don't** reload in the browser; the browser will silently poll the server in the background. After 20 seconds or so, you should see the **SHOW NEW UPDATES!** button appear. Before you tap it, have a think about where in the page `item-3` might be inserted. OK, now tap it!

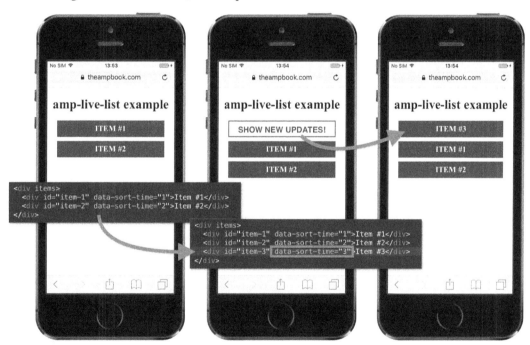

amp-live-list example: a new item with highest data-sort-time is inserted at top of the list

Did you get it right? Since `item-3` has the highest timestamp so far, it's inserted at the top of the list.

Now uncomment `item-4` and save the file, and again, **don't** reload in the browser; just wait for `amp-live-list` to notice the change. When the update button appears, tap it. This time, we have `data-sort-time="1"`, so where will this one be inserted?

Since it has the (joint) lowest sort time of 1, you might expect it to be inserted at the bottom, below `item-2` which has a higher value of 2. However, items will be inserted above any item with the same sort time, and `item-1` has the same sort time as `item-4`, so `item-4` is inserted above `item-1`.

Now uncomment the next line. This also has `id="item-4"` but, this time, it has attribute `data-update-time="6"`. If this attribute is present and if the `id` exists, then the element will be updated in place automatically, without needing user interaction, so we should see `item-4` update without the update button appearing:

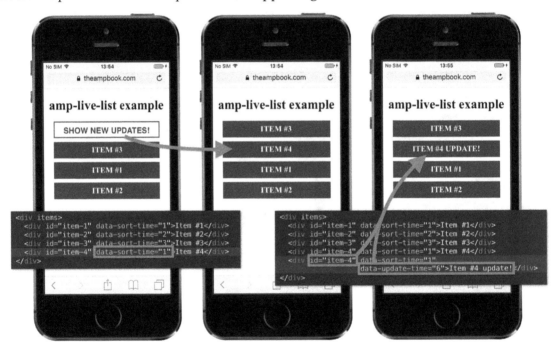

On tapping update button (left) a new item is inserted into list (middle). An automatic update occurs via data-update-time (right)

Finally, uncomment the last line. This has `id="item-1"` and also has the `data-tombstone` attribute. When `amp-live-list` sees this attribute on an item, it removes the item from the page, so we should see `item-1` disappear after a few seconds. Once again, this update will happen automatically without user interaction:

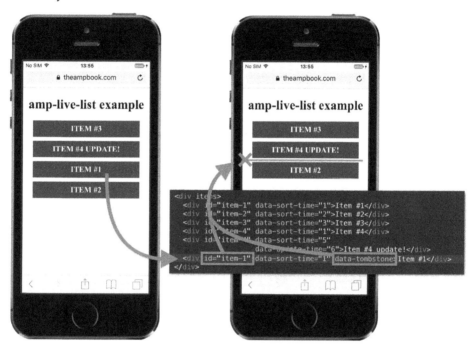

An item (ITEM #1) is removed from the list by adding the data-tombstone attribute

It can also be useful to illustrate how `amp-live-list` works by opening up the network tab of your browser developer tools. You should be able to see periodic XHR fetches to the same URL as `amp-live-list` polls for new data. Note that it keeps track of the last update time with the `amp_latest_update_time` parameter in the URL:

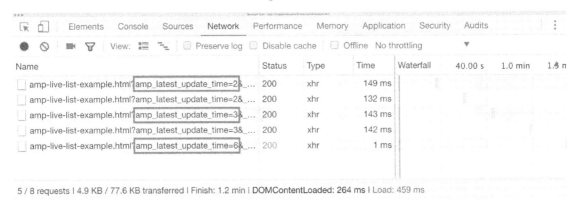

Network panel of Chrome developer tools shows amp-live-list polling the page for updates

A live Twitter search listing

As a slightly more practical example, let's build a simple Twitter search page that could be used to show updates for a particular hashtag or search term.

Since we're dealing with dynamic content, this is going to need some server-side processing. It will work like this:

1. The server will perform a search via the Twitter API.
2. The set of tweet statuses returned by the API will be output as `amp-live-list` child items, with the unique tweet ID used as the `id` of the `amp-live-list` items, and the tweet time used as the `data-sort-time`.
3. The `amp-live-list` component will then poll the server from the client's browser at 15-second intervals. This will cause the server to search via the Twitter API again, and build the AMP page again. The browser basically fetches this page in the background, but doesn't render it.
4. If `amp-live-list` detects any new tweets in the latest response from the server, the update button will be shown.
5. When the update button is tapped, any new item will be inserted into the DOM in the appropriate place based on the `data-sort-time` attribute.

We only really need to build the page and implement steps 1 and 2, and `amp-live-list` will do the rest. We'll hardcode the search term first, and then look at options for providing a search form (it's complicated slightly when the AMP is cache considered--we'll see why shortly).

We'll use a Twitter API library to perform the search and retrieve the tweets. Once we have the tweets, we'll use the `amp-twitter` custom element to display the tweet in the page. So each item in the `amp-live-list` will contain an `amp-twitter` element.

First, we'll set up the `amp-live-list` like this (`/ch7/amp-live-list-twitter.php`):

```
<amp-live-list id="tweet-list" data-poll-interval="15000" data-max-items-
per-page="10">
  <button update on="tap:tweet-list.update">Load new tweets</button>
  <div items>
  ...
  </div>
</amp-live-list>
```

Then the server will build the list of tweet items that looks like this:

```
<div items>
  <div id="898280450350751744" data-sort-time="1498046355">
    <amp-twitter width="640" height="480" layout="responsive"
              data-tweetid="898280450350751744">
    </amp-twitter>
  </div>
  ...
</div>
```

So far, so good! This works. So what about adding a form so the user can choose the search term?

Adding a search form to use with <amp-live-list>

The quickest way to add a form is like this (don't forget to include the `amp-form` extension script):

```
<form action="amp-live-list-twitter.php" method="get">
  Search twitter for: <input type="text" name="q">
  <input type="submit" value="Search">
</form>
```

Then the server just needs to parse the q request parameter, and pass it along to the Twitter API:

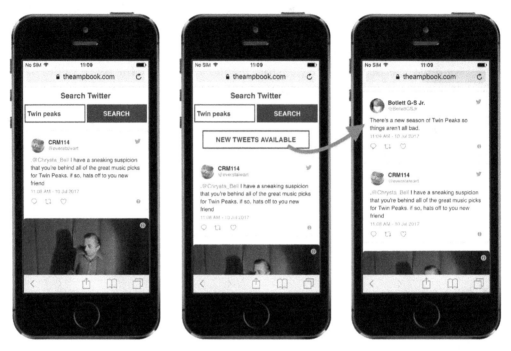

Twitter search with amp-live-list: initial search (left), update button appears for new content (middle), and newly inserted content (right)

And we're done! Or are we? Things can get a little complicated when the page is served from the AMP Cache.

Why is it more complicated with the AMP Cache?

When dealing with any dynamic content in AMP, it's always useful to consider how a page will work with the AMP Cache. Although most valid pages will work fine whether served from the cache or the original server, you should always test on both. This is particularly true for amp-live-list.

So what happens when an amp-live-list page is served from the AMP Cache? When the AMP Cache adds a server-generated page, it caches the result of what the server generated-- the AMP Cache can't generate any new pages. So when amp-live-list makes a request back to the AMP Cache, it has to go back to the original server for updates when the caching schedule permits. This means that it will get updates, but it might not be as quick as going directly to the original server.

There's another issue: AMP form action URLs can't point to the AMP Cache. So when a search keyword is submitted, the user is redirected to the original URL. This will work, and is a perfectly acceptable pattern, and the updates will probably be faster this way anyway. So, is there any way to get this to work with the AMP Cache? There are a few options:

- **Creating an index of prepared search links:** You can set up some predefined searches on an index page, for example,
  ```
  <a href="amp-twitter-search.php?q=brexit">Search for brexit tweets</a>,
  <a href="amp-twitter-search.php?q=amphtml">Search for amphtml tweets</a>,
  ```
  and so on.
  This would remove the form, but obviously restricts functionality. However, it could be fine for following hashtags or specific events, for example.

- **Using** `amp-bind` **to simulate a form:** You could simulate a form submission using `amp-bind` to modify the `href` of a **submit** link. This setup might look something like this:
  ```
  Search Twitter: <input type="text" name="searchterm"
  on="change:AMP.setState({searchterm: event.value})">
  <a href="searchpage.htm?q=brexit"
  [href]="'searchpage.htm?q='.searchterm">Submit</a>
  ```
  We'll look at `amp-bind` in detail in the next chapter.

- **Using the** `AMP-Redirect-To` **header:** A final option is to set up an `action-xhr` endpoint that the form submits to, and which redirects back, using the `AMP-Redirect-To` header, to the AMP Cache URL with the query appended.

It's hard to see the advantage of keeping this search on the AMP Cache. Since the data is dynamic, the cache will need to make requests to the origin server anyway for updates. But, because of the caching rules, it may be slower to update than serving directly from the original server. However, it may scale better than running it directly from your own server. If you need to do this, at least you know there are some options.

Implementing a live leaderboard

Another nice feature of `amp-live-list` is that updates can be applied automatically, without the need to click or tap a button. This is very useful for live-updating of scores that you might find in sport, such as football scores, or leaderboard style rankings that you would find in racing and election results.

Let's implement a live Grand Prix position leaderboard. To get the list items to update without having to press the update button, we need to make sure that we do the following:

- Don't change any item IDs after initial load: If you introduce new IDs, then the update button will be displayed.
- Include the `data-update-time` attribute: If the latest server update contains a value higher than the current value in the DOM for any item, then `amp-live-list` will replace the item with the new content.

 Note that `amp-live-list` won't re-sort already rendered items, even if you change the `data-sort-time`; `data-sort-time` is only used for new insertions.

On the initial page load, the source code might look like this, with the world's greatest F1 drivers listed (`/ch7/amp-live-list-leaderboard.php`):

```
<amp-live-list id="leaderboard" data-poll-interval="20000" data-max-items-
per-page="10">
  <div update on="tap:leaderboard.update"></div>
  <div items>
    <div id="item-1" data-sort-time="1" data-update-time="1">1. Sebastian
Vettel</div>
    <div id="item-2" data-sort-time="2" data-update-time="1">2. Esteban
Ocon</div>
    <div id="item-3" data-sort-time="3" data-update-time="1">3. Lewis
Hamilton</div>
    <div id="item-4" data-sort-time="4" data-update-time="1">4. Kimi
Räikkönen</div>
    <div id="item-5" data-sort-time="5" data-update-time="1">5. Ruadhan
O'Donoghue</div>
    <div id="item-6" data-sort-time="6" data-update-time="1"></div>
  </div>
</amp-live-list>
```

Note that we've included the `<div update...>` element with empty text because we don't ever intend to use the update button--the desired behavior is that the leaderboard positions are updated in place, without requiring the user to manually trigger the update. It's mandatory to include an update element, however, so we have to include it even if we don't intend to use it.

On the second iteration, the `amp-live-list` makes an XHR request to the original URL:

```
https://theampbook.com/ch7/amp-live-list-
leaderboard.php?amp_latest_update_time=1&__amp_source_origin=https%3A%2F%2F
theampbook.com
```

Note the `amp_latest_update_time=1` parameter. The server might respond with a partial reordering like the following (remember, `amp-live-list` is fetching the page in the background, but not rendering it; rather, it looks for differences to what is currently rendered):

```
<div items>
  <div id="item-1" data-sort-time="1" data-update-time="1">1. Sebastian
Vettel</div>
  <div id="item-2" data-sort-time="2" data-update-time="1">2. Esteban
Ocon</div>
  <div id="item-3" data-sort-time="3" data-update-time="1">3. Lewis
Hamilton</div>
  <div id="item-4" data-sort-time="4" data-update-time="2">4. Ruadhan
O'Donoghue</div>
  <div id="item-5" data-sort-time="5" data-update-time="2">5. Kimi
Räikkönen</div>
  <div id="item-6" data-update-time="1"></div>
  </div>
```

On the client, since `item-4` and `item-5` now have a `data-update-time` of 2, which is higher than 1, which was the last update time, and since these item IDs are already in the DOM, `amp-live-list` will now update these items with the new content, and the driver's positions are updated.

The next iteration might look like this:

```
<div items>
  <div id="item-1" data-sort-time="1" data-update-time="3">1. Ruadhan
O'Donoghue</div>
  <div id="item-2" data-sort-time="2" data-update-time="3">2. Sebastian
Vettel</div>
  <div id="item-3" data-sort-time="3" data-update-time="3">3. Esteban
Ocon</div>
  <div id="item-4" data-sort-time="4" data-update-time="3">4. Lewis
```

```
Hamilton</div>
  <div id="item-5" data-sort-time="5" data-update-time="2">5. Kimi
Räikkönen</div>
  <div id="item-6" data-sort-time="6" data-update-time="3"> FINAL
RESULT</div>
  </div>
```

In this case, the first four items would be updated, and the last item would remain untouched:

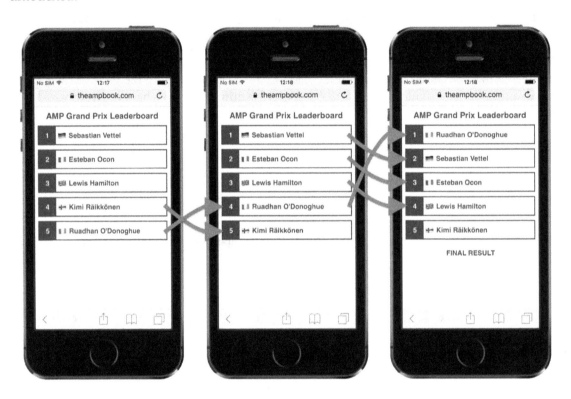

A Grand Prix leaderboard implemented with amp-live-list. Updates happen automatically (/ch7/amp-live-list-leaderboard.php)

Once again, there is server-side work to be done here. In this case, this could be someone manually updating a file or database that the server script reads. For the purposes of having a working demonstration, you can find an implementation that automatically updates the positions after a number of requests by the client in the source code for this chapter at `/ch7/amp-live-list-leaderboard.php`.

Summary

In this chapter, we covered a lot of ground. We saw how to dynamically fetch and update content in a number of different ways, both automatically, on page load, or by user-triggered actions. With `amp-list`, we were able to show the contents of a shopping cart without requiring the user to trigger its display. It also gave us a mechanism to delete items from the cart. With `amp-live-list`, we were able to build automatically-updating pages that polled the server for updates, and inserted new items into the page depending on the update time.

In the next chapter, we'll further improve the e-commerce experience by looking at a very special AMP component: `amp-bind`. The `amp-bind` component gives us a basic programming layer for AMP pages so that we can build even better, more interactive, and user-friendly pages.

8
Programming in AMP - amp-bind

In this chapter, we'll explore `amp-bind`, a programming layer for AMP. This will allow us to enhance our e-commerce experience and create even richer and more dynamic pages that would otherwise not be possible in AMP. Specifically, we'll look at the following topics:

- How to get started with `amp-bind`
- Improving the shopping cart so that we can remove items without a full page reload
- Adding filtering, sorting, and autosuggest to the product search form
- Improving the product carousel
- Two different approaches to dynamically configuring product options, and adding them to the cart

Introducing <amp-bind>

We've mentioned `amp-bind` a few times in the previous chapters; now it's time to see it in action. The `amp-bind` component makes it possible to program custom interactivity into your pages. You can think of it as a programming layer for your AMP pages, sort of a JavaScript-*lite*.

You can add `amp-bind` to your pages with the following script:

```
<script async custom-element="amp-bind"
src="https://cdn.ampproject.org/v0/amp-bind-0.1.js"></script>
```

State, expressions, and data-binding

There are three parts to `amp-bind`: stateful data, expressions, and data-binding. With `amp-bind`, element properties can be linked to custom JavaScript-like expressions which can reference custom state variables. This needs some explanation, so let's expand on it now.

Stateful data in <amp-bind> with <amp-state>

The `amp-bind` component introduces the notion of document *state*. You can think of this as mutable JSON variable storage.

Initializing state with <amp-state>

By default, the document state is empty, but we can add custom data with the `amp-state` component (`amp-state` is included with `amp-bind`). For example, we could set a state property for a customer's username like this:

```
<amp-state id="user">
  <script type="application/json">
    {
      "username": "ruadhan"
    }
  </script>
</amp-state>
```

Note the `id` of the `amp-state` element. This would result in the following state:

```
{
  user: {
    username: "ruadhan"
  }
}
```

Whenever we create a state using the `amp-state` element, we access data within the state using the `id` of the element with dot or bracket syntax. So, `user.username` (or `user[username]`), in this case, would evaluate to `ruadhan`.

A neat thing about `amp-state` is that it can be fetched from a server endpoint; you don't need to hardcode it directly in the AMP page. So we could retrieve data about a returning visitor with something like this:

```
<amp-state id="user" src="/ch8/user.json?client_id=CLIENT_ID(user)">
</amp-state>
```

Since the document state in `amp-bind` is JSON based, it can include nested JSON data, for example:

```
<amp-state id="user">
  <script type="application/json">
    {
      "username": "ruadhan",
      "address": {
        "street": "18 Camden Street Lower",
        "city": "Dublin",
        "country": "Ireland"
      }
    }
  </script>
</amp-state>
```

Updating state with AMP.setState()

We can set and update state properties with the `AMP.setState()` action. To set a property `username`, we could use the following:

```
AMP.setState({username: 'eadaoin'})
```

If the `username` property doesn't already exist, then it will be created and set to value `eadaoin`, and the state will be as follows:

```
{
  username: 'eadaoin'
}
```

Note that this is subtly different to the state when initialized with the `amp-state` element. When initialized with `amp-state`, the state will always be nested inside a property with name corresponding to the `id` of the `amp-state` element. In our earlier example, the `id` was `user`, and it resulted in this state:

```
{
  user: {
    username: "ruadhan",
    address: {
      ...
    }
  }
}
```

Thus, to update the `username` in the previous state, we would have to reference it via its parent like this:

```
AMP.setState({user: {username: 'eadaoin'}})
```

If we wanted to merge a new property called `firstname` into this state, we'd use the following:

```
AMP.setState({user: {firstname: 'Eadaoin'}})
```

And the state would then be as follows:

```
{
  user: {
    firstname: "Eadaoin"
    username: "eadaoin",
    address: {
      ...
    }
  }
}
```

`AMP.setState()` can also set more deeply nested JSON data. For example, we could use the following to set the country property:

```
AMP.setState({user:{address:{country:'Ireland'}}})
```

Conveniently, this can be written over multiple lines to help with code clarity:

```
AMP.setState(
  {
    user: {
      address: {
        country: "Ireland"
      }
    }
  })
```

Debugging state with AMP.printState()

You can output the current state to the developer console at any time. This can be useful in debugging an AMP page. To do this, type `AMP.printState()` into the developer console when in development mode (that is, with `#development=1` appended to the page URL):

Displaying AMP state in the browser developer console with AMP.printState()

Expressions in <amp-bind>

With `amp-bind`, we can execute JavaScript-like expressions from a set of whitelisted JavaScript functions that includes `Array`, `String`, and `Math` based operations. You can see a full list of whitelisted functions in Appendix C, or online at `ampproject.org/docs/reference/components/amp-bind#white-listed-functions`.

Expressions can access any state data in the document. To use a state property in an expression, just include the property name in the expression. Some example expressions are given as follows.

Text manipulation expression

A simple text concatenation could be performed with the following:

```
'Hello ' + user.username
```

This would evaluate to `Hello eadaoin`.

Arithmetic expression

We could increment a counter with an expression like this:

```
AMP.setState({counter: counter+1})
```

Branching if...else expression

We can implement a basic `if...else` expression like this:

```
(currentImage==0 ? 'show' : 'hide')
```

You will probably recognize this expression syntax--it's shorthand for `if...else` in a number of programming languages. It says "if `currentImage` equals 0 then evaluate to string `show`, otherwise evaluate to `hide`". This is a useful pattern for showing or hiding elements based on a state property.

For performance reasons, there are limitations to what is possible with `amp-bind` expressions; these include the following:

- No access to JavaScript globals such as `window` or `document`
- No custom functions or classes
- No `for` loops

Data-binding: linking expressions to element state

The final part of `amp-bind` is data-binding. This allows us to link expressions to the state of HTML and AMP-HTML elements in an AMP page. When the expression evaluates and produces a new value, then the state of any element to which it is bound is updated.

Data-bindings are made to element state with square bracket syntax on the attribute or property that is being bound, like this:

```
<element [property]="expression" ...>
```

There are four types of element state that expressions can be bound to:

- Text nodes: `[text]`
- CSS classes: `[class]`
- Element size attributes: `[width]`, `[height]`
- Whitelisted element attributes: `[attr]`, for example `[src]` for `amp-img`, and `[slide]` for `amp-carousel` elements (see Appendix D for a full list of these attributes, or online at `ampproject.org/docs/reference/components/amp-bind#element-specific-attributes`)

Using <amp-bind>

The `amp-bind` component is very powerful, so we'll start with a simple example: changing some text when a button is tapped. Then we'll see how to change CSS styles using `amp-bind`. After that, we'll build more complex examples: we'll combine `amp-list` and `amp-bind` so that we can remove items from the shopping cart without a page reload.

After that, we'll see how `amp-bind` can be used to configure options for products.

 The starting point for the first two examples in this chapter is `/ch8/amp-bind-start.html`. You can follow along with the examples by adding code to this file.

Changing text with <amp-bind>

In this example, we'll see how to change paragraph text by pressing a button. First, we'll use a paragraph element <p> with some default text:

```
<p>Hello World</p>
```

Next, we'll bind the text node of the p element to a simple expression:

```
<p [text]="'Hello '+username">Hello World</p>
```

The expression here is a string concatenation: `'Hello '+username`. The binding is created with `[text]=....`

Now let's add the button. We'll use the `tap` event to change the state with `AMP.setState()`:

```
<button on="tap:AMP.setState({username: 'ruadhan'})">Say hello</button>
```

Text replacement example with amp-bind (/ch8/amp-bind.html)

When the button is tapped, the state property `username` is set to `ruadhan`. Since the AMP state has changed, any bound expressions are evaluated. So `'Hello '+username` is now evaluated, and results in the string `Hello ruadhan`. This expression is bound to the text node of the `p` element, which is now updated, and results in the following:

```
<p>Hello ruadhan</p>
```

Setting default values for AMP state properties

If you happened to check the last example while in AMP development mode (`#development=1` appended to URL), you might have noticed an error similar to that shown in the following image (the error message will also appear in the browser developer console):

amp-bind "default value for ... does not match first expression result" error

This error is basically complaining about not having default values set for AMP state properties. You can define default values for your state properties with `amp-state`, but it's not required. However, if you have a property that's not initialized before it's used, then you'll see this error message.

To avoid this message, you can use this syntax: `(propertyName||'defaultValue')`. This will use the value `defaultValue` if `propertyName` does not have a value already. So to fix the preceding error in our example, we could change the `amp-bind` expression to the following instead:

```
<p [text]="'Hello '+(username||'World')">Hello World</p>
```

However, if you have a lot of properties, then your code can get a little messy since you'll have to use this syntax whenever you use any property. So, the recommended approach is to use <amp-state> to give default values to your state properties. So we could add this to the example:

```
<amp-state id="props">
  <script type="application/json">
  {
    "username": "World"
  }
  </script>
</amp-state>
```

This introduces its own small complication: now we must use props.username instead of username, so the expression would be as follows:

```
<p [text]="'Hello '+props.username">Hello World</p>
```

And when we use AMP.setState() to set the username, we need to nest it correctly:

```
<button on="tap:AMP.setState({props: {username: 'ruadhan'}})">Say
Hello</button>
```

Changing CSS class with <amp-bind>

We can also bind an element's class attribute to an expression with amp-bind. This allows us to modify an element's style by adding or removing CSS classes. A common pattern is to hide or show an element by applying an appropriate CSS class. We could achieve this with amp-bind.

First, let's set up some CSS classes to show or hide an element. We use the visibility: hidden property to hide the element; you could also use display:none here depending on your needs:

```
.hide {
  visibility: hidden;
}

.show {
  visibility: visible;
}
```

Next, we set up an image. Note the binding of the property `displayStatus` to the `class` attribute, and that we have defaulted it to the `show` class:

```
<amp-img src="..." width="600" height="400" layout="responsive"
        class="show"
        [class]="(displayStatus||'show')">
</amp-img>
```

Now we just need to use `AMP.setState()` to change the class. We'll add two buttons here, one to show the image, and one to hide it (we could do this with a single button too, but let's keep things simple for now):

```
<button on="tap:AMP.setState({displayStatus: 'show'})">SHOW IT</button>
<button on="tap:AMP.setState({displayStatus: 'hide'})">HIDE IT</button>
```

Now, when either button is tapped, the `displayStatus` state property is updated, and then any bindings are re-evaluated, so the new class is applied to the image, and it is then either hidden or shown:

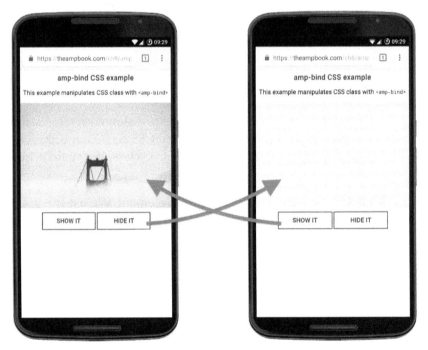

CSS class manipulation with amp-bind to show or hide an image (/ch8/amp-bind-css.html)

The astute reader might point out that the same could be achieved with the `element.toggleVisibility()` approach introduced in Chapter 4, *Engaging Users with Interactive AMP Components*. If *all* you need to do is toggle visibility of an element, then `amp-bind` is overkill!

Removing cart items with <amp-bind>

After that not-so-brief introduction to `amp-bind`, it's time to get back to the shopping cart. Earlier, we mentioned that a nice update to the cart would be if we could remove items via an XHR request without a full page reload. Let's build this now.

Recall that the shopping cart summary is fetched from the server via `amp-list` on page load. We're going to use `amp-bind` to trigger an `amp-list` fetch that will also remove an item from the cart.

The product page examples in this chapter will use `/ch8/product-start.html` as a starting point. You can follow along with the examples by adding code to this file.

User-triggered updates with <amp-list> and <amp-bind>

With `amp-bind`, we can trigger `amp-list` to update, without a page reload, based on a user action such as tapping a button or entering some text. To do this, we must bind to the URL of `amp-list` with the square bracket syntax, like this: `[src]`.

This `amp-bind`/`amp-list` combination is powerful pattern that we'll see several times in this chapter, so it's worth getting to know it well!

When the user clicks the remove link next to an item in the cart, then we'll add the `product_id` to the `amp-list` URL. When the URL changes, `amp-list` will automatically fetch the content at the new URL and render it.

Let's think about this in terms of state, expressions, and data bindings:

- **State**: We'll add a property to the AMP state to store the `product_id` of the item we want to remove; let's call it `removeProductId`.
- **Expression**: We'll create an expression that appends `removeProductId` to the `amp-list` URL: `'/cart.php?del='+removeProductId`.
- **Data-binding**: We'll bind this expression to the `amp-list` URL `src` attribute:
  `<amp-list [src]="'cart.php?del='+removeProductId">...</amp-list>`.
- **Trigger state change**: When the user taps the remove link, we'll set the value of the `removeProductId` state property to the ID of the associated product item like this:
  `<div on="tap:AMP.setState({removeProductId: '{{product_id}}'})">X</div>`.
  This will cause the expression to be re-evaluated. This, in turn, will update the `amp-list` `src` URL, and finally, this will trigger `amp-list` to fetch the new URL and render the server response.

The server backend (`/ch8/cart.php`) then functions the same as in the last chapter: it checks whether there is a `del` parameter included in the URL and deletes from the cart any item that matches. The new cart data is then returned as a JSON string and rendered by `amp-list` using the mustache template as before.

Ensuring that <amp-list> has a unique URL

There's a small catch in our solution: `amp-list` will only fetch new URLs. Let's say we decide to remove a product with ID `product1`. The URL would end up like this: `cart.php?del=product1`. This will remove the product with ID `product1` from the cart. Suppose then that we add `product1` back into the cart, and try to remove it again. Then the URL hasn't actually changed, so `amp-list` won't fetch the URL again and the product won't be removed.

To deal with this situation, we can add a random number to the end of the URL, so that the URL will be unique and `amp-list` will perform the fetch. Luckily, `amp-bind` gives us a way to achieve this with the `random()` function.

First, we'll need to update the URL to append the random number as a parameter. We'll use another state property called `rnd` for this:

```
<amp-list src="cart.php?client_id=CLIENT_ID(cart)&del=null&rnd=null"
    [src]="'cart.php?client_id=CLIENT_ID(cart)&del=' + removeProductId
+'&rnd=' + rnd">
    ...
</amp-list>
```

Now when we click the remove button, as well as setting the `removeProductId` property, we also need to set the `rnd` property with `AMP.setState()`:

```
<div on="tap:AMP.setState({removeProductId: '{{product_id}}', rnd:
random()}),add_cart_summary.hide,cart_summary.show">X</div>
```

In `AMP.setState({removeProductId: '{{product_id}}', rnd: random()})`, first `removeProductId` is set to the value `{{productId}}`, which is itself mustache syntax that substitutes in the `productId` value from the cart JSON data. Then `rnd: random()` sets the state property `rnd` to the result of JavaScript function `Math.random()`.

In `amp-bind`, we don't need to use the namespace for supported JavaScript functions. So, for example, use `random()` instead of `Math.random()`.

Since the state has changed, the expressions are re-evaluated, the URL is updated with the new `productId` and `rnd` values, and `amp-list` makes the server request:

Removing item from cart without page reload, with amp-bind and amp-list (/ch8/product-cart.html)

If we wanted, we could use the same method to add items to the cart, and remove the form altogether. Note that we'd have to add any product details we need to the `amp-list` URL. This is left as an exercise for the reader.

Improving search with <amp-list> and <amp-bind>

Earlier we noted that `amp-bind` and `amp-list` together was a potent combination--so what else can we do? Search is one place that it can help with, so let's revisit our product search form from `Chapter 6`, *Making contact - Forms in AMP*. We can improve it in two ways:

- Adding filtering and sorting, and removing the reliance on `submit-success`
- Adding autocomplete/autosuggest functionality

Sorting, filtering, and updating search results

In Chapter 6, *Making contact - Forms in AMP*, we implemented a product search form. It performed the search without needing a page reload using an XHR `amp-form` submission, and displayed the results with `amp-mustache` in the `submit-success` template. We noted, however, that the `submit-success` approach was clunky and limiting in terms of page layout: the search results were too tightly coupled with `amp-form`. With `amp-list` and `amp-bind`, we can loosen this coupling in a more flexible approach that also allows us to implement search and sort filters.

 The starting point for this search example is `/ch8/search-start.html`, and the finished code is at `/ch8/search.html`.

Using amp-list to show search results

The first thing we'll do is remove the `form` and the `submit-success` elements that we used last time, and instead use `amp-list` to fetch the search results. We'll keep the input field, and when the input changes, we'll set an AMP state property with the keywords entered. We'll bind this property to the `amp-list` `src` URL that will fetch the search results from the server. The search input field will look like this:

```
<input name="keywords" type="text" placeholder="Search"
       on="input-debounced:AMP.setState({keywords: event.value})">
<input type="submit" value="">
```

The magic happens in the `on` attribute. We're using an event we haven't seen before: `input-debounced`. This event is just like the `change` event, except that it waits 300 ms after the last change before firing. This makes it good for using with text input, since it waits for the user to stop typing before firing.

Next, we'll remove the `submit-success` container, and add this `amp-list`:

```
<amp-list width="auto" height="600" layout="fixed-height"
  src="search.php?keywords=&filter=&sort="
[src]="'search.php?keywords='+(keywords||'')+'&filter='+(filter||'')+'&sort
='+(sort||'')">
  ...
</amp-list>
```

The main thing to note here is that, as well as binding the `keywords` state property, we're also binding `filter` and `sort` to the `src` attribute. We'll use `filter` and `sort` for filtering the search by color, and sorting by price. Whenever any of these properties change, then `amp-bind` will update the `src` attribute, and `amp-list` will fetch the updated URL. The server will then return a JSON response with a list of products that satisfies the `keywords`, `sort`, and `filter` options. The server code is at `/ch8/search.php`.

Search results JSON response

Note also that, since we are now using `amp-list` to fetch the search results, we need to change the JSON structure of the results from what we had in Chapter 6 to be more like the structure we used in Chapter 7 to fetch related products. That is, we'll need to wrap the results in a single item array again, so that the JSON data will look like this (`/ch8/search-results-sample.json`):

```json
{
  "items":[
    {
      "keywords":"tshirt",
      "results":[
        {
          "name":"T-shirt: Super Pouvoir",
          "price":9.99,
          "color":"red",
          "description":"Super cool super power t-shirt",
          "image":"img\/tshirt-0-f-red-320.png"
        },
        ...
      ]
    }
  ]
}
```

The search results are displayed in the same `amp-mustache` template as before, so we won't repeat it here.

Filtering by color, and sorting by price

Now we just need to set up the `sort` and `filter` options for the user. We'll use `amp-selector` for these. First, the color `filter`:

```
<amp-selector class="style-chooser"
              on="select:AMP.setState({filter: event.targetOption})">
  <span class="none" option="none" selected></span>
  <span class="red" option="red" ></span>
  <span class="green" option="green"></span>
  <span class="blue" option="blue"></span>
  <span class="yellow" option="yellow"></span>
  <span class="black" option="black"></span>
</amp-selector>
```

When a color is selected, `AMP.setState()` sets the `filter` property to the chosen option.

The selector for sorting by price is similar, but with only two options this time, `up` (low-to-high), and `down` (high-to-low):

```
<amp-selector class="style-chooser"
              on="select:AMP.setState({sort: event.targetOption})">
  <span class="up" option="up"></span>
  <span class="down" option="down"></span>
</amp-selector>
```

 We won't go into the CSS styling for these option selectors here, but you can find the styles in the `search-start.html` file.

Because of our bindings earlier, whenever an option is selected, or indeed the keywords change, it updates the `amp-list` URL which fetches and displays the new search results, without a page reload:

Search with amp-bind: no sort or filter (left), sort by price high-to-low (middle), and filter by color blue (right)

Adding search autosuggest

Autosuggest (or autocomplete) is a nice enhancement to any search: as the user types, partial keyword matches are displayed for the user. Let's add this to our search. To achieve this, we'll do the following:

1. When the user enters text, we'll update a new state property: `autosuggest`.
2. We'll add another `amp-list` to display the suggestions, and we'll bind the `src` URL to the `autosuggest` property.
3. When the `autosuggest` property updates, the `amp-list` will perform a new fetch to the server which will respond with partial text matches.

First, the input text field:

```
<input name="keywords" type="text" placeholder="Search"
       on="input-debounced:AMP.setState({
               keywords: event.value,
               autosuggest: event.value}),
           autosuggest-list.show"
       autocomplete="off"
       value=""
       [value]="keywords || ''">
```

There are a few things going on here:

- When new debounced input is detected the following occurs:
  - Both `keywords` and `autosuggest` are assigned the input value
  - The suggestion list is shown with `autosuggest-list.show`
- We use `autocomplete="off"` to disable the browser's own autocomplete function.
- We bind the value of the input box to the `keywords` property. We'll see why this is necessary shortly.

Next, let's set up the autosuggest list. It will look like this:

```
<amp-list id="autosuggest-list" layout="fixed-height" height="120"
  src="search.php?q="
  [src]="'search.php?q=' + (autosuggest || '')"
  hidden>
  ...
</amp-list>
```

The binding of `autosuggest` to the `src` attribute is the main thing to note here--this causes `amp-list` to fetch the suggestions from the server. As usual with `amp-list`, the data fetched is a JSON payload that will be displayed with an `amp-mustache` template:

```
<template type="amp-mustache">
 <amp-selector id="option-selector" layout="container"
              on="select:AMP.setState({keywords: event.targetOption}),
                  autosuggest-list.hide">
   {{#results}}
     <div class="select-option no-outline"
          role="option" tabindex="0"
          option="{{.}}">
       {{.}}
     </div>
   {{/results}}
 </amp-selector>
```

```
</template>
```

In this template, we wrap the suggestions in an `amp-selector`, and use the `select` event to set the `keywords` property to the selected suggestion. Remember we bound the search input to the keywords property earlier? This is why: the keywords can be changed by choosing an autosuggest option here, as well as the normal way by typing into the search box. Now when the user selects an autosuggest option, this value will be copied into the search box, which will trigger the search results `amp-list` from earlier to fetch new search results as before.

The rest of the template iterates over the suggestions with `{{#results}}`... `{{/results}}`. Each option is displayed in its own `div` with the mustache syntax `{{.}}` (`{{.}}` displays the *current item*). The result is shown in the following image (full code at `/ch8/search-autosuggest.html`):

Suggestions and search results are fetched as user types (left, middle), and user selects a suggestion to complete search (right)

Improving the product image carousel with <amp-bind>

In Chapter 5, *Building Rich Media Pages in AMP*, we built a product image carousel. We used amp-selector to let the user choose the image to show in the carousel and we used its selected attribute to highlight the selected thumbnail. This all worked great if the user tapped the thumbnails to navigate the images. Recall, however, that if the user swiped through the images, then the highlighted thumbnail would not change, and the thumbnail would be out of sync with the visible carousel image:

Original product carousel from Chapter 5 showing thumbnails out of sync with main image

In this example, we're back using the product page again as starting point: /ch8/product-cart.html.

We can fix this by using `amp-bind` to change the selected thumbnail in the `amp-selector` whenever the user changes slide by swiping through the carousel. Lucky for us, `amp-carousel` exposes a `slideChange` event that we can use here. This event also exposes the current slide via `event.index`. This gives us a way to store the index of the new slide whenever the user swipes through the carousel; we'll store it in a state property called `currentImage`:

```
on="slideChange:AMP.setState({currentImage: event.index})"
```

We'll also bind the carousel's current slide to the `currentImage` property with `[slide]=currentImage`. So, the carousel element will look like this:

```
<amp-carousel id="product-carousel" width="600" height="600"
layout="responsive" type="slides"
  [slide]="currentImage"
  on="slideChange:AMP.setState({currentImage: event.index})">
  ...
</amp-carousel>
```

Now, since we know what `currentImage` is, we can also bind it to the selected thumbnail image of the `amp-selector` with `[selected]="currentImage"`. Previously, we used `goToSlide(index=event.targetOption)` to make the carousel go to the selected slide. But now that we know the carousel slide is bound to `currentImage`, we can just update `currentImage` instead with `on="select:AMP.setState({currentImage: event.targetOption})"`. So the amp-selector will now look like this:

```
<amp-selector class="carousel-thumbs" layout="container"
  on="select:AMP.setState({currentImage: event.targetOption})"
  [selected]="currentImage">
  <amp-img src="img/tshirt-0-f-red-120.png" width="60" height="60" alt="a
sample image" selected role="" tabindex="" option="0"></amp-img>
  ...
</amp-selector>
```

Since both the `amp-selector` and the `amp-carousel` are now bound to `currentImage`, if the carousel changes `currentImage`, then the `amp-selector` will be updated, and likewise if the `amp-selector` updates `currentImage`, then the carousel will be updated. Problem solved: the thumbnails will stay in sync with the visible carousel image!

 The full code for this example can be found at `/ch8/product-carousel.html`.

Configuring product options with <amp-bind>

Another great use for `amp-bind` within an e-commerce application is to configure product options. We can use AMP state to store the possible product options, as well as the user-selected configuration. We can bind this state to the product details UI, updating images and styles as appropriate when different options are selected.

Our e-commerce prototype store carries one type of product: *T-shirts*. Naturally then, configurable options might include *color*, *size*, and *style* (male or female).

As is usual in web development, there are multiple ways we can build this, and each with its own strengths and weaknesses. We're going to explore two ways to do it here: a simple, minimal approach; and a more complex but feature-rich approach. We show both here because the simple approach will be good enough to use for many applications, but there is always the possibility to use the complex version if you need to.

Product configuration: basic version

In this version (`/ch8/product-config-basic.html`), we're going to do away with the product carousel altogether, and we'll replace it with a single `amp-img`. We can do this because `amp-bind` allows us to bind to the `src` attribute of `amp-img`, and when we change the `src`, the new image will be fetched. Of course, a drawback is that the user won't be able to swipe through images.

When the user chooses a new option, a different color for example, then we'll change the image source to point to an image with the correct color, and the new image will be fetched and displayed. We'll do the same for the style of the t-shirt.

The trick here is to use `amp-bind` to build the URL of the image on the fly, based on the options. This requires that we have structured image filenames, with the options baked into the filenames. For example, a *green*, *female* style t-shirt would have the filename `tshirt-0-`**f-green**`-640.png`. The same t-shirt but *blue* and *male* style would be `tshirt-0-`**m-**`blue`-640.png.

We'll start off with the following `amp-state` to initialize the `style`, `color`, and `price`-- these values will be used if the user doesn't change any options:

```
<amp-state id="product">
  <script type="application/json">
    {
      "color":"red",
      "style":"f",
      "price":"8.99"
    }
  </script>
</amp-state>
```

Now when we bind to the `src` of the `amp-img`, we need an expression that will build the filename based on the selected options. This is just a string concatenation expression:

```
[src]="'img/tshirt-0-'+product.style+'-'+product.color+'-640.png'"
```

Pretty simple! That's all the code we need to replace the main carousel:

```
<amp-img src="img/tshirt-0-f-red-640.png" width="300" height="300"
layout="responsive"  on="tap:tshirt-lightbox" role="button" tabindex=""
[src]="'img/tshirt-0-'+product.style+'-'+product.color+'-640.png'"
></amp-img>
```

Choosing options with <amp-selector> and <amp-bind>

Next, let's set up two `amp-selectors` to let the user choose color and style. First the color option:

```
<amp-selector class="style-chooser"
  on="select:AMP.setState({product:{color: event.targetOption}})">
  <span option="red" selected></span>
  <span option="green"></span>
  <span option="blue"></span>
  <span option="yellow"></span>
</amp-selector>
```

We use `AMP.setState()` to change the `color` property of the state whenever a new selection is made and the `select` event is triggered.

The `style` selector is very similar. There is a difference, however. It's common for different options to have different prices. For example, a large size could be more expensive than a small. We'll implement a simple option-based pricing model here, where the price depends on only a single option: the `style`. If the price depends on more than one option then we need to store a map or array of options and prices. We can do this with `amp-state`; we'll see how to do this in the next example in this chapter. For now, we'll keep it simple. The male style t-shirt will have a different price to the female. Let's set the `price` property, as well as the `style`, when the `style` is changed:

```
<amp-selector class="style-chooser"
  on="select:AMP.setState({product:{style: event.targetOption, price:
(event.targetOption=='m'?'9.99':'8.99')}})">
  <span option="f" selected>F</span>
  <span option="m">M</span>
</amp-selector>
```

To set the price, we use a simple expression that checks the value of the selected option (m or f), and sets a price depending on its value:
`(event.targetOption=='m'?'9.99':'8.99')`.

Earlier, we bound the main product image `src` to `product.style` and `product.color` like this:

```
[src]="'img/tshirt-0-'+product.style+'-'+product.color+'-640.png'"
```

So now, whenever either of these change, the `src` is updated, and the appropriate image is displayed:

Setting style and color product properties with amp-bind and amp-selector (/ch8/product-config-basic.html)

Binding selection options to the shopping cart

We still need to pass the selections to the shopping cart. We can do this by binding the `value` attribute of hidden input fields in the add-to-cart form. Whenever any of the options are changed, then the hidden fields will automatically be updated, starting with the `color` and `style` options:

```
<input type="hidden" name="color" value="green" [value]="product.color">
<input type="hidden" name="style" value="f" [value]="product.style">
```

We need to tweak the `product_id` too, so that we can distinguish between different colors or styles of the same t-shirt. We'll use the same method that we used for the image URL, that is, we'll build the style and color into the `product_id`:

```
<input type="hidden" name="product_id" value="thsirt-0-f-green"
    [value]="'tshirt-0-'+product.style+'-'+product.color">
```

Next, we need to bind the value attribute of the price input field in the add-to-cart form, so that we set the correct price:

```
<input type="hidden" name="price" value="9.99" [value]="product.price">
```

We should also bind to the price that is displayed on the page, so the user knows how much they will be charged. This time, we'll bind to the text node of the price display:

```
<span class="item-price" [text]="'€'+product.price">€9.99</span>
```

That's it! When the user selects some options, and then submits the form, the options will now be sent to the server endpoint. It's up to the server to now store the user's cart. Once again, we won't go into the server details here, but you can see a PHP prototype implementation with the code for this chapter at /ch8/add-to-cart.php.

In this example, we're determining the product price on the client side. This is good enough for our prototype, but in a real application, you wouldn't rely on client-side submitted data to determine the price of a product. Rather, the server would maintain a database of prices and would validate any shopping cart submission against this database.

Selecting options and adding different product configurations to the cart

Product configuration: advanced version

The configurator we just implemented is good, but has a couple of drawbacks. We sacrificed the carousel and so we can't swipe through images. Also, there might be a lag when the user selects an option if the image hasn't already been loaded. These issues aren't deal-breakers, but they might not suit everyone.

This time round, we'll keep the carousel. In fact, we'll have two carousels, one for male style t-shirts, and one for female style, and only one carousel will be visible at a time. We'll also implement a more complex pricing model than the last example, so that the price will depend on more than one option. So we'll need to add another configuration option too: `size`.

Initializing product data with <amp-state>

We'll set it up so that the price depends on the size as well as the style. We'll use `amp-state` to initialize this information. Let's start with that (full code at `/ch8/product-config.html`):

```
<amp-state id="product">
  <script type="application/json">
    {
      "color":"red",
      "style":"f",
      "size":"s",
      "price":"8.99",
      "currentImage": "0",
      "m": {
        "sizes": {
          "l": "10.99",
          "m": "9.99",
          "s": "8.99"
        }
      },
      "f": {
        "sizes": {
          "l": "8.99",
          "m": "7.99",
          "s": "6.99"
        }
      },
      "colors": {
        "0":"red",
        "1":"black",
        "2":"blue",
```

```
        "3":"green"
      }
    }
  </script>
</amp-state>
```

In this setup, the properties `color`, `style`, `size`, and `price` will represent the *current* options, so whenever the user changes an option, we'll need to update one of these properties. Also note that we've given them initial default values of `red`, `f`, `s`, and `8.99` respectively. If the user doesn't change any options, these values will be used. There is one more property: `currentImage`. This will store the index of the visible carousel image, and will be used to keep the thumbnails in sync with the carousel, like we saw earlier.

Note also the nested prices. We can access these with dot notation in an expression. Say, for example, we want to get the price for a male (`m`), size large (`l`), then we'd use `product[m].sizes[l]`.

Now, because we'll be using `product.style` to store the currently selected `style` option, we'll have to substitute that into the expression. It will look like this:

```
product[product.style].sizes[product.size]
```

This would evaluate to `10.99` using the preceding `amp-state` data.

Creating the product carousels

Let's set up the two carousels. First, why do we need two? The reason is that there will be a different set of product images and preview thumbnail images, based on whether the user chooses the male or female `style` option. We'll only ever show one of them at a time, and we'll use an `amp-selector` to switch between them.

In the last example, we used an `amp-selector` to set the `style` property to value `m` or `f`. We do the same here, but note the different syntax for setting properties initialized with `amp-state`:

```
<amp-selector class="style-chooser"
  on="select:AMP.setState({product: {style: event.targetOption}})">
  <span class="female" option="f" selected>F </span>
  <span class="male" option="m">M </span>
</amp-selector>
```

Recall that with the `select` event of `amp-selector`, we can retrieve the selected option with `event.targetOption`. Thus, `AMP.setState({product: {style: event.targetOption}})` will set the current `style` to the option just selected by the user.

This time, we'll also bind the `class` of the carousel containers with an expression that checks the current `style` (m or f) and sets an appropriate CSS so that we can show or hide each carousel as necessary:

```
<div id="carousel-f" class="visible"
  [class]="(product.style=='f'?'visible':'hidden')">
  <amp-carousel>
  ...
  </amp-carousel>
</div>
```

The second carousel will have the following:

```
<div id="carousel-m" class="hidden"
[class]="(product.style=='m'?'visible':'hidden')">
```

The CSS is straightforward:

```
.hidden {display: none;}
.visible {display: block;}
```

By applying an initial CSS class of `visible` or `hidden`, we can set one to be visible and one hidden by default.

 Due to an AMP bug that affects Firefox desktop and mobile browsers at the time of writing, when switching between carousels (that is, hiding one and showing the other), the carousel can sometimes jump to the last image (`github.com/ampproject/amphtml/issues/9882`)

Adding a size option

We can use another `amp-selector` to set up our `size` option. It's very similar to the male or female `style` option selector we just saw. This one will have three options:

```
<amp-selector class="style-chooser"
on="select:AMP.setState({product: {size: event.targetOption}})" >
  <span class="small" option="s" selected>S</span>
  <span class="medium" option="m" >M</span>
  <span class="large" option="l">L</span>
</amp-selector>
```

This time, `AMP.setState({product: {size: event.targetOption}})` will set the current `size` to the option just selected.

Using <amp-selector> for image preview thumbnails

Next, let's build the preview thumbnails. This will be very similar to the code we saw earlier in this chapter when we improved the carousel with `amp-bind`. We'll use `amp-selector` and `amp-bind` to set the `currentImage` property.

We're also going to use these thumbnails to set the `color` option. Remember how we set up the colors with `amp-state` earlier:

```
"colors": {
  "0":"red",
  "1":"black",
  "2":"blue",
  "3":"green"
}
```

We can use `event.targetOption` here to give us the option that was selected--a number between `0` and `3` in this case. So, for example, if `event.targetOption` is 2, then `product.colors[event.targetOption]` would evaluate to `blue`. So now we can set the two properties with the following:

```
on="select:AMP.setState({product: {currentImage: event.targetOption, color:
product.colors[event.targetOption]}})"
```

So, the thumbnail preview and `color` option chooser code will look like this:

```
<amp-selector class="carousel-thumbs"
  on="select:AMP.setState({product: {currentImage:
event.targetOption,color: product.colors[event.targetOption]}})"
  [selected]="product.currentImage">
  <amp-img  src="img/tshirt-0-f-red-120.png" width="60" height="60"
option="0" selected></amp-img>
  <amp-img  src="img/tshirt-0-f-black-120.png" width="60" height="60"
option="1"></amp-img>
  ...
</amp-selector>
```

We'll have two of these, one for each carousel, and they will share the `currentImage` property so that if the user chooses a blue `color`, for example, and then switches the `style`, then the blue tshirt will still be selected in the second carousel. If we didn't do this, then changing the `style` could also change the `color`, and that would be a poor user experience:

Product configuration with amp-bind; the options *female, small, red* are chosen on the left, and *male, large, green* on the right

Keeping the thumbnails preview option in sync

Next, we need to ensure that the carousel displays the correct slide. We've seen how to do this earlier: we just bind the `[slide]` attribute of the carousel to the `currentImage` property with `[slide]="product.currentImage"`.

We also need to make sure that the highlighted preview thumbnail stays in sync with the carousel when the user swipes through images directly instead of tapping a thumbnail. We saw this earlier too:

```
on="slideChange:AMP.setState({product: {currentImage: event.index}})"
```

But we have an extra task this time: we need to update the `color` property as well as the current slide because changing slide changes the color too. We could set the color using `event.index` since it gives us a number between 0 and 3, corresponding to both the index of the slide **and** the index of the color we want:

```
AMP.setState({product:{color: product.colors[event.index]}})
```

Let's combine this with the `slideChange` action we already have:

```
on="slideChange:AMP.setState({product: {currentImage: event.index,color:
product.colors[event.index]}})"
```

So the carousel code will look like this:

```
<div id="carousel-f" class="visible"
[class]="(product.style=='f'?'visible':'hidden')">
  <amp-carousel class="product-carousel" width="600" height="600"
layout="responsive" type="slides"
  [slide]="product.currentImage"
  on="slideChange:AMP.setState({product: {currentImage: event.index,color:
product.colors[event.index]}})">
    <amp-img src="img/tshirt-0-f-red-640.png" width="300" height="300"
layout="responsive" on="tap:tshirt-lightbox" ... ></amp-img>
    ...
  </amp-carousel>
  ...
</div>
```

Keeping track of chosen options and price in the cart

We're almost there--just a few loose ends to tie up. We need to bind the options to the hidden fields of the form--this data will be sent to the server when the user adds a configured product to the cart. We've seen how to do basic options already:

```
<input type="hidden" name="color" value="red" [value]="product.color">
<input type="hidden" name="style" value="f" [value]="product.style">
<input type="hidden" name="size" value="s" [value]="product.size">
```

Next, we'll do the `product_id`. For this prototype, we'll want to list different product configurations separately in the cart (so that we can remove them separately, and show their prices separately). So we'll append the options to the `product_id` to create a unique ID for each configuration, such as `tshirt-0-`**f-red-s**:

```
<input type="hidden" name="product_id" value="tshirt-0-f-red-s"
[value]="'tshirt-0-'+product.style+'-'+product.color+'-'+product.size">
```

Finally, we need to bind the `price` to the initial `amp-state` price data we set up, based on the configuration options. We saw how to do that earlier with `product[product.style].sizes[product.size]`. So, for the `price` hidden form field:

```
<input type="hidden" name="price" value="6.99"
[value]="product[product.style].sizes[product.size]">
```

And for the price displayed on the web page for the user to see:

```
<span class="item-price"
[text]="'€'+product[product.style].sizes[product.size]">€6.99</span>
```

The result is shown in the next image, where products with different configurations have been added to the cart:

Different product configurations selected and added separately to cart, with different prices from AMP state setup (/ch8/product-config.html)

Summary

In this chapter, we introduced a programming layer for AMP with `amp-bind`. This allowed us to create even richer and more interactive pages than would otherwise be possible within the confines of AMP's restrictions. Through the techniques in this chapter, we were able to build professional-grade e-commerce experiences. We saw how to build XHR searches with sorting and filtering, as well as autosuggest partial search matches. We saw how to improve our shopping cart by supporting XHR adding and removal of items from the cart.

In short, `amp-bind` opens up a whole new dimension for your AMP pages. It's not quite JavaScript, but it's powerful enough to deliver most of the functionality you'll need. However, when even `amp-bind` is not enough, there's still another option: `amp-iframe`. In the next chapter, we'll learn some further techniques that will help us fill the gaps when AMP doesn't quite fit our needs. With `amp-iframe` we can include features and functionality not currently possible in AMP.

9
When AMP Is Not Enough - Enter the iframe

So far we've seen the breadth of features possible with AMP. Sometimes, however, AMP is just not enough. There might be some functionality that you really need, but despite AMP's extensive list of components, it's not supported. A solution may still be possible. Sometimes referred to as the *duct tape of AMP*, `amp-iframe` might be able to help.

In this chapter, we'll see how the `amp-iframe` component can be used to plug functionality gaps in AMP. In particular, we'll see how to:

- Add a Google map to an AMP page
- Implement a searchable map
- Use the geolocation feature of the user's device, and plot routes
- Add Disqus comments to an AMP page
- Add a checkout payment process to our e-commerce prototype

The <amp-iframe> component

The `amp-iframe` component allows you to add iframes to your AMP pages. In a well-attended talk at AMP Conf 2017, Sebastien Benz referred to iframes as the *duct tape of AMP* (watch: `youtu.be/Em-tZ4WMMps` [16:25]). This is an apt metaphor: like duct tape, iframes are incredibly useful, but just as duct tape is often not the prettiest solution, neither are iframes. Like duct tape, `amp-iframe` can stick things together, allowing us to combine features not supported in AMP. The prevailing advice, however, is that if there is a dedicated AMP component that implements the functionality you need, then you should use that instead of `amp-iframe`.

What about the risk to performance?

You might be wondering why third-party JavaScript or other non-validated content is permitted in AMP through iframes, with all the other restrictions in the name of performance. Malte Ubl, the AMP project lead, gives a couple of reasons why this is OK (`support.google.com/partners/answer/7336293`):

- Third-party JavaScript is restricted to a sandboxed iframe, so it can't block the main page render
- Even if style recalculations are triggered by third-party JavaScript, it will still be quick to execute as they operate on a small DOM

Restrictions on <amp-iframe>

In case you get too carried away, however, there are several restrictions that AMP imposes on iframes to ensure that they don't interfere with performance:

- **Must not be near the top of the page:** No `amp-iframe` should be placed within the first 600 pixels, or first 75 percent of the viewport, whichever is smaller. If you **do** place an iframe within this distance from the top of the viewport, then the iframe won't be displayed. There is a way to circumvent this restriction: using *placeholders.</li>*
- **Must be served from a separate domain**: iframe content must be served from a different domain to the main AMP page. This is to ensure uniform behavior of AMP pages whether they're served from the AMP cache or from the original domain. If served from the same domain it might result in code that takes advantage of possible communication between the parent page and the `amp-iframe` page. Such communication would never be possible when the AMP page is served from the cache because the `amp-iframe` page will never live in the cache.

  This might be viewed as being overly restrictive, but it actually conforms to the philosophy that underpins AMP: that is, to restrict behavior that could degrade performance or user experience.

  The downside is that it adds some complexity to the deployment of AMP applications that use `amp-iframe`: at the very least you'll need to set up a subdomain or domain alias that the iframe page can be accessed from. In practice, however, this isn't very difficult.

- **Secure origins:** `amp-iframe` content must be served from secure (HTTPS) URLs.
- **Iframe sandboxing:** An `amp-iframe` will be maximally sandboxed by default. It can be made less restrictive by adding specific values to the `sandbox` attribute.
- **Data sharing with parent page:** An `amp-iframe` can't access the data from the parent AMP page. Data **can** be sent to the parent page from the iframe page with the `postMessage` function.

 You shouldn't use `amp-iframe` for ads as it breaks ad clicks and recording view-ability information. Instead, use one of the supported ad formats, or integrate the required ad network.

Configuring the iframe

The `amp-iframe` component is included with the following script:

```
<script async custom-element="amp-iframe"
src="https://cdn.ampproject.org/v0/amp-iframe-0.1.js"></script>
```

By default, the iframe will have maximum sandbox restrictions, but these can be relaxed by adding any of the following values to the `sandbox` attribute of the iframe: `allow-scripts`, `allow-same-origin`, `allow-popups`, `allow-modals`, and `allow-forms`.

For most `amp-iframe`s you will probably want to include the following:

```
sandbox="allow-scripts allow-same-origin"
```

In all the examples in this chapter, we'll also specify a placeholder element so that we can place the iframe at the top of the page if we want. In the following code, we use a simple gray `amp-img` as a placeholder:

```
<amp-iframe src="..." sandbox="allow-scripts allow-same-origin">
  <amp-img src="img/placeholder.png" layout="fill" placeholder>
  </amp-img>
</amp-iframe>
```

iframe resizing

Like all AMP elements, `amp-iframe` must define its static layout, but it's also possible to resize an `amp-iframe` at runtime. This is useful if the iframe contains dynamic content that you don't know the size of in advance (we'll see this in the Disqus example later). The `resizable` attribute can be added to the `amp-iframe` element to indicate that it can be resized:

```
<amp-iframe src="" ... resizable ...>
```

A request can be sent from the iframe to the AMP page container to request a resize. The requested height is specified in the `height` property. It could simply be a numeric value representing the pixel height, or it could be computed by JavaScript in the iframe code itself, like this, for example:

```
window.parent.postMessage({
  sentinel: 'amp',
  type: 'embed-size',
  height: document.body.scrollHeight
}, '*');
```

Note that a resizable `amp-iframe` must include an `overflow` element. This is essentially a button that will appear if the AMP runtime can't accommodate a resize request immediately. This might happen, for example, if resizing would affect the user's experience adversely by causing a page reflow or interrupting scrolling. The markup for a resizable `amp-iframe` would look something like this:

```
<amp-iframe height="400" layout="fixed-height"
            sandbox="allow-scripts allow-same-origin"
            resizable
            src="https://alt.theampbook.com/ch9/iframe.html#somehash">
  <amp-img layout="fill" src="img/placeholder.png" placeholder></amp-img>
  <div overflow tabindex="0" role="button" aria-label="Show all">Show
all!</div>
</amp-iframe>
```

When the user taps the overflow button, however, the iframe will be resized **immediately**, since it was a user-triggered action.

Google Maps in AMP

The Google Map is the cornerstone of many *Contact* or *Find us* pages on the web. In the following sections, we'll see how to add a Google Map to an AMP page with `amp-iframe`. After that, we'll see how to:

- Add a search function to a map
- Use the Geolocation API to determine the location of the user's device and center the map on this location
- How to draw a route on the map between the device location and another location

We'll start off with the Google Maps *Embed* API, which just requires you to configure a URL to request a map to display in the iframe. We can achieve quite a lot with the Embed API, but we'll get to a point where we'll need to use the more powerful Google Maps *JavaScript* API, which allows us to build and configure maps through JavaScript programming.

 Note that you're not limited to using Google Maps in AMP. You could equally use any map tile provider, such as OpenStreetMap, along with any JavaScript API you like, such as the wonderful `leaflet.js`.

Getting a Google Maps Embed API key

For the examples in this chapter, you'll need an API key for each of the Maps APIs. You can sign up for a free Google Maps Embed API key here: `developers.google.com/maps/documentation/embed/get-api-key`. Just get the Embed API key for now, you can get the JavaScript API key later.

Note that you're not required to *restrict* your key, but you should! This means that its use will be restricted to the domains that you specify. If you restrict your key, be sure to add `ampproject.org` to the list of domains permitted to make requests with your key. This means your pages will still work when served via the AMP cache. You can find out how to do this at the preceding URL.

Using the Google Maps Embed API

Now we're ready to add a map to our AMP pages. The Google Maps Embed API is probably the easiest way to get going with maps since it doesn't require any JavaScript programming, and is designed specifically to be used with iframes.

The starting point for the map examples in this chapter is `/ch9/iframe-map-start.html`. You can follow along with the examples by adding code to this file.

The Embed API is all about building the correct URL to request the map you want. We can start with the following code to embed a map within an AMP page:

```
<amp-iframe height="400" width="auto"
            layout="fixed-height"
            sandbox="allow-scripts allow-same-origin allow-popups"
            frameborder="0" allowfullscreen
src="https://google.com/maps/embed/v1/place?q=place_id:ChIJK_hq7580Z0gRc-q7
KyQHvqo&key=YOUR_KEY">
    <amp-img src="img/placeholder.png"
             placeholder layout="fill"></amp-img>
</amp-iframe>
```

Note that we use `layout="fixed-height"` and set `height="400"`; fixed height layouts work well with maps.

Google Maps Embed API map displayed with amp-iframe (/ch9/iframe-map.html)

In the preceding code, the `src` attribute contains a URL that points to the Embed API. The Embed API URL is constructed like this:

```
https://google.com/maps/embed/v1/MODE?key=YOUR_KEY&parameters
```

Where:

- `MODE` is one of `place`, `search`, `directions`, `view`, or `streetview`
- `YOUR_KEY` is the API key you got earlier
- `parameters` will depend on the `MODE` used and can include things such as `place_id`, `center`, and `zoom`

In the preceding example, we used `place` for the `MODE`, and we included parameter `q=place_id:....` This results in a map, centered on `place_id`. Using this URL as the `src` attribute of an `amp-iframe` element is a nice, simple way to get a map into an AMP page.

You can get the `place_id` for a location or address by entering the address into this page: `developers.google.com/places/place-id`.

Fullscreen maps

In the last example, we used a fixed height iframe. It's often useful to have a fullscreen map to make the most of the small screens on mobile devices. This means we need a fullscreen iframe.

One way to achieve this is to set CSS `height` to `100vh` (100 percent viewport height). This is problematic, however, because mobile devices hide (Android) or shrink (iOS) the address bar when the user scrolls down. This means that the viewport height changes slightly, making things tricky when sizing the map. So if we use CSS `height: 100vh;` then the browser includes the address bar in the height. So on initial load, the bottom of the map will be truncated until the user scrolls, and then the address bar disappears, and the map moves up and can be seen in full. As a user experience, it's a little clunky.

An alternative approach would be to ensure that the address bar doesn't disappear as the user scrolls, and then the viewport will always be the same size. We can achieve this with some CSS like this:

```
<style amp-custom>
  html {overflow:hidden;}
  body {height:100%;overflow-y:scroll;}
  .fullsize {position:fixed;width:100%;height:100%;}
</style>
```

Then in our iframe, we apply the `fullsize` class, and use the AMP `fill` layout:

```
<amp-iframe class="fullsize" layout="fill">
  ...
</amp-iframe>
```

Next, it can be useful to provide some navigation or other controls, in a header or footer. This could be an overlay, such as the shopping cart overlay we used in the last couple of chapters. We can implement a header like this:

```
.header {
  position:fixed;
  height: 100px;
  width: 100%;
  background-color: rgba(255,255,255,0.85);;
  z-index:9999;
  box-shadow: 0px 2px 6px rgba(0,0,0,.3);
}
```

This CSS will give us a nice, semi-translucent header bar that *floats* over the map. Now we just need to apply it to an HTML element (`/ch9/iframe-map-overlay.html`)

```
<div class="header" >
  <h1>amp-iframe fullscreen</h1>
</div>
```

Note that if you use an overlay like this, it might obscure buttons or other features on the map, so you should provide a way to show or hide the overlay like we did with the shopping cart in the previous chapter.

If you prefer a separate header that doesn't obscure the map, you can use this CSS for the `fullsize` class instead (`/ch9/iframe-map-full.html`).

```
.fullsize {
  position:fixed;
  width:100%;
  height:calc(100% - 100px);
  top:100px;
}
```

Fixed size amp-iframe with Google Map (left), fullscreen map with overlay (middle), and non-overlay header (right)

Other features of the Google Maps Embed API

There's lots we can do with the Embed API--too much to list here. You can see the full documentation at `developers.google.com/maps/documentation/embed/guide`. For now, we'll just show a couple of cool things and you can explore the rest yourself later.

Centering a map on a place name

We used a `place_id` earlier, but you don't necessarily need to use a `place_id`. With the Embed API you can put a place name into the `q` parameter of the URL, for example,

```
https://google.com/maps/embed/v1/place?q=18+Camden+Street+Lower,Dublin&key=KEY
```

Centering a map on a lat/lng location

Alternatively, if you already have the lat/lng coordinates, you can use them with the `center` and `zoom` parameters in `view` mode:

```
https://google.com/maps/embed/v1/view?center=53.3786,-6.0570&zoom=13&key=KEY
```

Showing directions and routes

If we have two locations, we can also plot a route between them, using the `directions` mode with `origin` and `destination` parameters:

```
https://google.com/maps/embed/v1/directions?origin=dublin+airport&destination=rathmines+dublin&key=KEY
```

If you're not sure what URL to use, there is a handy page that will build the URL for you at `developers.google.com/maps/documentation/embed/start`.

Searching for a location

We can combine our knowledge of forms from `Chapter 6`, *Making contact: Forms in AMP* with what we've just learned to create a *searchable* map. For this we can use the `search` mode of the Embed API:

```
https://google.com/maps/embed/v1/search?q=SEARCH_QUERY&key=YOUR_KEY
```

We'll need to build a search form in AMP so that the user can input some keywords--a place name or address--to search for. There are a few different ways we might build a search like this: with or without `amp-form`, `amp-bind`, or a server backend.

Map search with <amp-form> and server backend

In this first approach, we'll set up an `amp-form` in a server generated page. The page will make a `GET` submission to itself, and parse the submitted query. Then it will dynamically replace the Google Map URL with the search query. The form will look like this (`/ch9/search-map.php`):

```
<form action="search-map.php" method="get" target="_top">
  Find location: <input type="text" name="q" placeholder="e.g. Dublin">
  <input type="submit" value="search">
</form>
```

We can retrieve the search query with the following code:

```
<?php $query = isset($_GET['q'])?$_GET['q']:''; ?>
```

And finally, the `amp-iframe` that will contain the map:

```
<amp-iframe height="400" layout="fixed-height"
    sandbox="allow-scripts allow-same-origin"
    allowfullscreen
src="https://google.com/maps/embed/v1/search?q=<?=$query?>&key=YOUR_KEY">
  <amp-img layout="fill" src="img/placeholder.png" placeholder></amp-img>
</amp-iframe>
```

The only thing to note here is the echoing of the `$query` parameter into the `src` URL, highlighted in the preceding code. In this code, it's possible to send an empty string to the Embed API, which will cause an error:

```
The Google Maps API server rejected your request. Invalid request.
Invalid 'q' parameter.
```

To avoid this, we check if `$query` is an empty string, and set a default if it is:

```
https://google.com/maps/embed/v1/search?q=<?=($query==''?'planet
earth':$query) ?>&key=KEY
```

And that's it, we have a searchable map. One thing to note is that, if this page is served from the AMP cache, then, when the user submits the search, they will be brought to the origin server for the search results, and for subsequent searches. If you really wanted, you could ensure that the results page was also served from the cache by using the techniques discussed in Chapter 7.

The result, a searchable Google Map in an AMP page, is shown in the following image:

Server-based map search with amp-iframe, amp-form, and Google Maps (/ch9/search-map.php)

Map search without server backend

Why go to the trouble of setting up server generated page and form submission when AMP, with the help of `amp-bind`, gives us everything we need already? Yes, we can do this without the server script!

Along with the usual AMP boilerplate, we'll start with some initial data, set by `amp-state` (`/ch9/search-map.html`):

```
<amp-state id="props">
  <script type="application/json">
  {
    "input":    "planet+earth"
  }
  </script>
</amp-state>
```

We're going to use `props.input` to store the user's search keywords. When the user enters some text we'll use the `on="change:..."` event to update `props.input`. We'll also bind `props.input` to the query parameter of the iframe `src` URL, so when the query changes the map will be updated. In this way the search will happen automatically, so we don't need to submit the form. In fact, we don't need a `form` element at all. We'll just keep the input field:

```
Find location:
<input type="text" name="q" placeholder="e.g. Dublin"
       on="change:AMP.setState({props: {input: event.value}})">
<input type="submit" value="SEARCH">
```

Now we just have to bind to the `src` attribute of the `amp-iframe`:

```
<amp-iframe height="400" layout="fixed-height" layout="responsive"
sandbox="allow-scripts allow-same-origin"
  src="https://google.com/maps/embed/v1/search?q=planet+earth&key-KEY"
[src]="'https://google.com/maps/embed/v1/search?q='+props.input+'&key=KEY
'">
 ...
</amp-iframe>
```

Now when the user hits enter, the keywords are submitted as a search to the map. And that's it, we're done!

Or are we...? If we send an empty string to the embed API we'll see the same error message as earlier. To prevent this from happening, we need to ensure `props.input` isn't an empty string. To do this, we'll check `event.value`, and if it's an empty string, we'll set it to a default value, `'planet earth'`:

```
[src]="'https://google.com/maps/embed/v1/search?q='+(props.input==''?'plane
t earth':props.input)+'&key...
```

And now we're really done. We've removed the need for the server round-trip request, and saved ourselves a full page load. The entire page can be served from the AMP cache!

 In these examples, you could also use the `input-debounced` event that we saw in the last chapter, instead of the `change` event. Then the search will be submitted as the user types. This may or may not be suitable for your application.

Geolocating the users device

The previous examples have dealt with fixed locations on a map. But what if, instead, we wanted to center the map on the user's device location? This might be useful for *geofencing* or location-based applications, such as *near-me* type apps like bike- or car-sharing.

In the last example, we used the Google Maps Embed API URL directly in the `src` of the `amp-iframe`. This time we'll need to create our own page that executes the JavaScript necessary to access the browser's Geolocation API, and then center the map on that location.

We'll use the Google Maps *JavaScript* API instead of the Embed API this time round. Although they both use Google Maps, they work differently: with the Embed API you retrieve a map via URLs, while with the JavaScript API maps are built with JavaScript.

This next example will also highlight a strength of `amp-iframe`: we can execute our own custom JavaScript code.

Using the Google Maps JavaScript API

First, we need to create another, non-AMP page to hold the Google Map. This page will contain JavaScript code that will:

1. Use the Google Maps JavaScript API to build the map.
2. Use the HTML5 Geolocation API to obtain the position of the user's device.
3. Center the map on this location.

Then we'll use the URL of this page as the `src` attribute of the `amp-iframe` in the AMP page.

The code for the map in this example is a modified version of sample code available on the Google Maps documentation page here:

```
developers.google.com/maps/documentation/javascript/geolocation.
```

Before we begin, we need to get a key (it's free!) for the Google Maps JavaScript API. You can follow the same process to get a key for the JavaScript API as you did for the Embed API, but get it from this page:

```
developers.google.com/maps/documentation/javascript/get-api-key.
```

Building the map

First, we need to include the Google Maps API script before we can use it in a web page. The best place to put this is at the bottom of the page, just before the closing `</body>` tag (`/ch9/geomap.html`):

```
<script async defer
src="https://maps.googleapis.com/maps/api/js?key=KEY&callback=build Map">
</script>
```

Note that we need to provide the API key, as well as the name of a callback function. For the `callback` parameter, we've passed in the value `buildMap`, so we'll put the map code in a function with this name.

Next, we need to provide an HTML container `div` for the map. This goes inside the opening `<body>` tag:

```
<div id="map"></div>
```

Note the `id`, we'll tell the Google Maps API to put the map into this `div` based on the `id`.

We can create the map with the following JavaScript code, that we've put inside the `buildMap` callback function:

```
function buildMap() {
  map = new google.maps.Map(document.getElementById('map'), {
    center: {lat: 53.0982471, lng: -9.7358862},
    zoom:2
  });
  ...
}
```

Note that we've given initial values for:

- `center`: The center of the map, a `lat/lng` object literal like this `{lat: 53.098, lng: -9.735}`
- `zoom`: An integer in the range 0-22, where 0 is maximally zoomed out

Later, when we've determined the user's location, we'll update `center` and `zoom`.

Using the HTML5 Geolocation API

Accessing the device location with the HTML5 Geolocation API is straightforward. First check for Geolocation API support with:

```
if (navigator.geolocation) {
  // Do something
}
```

Then, if supported, we can retrieve the location with the `getCurrentPosition()` method like this:

```
navigator.geolocation.getCurrentPosition(function(location) {
  // Do something with location data
});
```

This method takes a callback function, which has access to the user's location as `location.coords.latitude` and `location.coords.longitude`. In this function we can now do something with the location, such as centering the map on the location, and zooming in a little:

```
navigator.geolocation.getCurrentPosition(function(location) {
  var position = {
    lat: location.coords.latitude,
    lng: location.coords.longitude
  };
  map.setCenter(position);
  map.setZoom(16);
}
```

Now the main work is completed. The full code is at `/ch9/geomap.html`. The remainder of the code handles errors and styling.

 Note that the device location can't be accessed without user permission. Therefore, whenever you use the HTML5 Geolocation API, the user will be prompted for permission before the location data can be used.

There is one more thing we need to do, however. Earlier we mentioned that `amp-iframe` content must be served from a separate domain to the AMP page it's embedded in. We'll need to set this up before our example will work.

Serving iframe content from a different domain

Setting this up will depend on your own environment, so we can only give general guidelines here. One way to do this is to add a domain alias to your hosting setup so that you can access the main AMP page at `https://domain.com/amp-doc.html`, and the iframe source could be at `https://domainalias.com/iframe-content.html`. In the examples for this chapter, the iframe content is served from `https://alt.theampbook.com` and the main AMP documents are served from `https://theampbook.com`.

If you are working locally you'll need to do something similar. Note that the iframe must be served from an HTTPS URL, unless it's served from `localhost`. So your options for `localhost` would be either:

1. AMP page at `http://domainalias.localhost/amp-doc.html`, iframe content at `http://localhost/iframe-content.html`. OR

2. You could generate and install a self-signed SSL cert and serve your AMP page from `http://localhost/amp-doc.html`, and serve your iframe content from `https://domainalias.localhost/iframe-content.html`.

It's probably easier to do the former.

Adding the iframe map content to the AMP page

We're almost done. Now we just need to create the AMP page. This page will be very similar to the previous `amp-iframe` examples we've seen already. All we need to do is point the `src` URL of the `amp-iframe` at the `geomap.html` file:

```
<amp-iframe height="400" layout="fixed-height"
        sandbox="allow-scripts allow-same-origin"
        allowfullscreen
        src="https://alt.theampbook.com/ch9/geomap.html">
  <amp-img layout="fill" src="img/placeholder.png" placeholder></amp-img>
</amp-iframe>
```

Note the domain we've used here: `alt.theampbook.com`. This should match the domain that you set up for your iframe content.

If you open up the example in your browser, it should look like the following image (full-screen version at `/ch9/iframe-geomap-full.html`, and fixed-height version at `/ch9/iframe-geomap.html`):

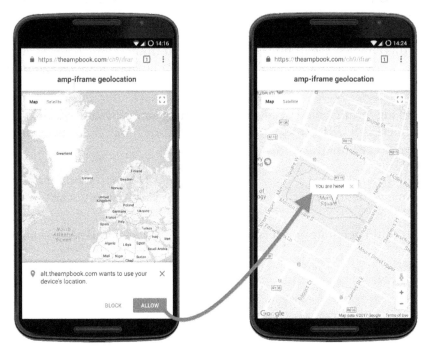

amp-iframe requesting device's location (left), and centering a map based on its location (right)

Showing a route from the current location

Let's try one more example: we'll let the user search for an address or area, and then display a route from the user's device location to that address. Again, this would be useful for any location-based app. This example will build on the earlier examples as follows. In the AMP page we will:

1. Add a search form as we did in our serverless map search earlier.
2. Append the search query to the `src` URL of the `amp-iframe` as we did earlier.

In the iframe source we will:

1. Geolocate the user's device as before.
2. Geocode (get the lat, lng coordinates) for the location with Google's Geocoding API.

3. Compute a route between the user's location and the search location with the `DirectionsService` object of the Maps API.

4. Display the route on the map.

It sounds like a lot of work, but it's not really.

On the AMP side, there's not too much to do--we just need to set up the iframe as before. It's almost identical to the `search-map.html` example we saw earlier, but pointing to a new file, `directions.html`, this time:

```
<amp-iframe height="400" layout="fixed-height"
            allowfullscreen
            sandbox="allow-scripts allow-same-origin"
src="https://alt.theampbook.com/ch9/directions.html?q=planet+earth"
[src]="'https://alt.theampbook.com/ch9/directions.html?q='+props.input"
        >
   <amp-img layout="fill" src="img/placeholder.png" placeholder></amp-img>
</amp-iframe>
```

You can see the full code for the AMP page at `/ch9/iframe-directions.html` (and `/ch9/iframe-directions-full.html` for a full-screen version).

Now for the iframe content. We only have small modifications to make from the last example. In the `buildMap` function, we create a `Geocoder` object with:

```
geocoder = new google.maps.Geocoder();
```

We can then translate the keywords query (`queryParams.q`) into a lat/lng location like this:

```
geocoder.geocode( { 'address': queryParams.q}, function(results, status) {
  if (status == 'OK') {
    destination = results[0].geometry.location;
    // Now calculate and display the route
  }
});
```

We want to get the directions and display a route between the user's position, and the location we just geocoded. First, we set up the `DirectionsService` and `DirectionsRenderer` objects and associate with the map:

```
var directionsService = new google.maps.DirectionsService;
var directionsDisplay = new google.maps.DirectionsRenderer;
directionsDisplay.setMap(map);
```

Next, we write a function to calculate the route and display it with the
`DirectionsService` and `DirectionsRenderer` objects:

```
function calculateAndDisplayRoute(directionsService, directionsDisplay,
start, end) {
  directionsService.route({
    origin: start,
    destination: end,
    travelMode: 'DRIVING'
  }, function(response, status) {
    if (status === 'OK') {
      directionsDisplay.setDirections(response);
    }
  });
}
```

All we need to do now is call this function and pass in the start and end locations:

```
calculateAndDisplayRoute(directionsService, directionsDisplay, position,
destination);
```

That's it! You can see the result in the following image:

Using amp-iframe and Google Maps to build a route-finding application (/ch9/iframe-directions-full.html)

Disqus comments in AMP

Disqus is one of the most popular comments platform in the world. It's a third-party service that hosts and manages comments for pages on your website. To integrate Disqus in a non-AMP website you would copy the Disqus-provided JavaScript code into your web page, configure it, and you're done. With AMP, we have a little bit more work to do, but with `amp-iframe` we can achieve it.

Configuring Disqus for your site

If you don't already have your site registered with Disqus, you need to do this now. Visit this page `disqus.com/admin/install` and click the **+Create a Site** button on the left. Fill out the name of your site and optionally configure the URL, and then click **Create Site**.

On the next screen, Disqus offers plugins for many common CMSes or platforms such as WordPress and Drupal. We're doing a manual install so you can scroll past all of these to the bottom where you should see a link to `Universal Code/Manual install` sample code:

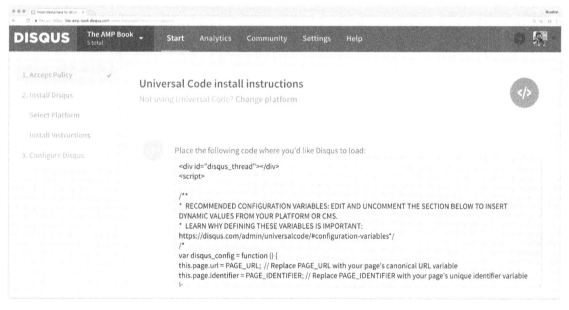

Disqus set up

We now need to make a couple of minor substitutions to get Disqus up and running. Make the following changes:

- Uncomment the section beginning with `var disqus_config=...`
- Replace `PAGE_URL` with `window.location`
- Replace `PAGE_IDENTIFIER` with `window.location.hash`

Your code should look like this (substitutions highlighted):

```
<div id="disqus_thread"></div>
<script>
  var disqus_config = function () {
    this.page.url = window.location;
    this.page.identifier = window.location.hash;
  };
  (function() {
    var d = document, s = d.createElement('script');
    s.src = '//theampbook.disqus.com/embed.js';
    s.setAttribute('data-timestamp', +new Date());
    (d.head || d.body).appendChild(s);
  })();
</script>
```

This code should be saved in a non AMP file on your server, let's call it `disqus.html`. We just need to add basic `<html>` and `<body>` tags around the content, like this:

```
<html>
  <head><title>Disqus comment thread</title></head>
  <body>
    <div id="disqus_thread"></div>
    ...
  </body>
</html>
```

Resizing the iframe

We'll need to send a message to the iframe parent in the AMP page so that it's sized correctly based on the amount of comment data there is. We can achieve this with another script:

```
<script>
  window.addEventListener('message', receiveMessage, false);
  function receiveMessage(event) {
    if (event.data) {
      var msg;
      try {
        msg = JSON.parse(event.data);
      } catch (err) {}
      if(!msg) return false;
      if(msg.name === 'resize') {
        window.parent.postMessage({
          sentinel: 'amp',
          type: 'embed-size',
          height: msg.data.height
        }, '*');
      }
    }
  }
</script>
```

Adding the Disqus <amp-iframe>

Now we're ready to add the `amp-iframe` element into the AMP page. Apart from the usual boilerplate, we can add the Disqus comments by adding the `amp-iframe` and setting the `src` URL to point to the Disqus content page we just built:

```
<amp-iframe src="https://alt.theampbook.com/ch9/disqus.html" width="200"
height="600" layout="responsive" resizable>
```

Again we have the `resizable` attribute, and we set an initial height of `600` px. You can see the full code for this example at `/ch9/iframe-disqus.html` and `/ch9/disqus.html`.

Disqus comments in AMP using amp-iframe, loading (left) and loaded (right)

Building a checkout process with the Payment Request API

There is one more `amp-iframe` application that's worth exploring here. Earlier in the book, we built an e-commerce prototype, with configurable product options, a product image carousel, and a shopping cart. But what e-commerce prototype would be complete without a checkout process? Let's see how AMP can accommodate us here.

Completing the e-commerce prototype is difficult in AMP due to JavaScript restrictions. However, it's possible to build a checkout solution combining `amp-iframe` with a recent HTML5 API: the Payment Request API. First, what is the Payment Request API?

The HTML5 Payment Request API

Traditionally, making payments on the web has been difficult, especially on mobile, where it takes users a long time to enter the required personal, delivery, and credit card information to complete a transaction. The HTML5 Payment Request API is an API designed to make this process more seamless for the user.

The Payment Request API provides the UI to collect all the necessary data from the user, and the data is stored securely in the browser for future use with other web apps, without requiring the user to manually re-enter.

 Note that the Payment Request API doesn't actually process payments; you still need to integrate a payment solution such as Stripe or PayPal.

Using the Payment Request API with <amp-iframe>

While AMP doesn't support the Payment Request API natively, it offers support through `amp-iframe` via a dedicated attribute: `allowpaymentrequest`. When this attribute is included, then the iframe is permitted to pop up the payment request UI that will allow the user to enter any personal, delivery, and credit information required.

To implement the checkout process, we'll add a checkout button using an `amp-iframe` that includes this attribute. The iframe source will then contain the JavaScript that actually triggers the payment request UI when the button is clicked. So, we'll add the button to our product page (`/ch9/product.html`) with the following `amp-iframe`:

```
<amp-iframe width="130" height="42"
        sandbox="allow-scripts allow-same-origin allow-top-navigation"
        allowpaymentrequest
        frameborder="0"
        noloading
        src="https://alt.theampbook.com/ch9/checkout.html">
  <button placeholder disabled>Checkout</button>
</amp-iframe>
```

Note that we provide a placeholder button that will be replaced by the real button when the `amp-iframe` source has loaded. We also include the `noloading` attribute since we don't require the loading indicator in this case.

Preparing the payment request

The next thing we need to do is set up the iframe source page. This will be a non-AMP page that:

1. Displays a checkout button.
2. Fetches the user's cart from the server.
3. Executes the JavaScript we need to set up the payment request.

There's some JavaScript to work through in this example. We'll only highlight the important parts here and you can see the full code for the `amp-iframe` at `/ch9/checkout.html`.

The first part is easy. We can add a button like this:

```
<button id="btn-pay">Checkout</button>
```

Before we do anything with the Payment Request API, we should check for support using `window.PaymentRequest`. If it's not supported, the user should be redirected to a non-AMP alternative checkout:

```
if (!window.PaymentRequest) {
  // Not supported, redirect to alternative checkout
  top.window.location.href =
'https://theampbook.com/ch9/alternative-checkout.html';
  return;
}
```

Next, we'll need to retrieve the user's cart from the server. We can make an XHR request to achieve this:

```
fetch('cart.php', {credentials: 'include'})
```

This request will respond with a JSON payload that contains the user's cart. We need to extract the cart contents and price from this response so that we can use them with the payment request. The Payment Request API expects a `details` object which includes the total price and the list items to be displayed. Each item will include a `label` property and an `amount` object, which specifies the price of the item and the currency. We create a display item like this for each of the items in the cart:

```
fetch('cart.php', {credentials: 'include'})
```

```
  .then((resp) => resp.json()) // Transform the data into json
  .then(function(cart) {
    var cart = cart.cart[0];
    cartTotalPrice = cart.cart_total_price;
    cart.cart_items.map(function(item) {
      cartItems.push({"label":item.product_name+' €'+item.price+' x
'+item.quantity,"amount":{"currency":"EUR",
"value":item.price*item.quantity}});
    });
})
```

Now let's wrap this data up into the `details` object that the API expects:

```
var details = {
  total: {label: 'Total', amount: {currency: 'EUR', value:
cartTotalPrice}},
  displayItems: cartItems
};
```

The API also expects a `methodData` object, and an `options` object. The `methodData` object specifies acceptable payment methods:

```
var methodData = [{supportedMethods: ["visa", "mastercard"]}];
```

And the options object allows further configuration options such as requiring email and shipping information. Let's keep things simple for this example:

```
var options = {
  requestShipping: false,
  requestPayerEmail: false,
  requestPayerPhone: false
}
```

Now we're ready to build the `PaymentRequest` object:

```
var paymentRequest = new PaymentRequest(methodData, details, options);
```

Next, we call the `show()` method to display the payment UI:

```
paymentRequest.show();
```

This will trigger the payment UI, and it should look something like this, depending on what has been added to the cart:

Checkout process: checkout button in amp-iframe (left), Payment Request UI (middle), and payment details (right)

The `show()` method returns a `Promise` to a `PaymentResponse` object. This promise is resolved when the user clicks the **PAY** button and accepts the payment request. If necessary, the Payment Request API will pop up a CCV entry dialog, which allows the user to confirm their credit card (shown in the next image). Once the promise is resolved successfully we can send the payment data contained in the response to the payment provider. First, we grab the data:

```
var paymentInfo = {
  methodName: paymentResponse.methodName,
  details: paymentResponse.details
}
```

Then we prepare the request that we'll make to the payment provider:

```
var params = {
  method: 'POST',
  credentials: 'include',
```

```
    headers: {
      'Content-Type': 'application/json'
    },
    body: JSON.stringify(paymentInfo)
  };
```

And finally, we send the data to the payment provider. This is where you'd integrate the API of a payment gateway such as *Stripe* or *Paypal*. In this example, we just simulate payment by fetching a page that always returns an HTTP 200 response:

```
  return fetch('process-payment.html', params).then(function(response) {
    if(response.status == 200) {
      top.window.location.href =
  'https://theampbook.com/ch9/checkout-complete.html';
    }
    else {
      return paymentResponse.complete('fail');
    }
  })
```

Importantly, after a successful checkout process, the `amp-iframe` can redirect the user to a confirmation page with:

```
top.window.location.href = 'https://...'.
```

Checkout process: CCV prompt (left), processing payment (middle), and order completion (right)

This completes our e-commerce prototype--we've built a seamless checkout process with minimal coding.

Summary

In this chapter, we saw how to extend AMP beyond what it supports through its core and extended components. We saw that with `amp-iframe` we can include all kinds of functionality. We focused on maps, comment systems, and checkout and payment functionality in this chapter since these are features common in e-commerce and news and blog type sites. Significantly, together with the HTML5 Payment Request API and `amp-iframe` we were able to complete our e-commerce prototype. However, `amp-iframe` is by no means limited to these features. You're only limited here by your imagination!

In the next chapter, we'll turn our attention towards *analytics* and *ad support* in AMP, two important topics that can help measure the performance of a site, as well as provide a monetization model, respectively.

10
Ads and Analytics in AMP

In this chapter, we'll cover ads and analytics support in AMP. While perhaps not the most exciting topics, they are important nonetheless. Analytics can offer insights into how well a website is performing against its goals, and into user behavior and interaction with the site. Ads offer a monetization model for many sites for which there may be no other revenue source available.

We'll start off with analytics and see how to add different types of tracking to our web pages. We'll see how to do the following:

- Track different types of events, such as pageviews, clicks, scrolling, and social sharing
- Apply this to our e-commerce cart, and see how to track addition and removal of products from the cart
- Unify sessions across the AMP cache and the original domain

We'll then look at ad support in AMP, and review the types and formats of ads that can be added to AMP pages.

Analytics support in AMP

AMP offers two main components for analytics tracking: `amp-pixel`, and `amp-analytics`. With `amp-pixel`, we can do simple pixel-tracking pageview analytics. If we want to do anything more advanced, such as click- or scroll-tracking, then we need to look at `amp-analytics`.

Pixel tracking with <amp-pixel>

The `amp-pixel` component offers simple pixel-tracking analytics. It's a core component, so there's no need to include any script. With `amp-pixel` you simply provide a URL that will register a pageview, for example:

```
<amp-pixel
src="https://a.theampbook.com/?idsite=1&rec=1&action_name=TITLE&url=CANONIC
AL_URL&rand=RANDOM">
```

Note the following:

- The `src` attribute URL must be HTTPS enabled
- Standard variable substitutions are supported, so `TITLE`, `CANONICAL_URL`, and `RANDOM` will all be replaced above

We'll see shortly that the `amp-analytics` component has built-in support for Google Analytics, but if you wanted to keep things super-lightweight, and if you have no need for features other than pageview counting, then you could even use `amp-pixel` with Google Analytics like this (`/ch10/ga-pixel.html`):

```
<amp-pixel
src="https://ssl.google-analytics.com/collect?v=1&tid=UA-12345678-1&t=pagev
iew&cid=CLIENT_ID(analytics)&dt=TITLE&dl=CANONICAL_URL&z=RANDOM"></amp-
pixel>
```

While `amp-pixel` is fine for simple pageview counting, if you want to do anything else, such as click-tracking, then you need `amp-analytics`.

Full analytics tracking with <amp-analytics>

We can implement more advanced page, event, and user-interaction tracking with the `amp-analytics` extended component. It can be used to track what users saw, clicked on, and scrolled through. It's included with this script:

```
<script async custom-element="amp-analytics"
src="https://cdn.ampproject.org/v0/amp-analytics-0.1.js"></script>
```

The configuration of `amp-analytics` is via a JSON configuration object. This can be specified inline or loaded from a remote endpoint. We'll see, later, that remote configurations can be very useful.

Configuring <amp-analytics>

The basic structure of the `amp-analytics` configuration object is like this:

```
{
  "requests": {
    request-name: request-value,
    ...
  },
  "vars": {
    var-name: var-value,
    ...
  },
    "triggers": {
      trigger-name: trigger-object,
      ...
    }
}
```

The code can be broken down as follows:

- `requests` contains a list of request types, each with an associated URL template where the analytics request will be sent
- `vars` contains a list of variables and values that will be submitted with the analytics request
- `triggers` defines how analytics requests are fired, by mapping events to one of the defined requests

Let's look at these in more detail with the help of an example (`/ch10/amp-analytics.html`):

```
<amp-analytics>
  <script type="application/json">
  {
    "requests": {
      "pageview":
"https://a.theampbook.com/?url=${canonicalUrl}&title=${title}&acct=${account}"
    },
    "vars": {
      "account": "UA-XXXXX-Y"
    },
    "triggers": {
      "trackPageview": {
        "on": "visible",
        "request": "pageview",
```

```
        "vars": {
          "foo": "bar"
        }
      }
    },
    "extraUrlParams": {
      "a": "1",
      "b": "2"
    }
  }
  </script>
</amp-analytics>
```

This example provides a good starting point as it highlights several important aspects of the analytics capabilities and configuration in AMP. Let's breakdown the configuration data:

Custom vendor pageview analytics request with amp-analytics

Requests

The `requests` object contains any URL endpoints for delivering analytics data. In the example, all `pageview` requests will be sent to the following URL:

```
https://a.theampbook.com/?url=${canonicalUrl}&title=${title}...
```

Note that we use `${...}` syntax for platform variable substitutions with `amp-analytics`, instead of the capitalized syntax we used with `amp-pixel`: `${title}` instead of `TITLE`, for example.

If we wanted to send `click` requests to a different URL or to configure different URL parameters, we can add another property to the `requests` object like this:

```
"requests": {
  "pageview":
"https://a.theampbook.com/?url=${canonicalUrl}&title=${title}&acct=${accoun
t}",
  "click":
"https://a.theampbook.com/?url=${canonicalUrl}&clickTarget=${clickTarget}&a
cct=${account}"
}
```

Variables

We can add arbitrary variables in the `vars` object, and we can then reference them in the request URLs. In the preceding example, we specified a property `account` as `"account"`: `"UA-XXXXX-Y"`, and in the URL, we can reference this property as `${account}`.

We can also use the `extraUrlParams` object to add arbitrary parameters to the URL automatically. We can add the following to the configuration:

```
"extraUrlParams": {
  "a": "1",
  "b": "2"
}
```

This would add `a=1&b=2` to the end of the analytics request URL without having to add `a=${a}&b=${b}` to the URL manually.

Triggers

We can define how and when analytics requests are made with triggers. They are essentially mappings between events and analytics requests and are defined in the `triggers` object. In the example earlier, we have one trigger:

```
"trackPageview": {
  "on": "visible",
  "request": "pageview",
  "vars": {
    "foo": "bar"
  }
}
```

It has the following properties:

- **Name**: `trackPageView`. You can use any alphanumeric string here.
- **Event listener**: `"on":"visible"`. The full list of possible events for triggers is `render-start`, `ini-load`, `visible`, `click`, `scroll`, `timer`, and `hidden`.
- **Request type**: `pageview`. This maps to a request type defined in the `requests` section of the config. This trigger is mapped to the `pageview` request.
- **Variables**: `"foo": "bar"`. We can also add variables at this point, in the `vars` object. Values can even be substituted dynamically from platform variables, or even from element-level data attributes. We'll see this shortly.

Loading configuration remotely

Configuration can be loaded from a remote URL with the `config` attribute. For instance, you can load a *Google Tag Manager* configuration with the following:

```
<amp-analytics
config="https://www.googletagmanager.com/amp.json?id=GTM-XXXXXX&gtm.url=SOU
RCE_URL" data-credentials="include">
  <script type="application/json">
  {
    "vars": {
      "foo": "bar"
    }
  }
  </script>
</amp-analytics>
```

The remote configuration can be combined with an inline configuration object too, as in the preceding example. Note that a remote configuration will:

- Take precedence over any inline configuration for conflicting properties
- Only be downloaded if the page is visible in the viewport

Transport configuration

We can also configure the transport mode of the analytics request by adding the transport object. There are three transport modes, all enabled by default. They're listed in order of precedence here:

- `beacon`: Uses `navigator.sendBeacon` to make a `POST` request with an empty body

- `xhrpost`: Uses `XMLHttpRequest` to make a `POST` request with an empty body
- `image`: Generates an `img` tag that makes a `GET` request

In the following example configuration, only `xhrpost` and `image` are enabled. If neither is supported by the client, then no analytics request would be made:

```
"transport": {
 "beacon": false,
 "xhrpost": true,
 "image": true
}
```

Using amp-analytics with built-in vendors

The `amp-analytics` component has built-in configurations for many vendors so that you don't need to manually configure all the details. You can specify a vendor by adding the `type="VENDOR_NAME"` attribute for a supported vendor. A list of supported vendors can be found here: `ampproject.org/docs/guides/analytics/analytics-vendors`.

Of course, Google Analytics, being one of the most widely used analytics solutions, has a built-in configuration. We can rewrite the `amp-pixel` pageview tracking example we saw earlier with `amp-analytics` built-in configuration like this (`/ch10/ga.html`):

```
<amp-analytics type="googleanalytics" id="ga1">
  <script type="application/json">
  {
    "vars": {
      "account": "UA-XXXXX-Y"
    },
    "triggers": {
      "trackPageview": {
        "on": "visible",
        "request": "pageview"
      }
    }
  }
  </script>
</amp-analytics>
```

The main benefit of built-in vendors is that certain aspects of the configuration are already taken care of for you. In this case, we don't need to manually configure the `requests` object; it's already set up.

Using Google Analytics with <amp-analytics>

Let's take a look specifically at how to use Google Analytics in AMP. Much of what follows here will be applicable to other vendors, but you'll need to familiarize yourself with the requests and variables supported by those vendors. The following request types are supported in Google Analytics for AMP:

- `pageview` for tracking pageviews
- `event` for tracking events, such as clicks or scrolls
- `social` for tracking social interactions

We've already seen how to do pageview tracking both with `amp-pixel` and `amp-analytics`, so we'll jump straight to click tracking.

Click and tap tracking

It's often useful to track what a user has clicked or tapped on. We can target elements to track using CSS selector style syntax. For example, suppose we had a simple button in our page like this:

```
<button>Click me!</button>
```

Then we could track its clicks with the following (`/ch10/ga-click-button.html`):

```
{
  "vars": {
    "account": "UA-XXXXXXXX-X"
  },
  "triggers": {
    "buttonClickTracker": {
      "on": "click",
      "selector": "button",
      "request": "event",
      "vars": {
        "eventCategory": "Click tracking",
        "eventAction": "click button",
        "eventLabel": "Click me button",
      }
    }
  }
}
```

Note the variables `eventCategory`, `eventAction`, and `eventLabel`. We can add any variables we want here, but these particular ones are supported in the `event` request type of Google Analytics, and will be sent with the request and parsed at the Google Analytics end.

As the click events are sent to Google Analytics, you can see them being registered in real time under **Realtime** | **Events**, or view them over a date range under **Behavior** | **Events** | **Overview**:

Observing realtime click events from AMP pages in Google Analytics (*Realtime > Events*)

In the preceding image, each blue bar on the right represents a single click event, while the number **22** is a count of the total number of clicks recorded. The **Click tracking** category and **click button** action entries come directly from the `eventCategory` and `eventAction` variables in the analytics configuration we just set up.

Variable substitution in <amp-analytics>

In the last example, the `vars` variables were given static values, but there are some interesting things we can do with variable substitution here. For example, suppose we had two buttons. Instead of setting up two separate click handlers, it would be better if we could just substitute in the button ID dynamically.

With data attributes, we can define arbitrary element-level variables to use in the configuration. Any data attribute with the format `data-vars-variable-name` will be made available as `${variableName}` in the analytics configuration. So we can update our button like this:

```
<button data-vars-button-id="Click me button">Click me!</button>
```

And we can then update the configuration object to use the button like this:

```
"eventLabel": "${buttonId}"
```

If you check the browser developer tools, you can confirm that the button ID is sent with the analytics request.

There's another trick here too. If we change the data attribute name to match a variable name in the `vars` object, then the assignment will happen automatically. So we can change the button, and add a second button, like this:

```
<button data-vars-event-label="Click me button">Click me</button>
<button data-vars-event-label="Another button">Click me too!</button>
```

Now we can drop the `eventLabel` assignment from the configuration altogether, leaving just the other variables:

```
"vars": {
 "eventCategory": "Click tracking",
 "eventAction": "click button",
}
```

The variable name will now be matched and substituted into the request URL, which is preconfigured because we're using `type="googleanalytics"`:

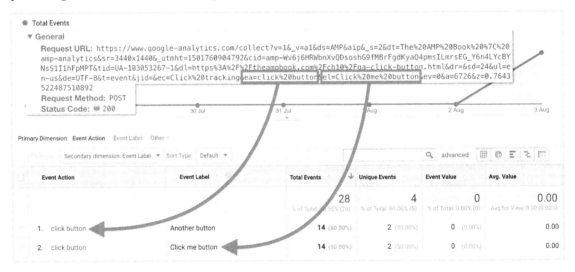

Click event URL (inset) and viewing button click events in Google Analytics (/ch10/ga-click-button.html)

We can see this substitution in a vendorless configuration too, where we have to specify the request URLs explicitly (`/ch10/novendor-click.html`):

```
{
  "requests": {
    "event":
"https://a.theampbook.com/?url=${canonicalUrl}&title=${title}&acct=${account}&buttonId=${buttonId}"
  },
  "triggers": {
    "buttonClickTracker": {
      ...
    }
  }
}
```

In the `button` element, `data-vars-button-id="Click me button"` will match `${buttonId}` in the event request URL, and its value, `"Click me button"`, will be automatically substituted.

Tracking outbound link clicks

Another useful thing to track is clicks on outbound links. We could use the following configuration to track clicks on links:

```
"triggers": {
  "outLinkClicks": {
    "on": "click",
    "selector": "a",
    "request": "event",
    "vars": {
      "eventCategory": "outbound",
      "eventAction": "click",
      "eventLabel": "${outboundLink}"
    }
  }
}
```

Then, we can annotate each outbound link with a data attribute:

```
<a href="http://example.com"
   data-vars-outbound-link="http://example.com">Some link</a>
```

A drawback of this approach is that a request will be sent whether or not it's an outbound link, although only the links we've annotated will contain an `eventLabel` value.

We could remedy this by targeting only the actual outbound links with a more specific selector:

```
"selector": "a:not([href*='theampbook.com']"
```

This would target any link with `href` that does not contain the string `theampbook.com` (`/ch10/ga-click-link.html`).

Scroll tracking

Another useful user interaction to track is scrolling. We can use the `scroll` event for this. This event fires as a user scrolls through a page. This could be useful in article or blog style pages to determine whether users are reading all the way through your content.

The `scrollSpec` object allows you to specify through what percentage of the page the user must scroll before the event will fire. Vertical and horizontal percentages are specified in the `verticalBoundaries` and `horizontalBoundaries` properties respectively. In the following configuration (`/ch10/ga-scroll.html`), the scroll trigger will be fired when the page is scrolled vertically to 25 percent, 50 percent, 75 percent, and 100 percent. Boundaries are rounded to the nearest multiple of five for performance:

```
"triggers": {
  "scrollTracking": {
    "on": "scroll",
    "scrollSpec": {
      "verticalBoundaries": [25, 50, 75, 100]
    },
    "request": "event",
    "vars": {
      "eventCategory": "Scroll completion",
      "eventAction": "Scrolled ${verticalScrollBoundary}%",
      "eventLabel": "${ampdocUrl}"
    }
  }
}
```

Note that we have sent some variables too. In particular, we make use of the platform variable ${verticalScrollBoundary}, which will substitute the scroll boundary that triggered the event automatically:

Viewing scroll events in Google Analytics (/ch10/ga-scroll.html)

Tracking time on a page with timer triggers

Timer triggers can be used to track the amount of time a user spends on a page. Google Analytics can already track time spent on a page using the difference between the pageview timestamps. However, if there is only one pageview, then Google Analytics can't track time accurately. That's where timer triggers come in. The following will send events every 15 seconds, to a maximum of 600 seconds (/ch10/ga-timer.html):

```
"triggers": {
  "pageTimer": {
    "on": "timer",
    "timerSpec": {
      "interval": 15,
      "maxTimerLength": 600
    },
    "request": "event",
    "vars": {
      "eventCategory": "pagetime",
      "eventAction": "Engaged ${totalEngagedTime}",
      "eventLabel": "${ampdocUrl}"
    }
  }
}
```

In this example, note the following:

- We use the `event` request type here for the `timer` trigger
- We use the `timerSpec` object to set `interval` and `maxTimerLength` properties that define the behavior of the timer
- We included the `${totalEngagedTime}` platform variable along with the request--this is the time in seconds since the page became visible in the viewport
- We also use the `${ampdocUrl}` platform variable as the `eventLabel` variable

Tracking social interaction

Another common analytics task is to track social engagement. The following example shows how we might track Twitter shares, based on clicks of an element with ID `twitter-share`:

```
"triggers": {
  "twitterShares" : {
    "on": "click",
    "selector": "#twitter-share",
    "request": "social",
    "vars": {
      "socialNetwork": "twitter",
      "socialAction": "tweet",
      "socialTarget": "${ampdocUrl}"
    }
  }
}
```

The Google Analytics `social` request has the following variables:

- `socialNetwork`: The network on which the action occurs, such as Facebook or Twitter
- `socialAction`: The social action, such as *like*, *send*, or *tweet*
- `socialTarget`: The target of the social action, typically a URL but can be any text

Earlier, we saw that variables can be injected into the `amp-analytics` configuration where a data attribute with format `data-vars-variable-name` will be made available as `${variableName}`, or **substituted automatically** if it matches a predefined variable name. So, if we add `data-vars-social-action`, `data-vars-social-network`, and `data-vars-social-target` to the `amp-social-share` element, then the analytics configuration can automatically accommodate different social networks:

```
<amp-social-share type="linkedin" width="60" height="44"
  data-param-text="Hello LinkedIn World"
  data-param-url="https://example.com/">
  data-vars-social-action="share"
  data-vars-social-network="LinkedIn"
  data-vars-social-target="https://example.com/"
</amp-social-share>
```

In the configuration, we can now drop the `vars` section altogether, as it will be automatically populated:

```
"triggers": {
  "socialShares" : {
    "on": "click",
    "selector": "amp-social-share",
    "request": "social"
  }
}
```

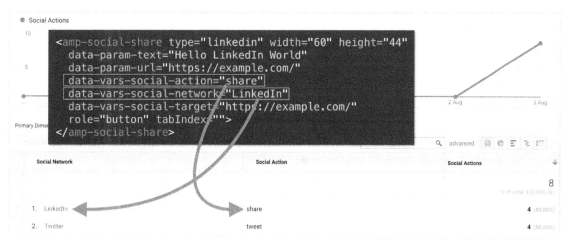

Tracking social interactions in AMP and Google Analytics (/ch10/ga-social.html)

This view uses a custom report. You can get this report for your Google Analytics account at this URL: `https://analytics.google.com/analytics/web/template?uid=FpmnKOfgRia3iAwNbbow7Q`.

Analytics for e-commerce

Let's apply some of this to our e-commerce prototype. We could track which items were added to the shopping cart and which were removed. We could also track whether the carousel is being used, or whether product images and descriptions are being clicked and read. There's lots we could measure!

Tracking the addition of items to the cart

To track when products are added to the cart, we just need to target the add-to-cart button. If we pass through the product ID as well, this would allow us to identify the *most-added* items in our analytics. First, let's set up a `click` trigger on the **add-to-cart** button, which has the CSS class `btn-add-to-cart`:

```
"triggers": {
  "addToCart": {
    "on": "click",
    "selector": ".btn-add-to-cart",
    "request": "event",
    "vars": {
      "eventCategory": "Cart",
      "eventAction": "Product added"
    }
  }
}
```

Next, we'll add a `data-vars` attribute to the `add-to-cart` button. Recall from `Chapter 8`, *Programming in AMP - amp-bind*, that, when we implemented the cart, we used an `amp-mustache` template variable, `{{product_id}}`, to populate the product ID of the item we were adding to the cart. We'll use this to populate the data attribute:

```
<input class="btn-add-to-cart" type="submit"
  ...
  data-vars-event-label="{{product_id}}">
```

This will automatically be submitted with the analytics request, and we don't need to explicitly add it to the configuration:

Developer tools showing an analytics request that tracks products added to the cart in AMP (/ch10/ga-cart.html)

Tracking the removal of items from the cart

We can use a similar setup too when items are removed from the cart. This time, we need to target the `remove-from-cart` link. First, the trigger: the remove link has the CSS class `cart-del`, so we can use this to target the link:

```
"triggers": {
  ...
  "remove from cart": {
    "on": "click",
    "selector": ".cart-del",
    "request": "event",
    "vars": {
      "eventCategory": "Cart",
      "eventAction": "Product removed"
    }
  }
}
```

And now we add the data attribute that will populate the `eventLabel` variable to the delete link to pass the product ID to the analytics request:

```
<div class="cart-del"
    ...
    data-vars-event-label="{{product_id}}">X</div>
```

Tracking which products were added to and removed from the cart in Google Analytics (/ch10/ga-cart.html)

Session stitching AMP Cache and original domain

A side effect of serving content from the AMP Cache is that, since it's a separate domain, user sessions from the original domain and the AMP Cache aren't automatically unified in analytics. That is, the same visitor to each of the domains will be treated as two different users and is assigned two different client IDs. However, with a little creativity, we can work around this.

> The solution presented here is based on an approach by Simo Ahava and Dan Wilkinson (`simoahava.com/analytics/google-analytics-client-id-amp-pages/`)

Earlier, it was mentioned that the `amp-analytics` configuration could be fetched from a remote (HTTPS) server endpoint. This is key to setting up cross-domain session stitching. We'll point our `amp-analytics` to a configuration script on our main server. This script will do a number of things:

1. **Check for the Google Analytics `_ga` cookie**
   If user has visited before and the cookie is found, it will do the following:
   - Parse the client ID from the cookie
   - Pass this cookie to the domain that made the request

If the cookie is not found, it will create a client ID in the `_ga` format, a 32-bit integer with dot-separated timestamp like this: `1234567890.1234567890`.

2. **Set the** `vars.clientId` **property**
   We need to add a property called `clientId` to the `vars` object in the AMP configuration. This will correspond to the client ID of the `_ga` cookie in step 1:

```
{
  "vars": {
    "clientId": "1234567890.1234567890"
  }
}
```

For this to work from the AMP Cache, we need to enable a CORS request for the `amp-analytics` configuration script on our origin server. We achieve this by including the following headers:

```
Access-Control-Allow-Origin: https://yourdomain-tld.cdn.ampproject.org
AMP-Access-Control-Allow-Source-Origin: https://yourdomain.com
Access-Control-Allow-Credentials: true
Access-Control-Expose-Headers: AMP-Access-Control-Allow-Source-Origin
```

You can host your entire configuration on the server, or just the `vars.clientId` property: the remote configuration will be merged with an inline configuration. For flexibility, it's recommended to do most of your configuration in the AMP page, and only emit the `vars.clientId` property from the remote configuration.

If you implement this on your own domain, to see and appreciate the results, you can do the following:

1. Load up Google Analytics and go to **Realtime** | **Overview** for your domain.
2. Visit `https://yourdomain.com/ga-session.html`.
3. Confirm the pageview in Google Analytics (see the following screenshot).
4. Visit the AMP cache version:
   `https://yourdomain-com.cdn.ampproject.org/c/s/yourdomain.com/ga-session.html`.

5. Confirm the pageview in Google Analytics, but observe that the number of visitors has remained the same: Google Analytics has identified that the two visits on the different domains were from the same client ID; the sessions have been unified--mission accomplished!

Session stitching: Google Analytics shows one user for two hits, one on each domain

The full code for this example can be seen at /ch10/ga-session.html, and the server script that performs the client ID stitching is at /ch10/session-stitch.php.

Session stitching with Google Tag Manager

This approach will also work if you use **Google Tag Manager** (**GTM**) to manage analytics and tracking tags on your main website. There are two extra steps, however. First, in our server script, we need to fetch the GTM configuration (you can cache this on your server too).

Then, once the GTM configuration has been retrieved, we need to perform a string replacement of all instances of "CLIENT_ID" with the "${clientId}" variable that AMP understands, but otherwise the procedure is the same.

You can see the code to achieve this at /ch10/session-stitch-gtm.php. You can follow the same steps as previously to confirm that it's working as expected.

Ads in AMP

Ads are well supported in AMP, as you might expect since AMP is backed by Google. The main component used for including ads in your pages is amp-ad. As with other AMP components, this has been designed with performance in mind. It's particularly important for ads to perform well since ads are often the cause of poor web page performance and slow load times. Indeed, if AMP determines that a third-party ad is affecting performance, it can stop animations or even remove them from the page.

The <amp-ad> component

The amp-ad component is included with the following script:

```
<script async custom-element="amp-ad"
src="https://cdn.ampproject.org/v0/amp-ad-0.1.js"></script>
```

Many ad platforms are supported; you can see a list here: ampproject.org/docs/reference/components/amp-ad. Since *Adsense* is one of the most widely used ad networks, let's take a look at that.

Embedding an Adsense ad

We can embed an Adsense ad with markup like this (/ch10/ad-adsense.html):

```
<amp-ad
  layout="fixed-height"
  height=100
  type="adsense"
  data-ad-client="ca-pub-1234567891234567"
  data-ad-slot="1234567890">
</amp-ad>
```

Note the use of the following:

- type="adsense": This specifies the built-in ad network to use. If we wanted to use a *DoubleClick* ad, we'd use type="doubleclick", and so on.
- data-ad-client and data-ad-slot: These are Adsense-specific variables that determine which ad unit will be displayed. You'll need to get these from your Adsense account. Other networks will use different properties.

Ad placement

While there are no restrictions on ad placement in AMP, if it's above the fold, it's recommended to use a fixed-height ad, as shown in the previous example code.

For below the fold placement, it's recommended to use 300x250 size, with a responsive layout, so that it resizes appropriately for the device viewport:

```
<amp-ad layout="responsive"
        width="300"
        height="250"
        type="adsense"
        data-ad-client="ca-pub-1234567891234567"
        data-ad-slot="1234567890">
</amp-ad>
```

Fixed-height, above-the-fold ad (left) and responsive below-the-fold ad (right) (/ch10/ad-adsense.html)

Ad placeholder

Like many elements in AMP, amp-ad supports a placeholder child element. This will be displayed while the ad loads, if supported by the ad network:

```
<amp-ad width="300" height="250" type="adsense">
  <div placeholder>Ad loading...</div>
</amp-ad>
```

Ad fallback

If an `amp-ad` slot is not filled, then the element will not be displayed unless a fallback element has been defined. In this case, the fallback will be displayed instead of the ad. If no fallback is specified and the ad request goes unfilled, then the ad container will collapse. This may or may not be desirable, depending on your application:

```
<amp-ad width="300 height="250" type="adsense">
  <div fallback>No ad this time</div>
</amp-ad>
```

Sticky ads

AMP provides a component to fix an ad to the bottom of the page: `amp-sticky-ad`. It's included with this script:

```
<script async custom-element="amp-sticky-ad"
src="https://cdn.ampproject.org/v0/amp-sticky-ad-1.0.js"></script>
```

The following applies to `amp-sticky-ad`:

- It must have a single child that is an `amp-ad` element
- It must have `layout="nodisplay"`
- It can have a maximum height of 100px
- It will pad the end-of-page content so that all content is viewable

> Sticky ads violate Adsense policies, so if you use an Adsense `amp-ad` with `amp-sticky-ad`, no ad will be displayed. You can, however, use sticky ads with other ad networks, such as DoubleClick.

The following code will display a DoubleClick ad as a sticky ad (`/ch10/ad-sticky.html`):

```
<amp-sticky-ad layout="nodisplay">
  <amp-ad width="320"
          height="50"
          type="doubleclick"
          data-slot="/12345678/sticky_ad">
  </amp-ad>
</amp-sticky-ad>
```

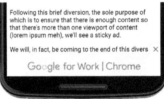

A sticky ad displayed at the bottom of the viewport with amp-sticky-ad (/ch10/ad-sticky.html)

Getting creative with ads

So far, we've seen how to embed ads directly into AMP pages. However, we can also combine and embed `amp-ad` with other AMP components.

Carousel ads

A very common ad use case is to include ads within an image carousel. We saw how to build image carousels in Chapter 5, *Building Rich Media Pages in AMP*. We could easily use an ad as one of the items in a carousel like this (`/ch10/ad-carousel.html`):

```
<amp-carousel height="300" layout="fixed-height"
              type="carousel">
  <amp-img src="img/jellyfish1.jpg"
           width="300" height="300">
  </amp-img>
  <amp-ad width="300" height="300" layout="fixed"
          data-ad-client="ca-pub-1234567891234567"
          data-ad-slot="1234567890">
  </amp-ad>
  <amp-img src="img/jellyfish2.jpg"
           width="300" height="300">
  </amp-img>
</amp-carousel>
```

This will work both with carousel `type="slides"` and `type="carousel"`.

Flying carpet ads

Another interesting way to deliver ads is with the `amp-fx-flying-carpet` component. We haven't seen this component before. It works by wrapping its children in a fullscreen container, but only displays a fixed-height portion of this container at a time, so that the user must scroll through the page to reveal the hidden portion of the content. It can be used with any AMP content, not just ads.

There are two restrictions on `amp-fx-flying-carpet` placement:

- It must be outside the first 75 percent of the first vertical viewport
- Its top must be above the top of the last viewport, that is, there must be enough content after it so that it can be viewed

An example (`/ch10/ad-flying-carpet.html`) can be seen in the following image:

Only a portion of a flying carpet ad will be viewable at any time

To set this up, first we need to include the `amp-fx-flying-carpet` script:

```
<script async custom-element="amp-fx-flying-carpet"
src="https://cdn.ampproject.org/v0/amp-fx-flying-carpet-0.1.js"></script>
```

Next, we just need to wrap the `amp-ad` element within the `amp-fx-flying-carpet` element:

```
<amp-fx-flying-carpet height="300px">
    <amp-ad
      layout="responsive"
      width="300"
      height="600"
      type="adsense"
      data-ad-client="ca-pub-1234567891234567"
      data-ad-slot="1234567890">
    </amp-ad>
</amp-fx-flying-carpet>
```

The height of the `amp-fx-flying-carpet` element will determine the portion of the ad that's viewable at any time.

Summary

In this chapter, we explored ads and analytics in AMP. While many analytics platforms are supported out-of-the-box, AMP is also able to accommodate analytics providers that don't have built-in support: all you need to know is the analytics URL endpoint, and the format of data that's expected, and you can track page views and events with any provider. We also saw that it's pretty simple to integrate ad platforms into your AMP pages, and saw a variety of different ad types.

We're coming close to the end of our journey in AMP. In the next chapter, we take a look at how AMP can fit in with your non-AMP web properties and we'll review different deployment options.

11
AMP Deployment and Your Web Presence

So far in this book, we've described how to build AMP pages, but we haven't really discussed how to deploy AMP pages within the wider context of the rest of your non-AMP web presence.

In this chapter, we will take a look at different deployment patterns and complementary web technologies that can be used to integrate AMP pages into a coherent web presence. This will include the following:

- Canonical AMP pages
- Patterns for how AMP and Progressive Web Apps can work together
- How to serve AMP pages to all mobile visitors, not just those arriving via Google
- AMP and WordPress

Canonical AMP pages

This is the simplest approach: You have a single website, built on AMP. Because AMP supports responsive design, it will work on the desktop too. We've already seen examples of responsive web pages throughout this book, so we won't go into much detail here. The important thing to remember about canonical AMP pages is that the canonical link should point to itself:

```
<link rel="canonical" href="https://example.com/theampdoc.html"/>
```

While we've seen throughout this book that AMP is both flexible and powerful, there will always be scenarios that it won't be possible to solve with AMP alone. If this applies to your project, then using canonical AMP as your sole web solution won't be an option, and you should consider some of the other options covered in this chapter.

Progressive Web Apps and AMP

The term **Progressive Web App** (**PWA**) is used to describe web apps that make use of modern browser features to deliver rich, app-like experiences. Typically, a PWA will exhibit some or all of the following characteristics:

- **Progressive**: Works on all devices, with progressively enhanced functionality
- **Responsive**: Has a flexible layout that fits any form factor
- **Connectivity-independent**: Will function under poor network conditions, and even offline
- **App-like**: Feels like an app, with an app shell, and fetches new content mostly without full page refreshes
- **Discoverable**: Identifiable as an app while also being indexable by search engines on the web
- **Installable**: Can be added to the home screen of a device

The reason PWAs have gained prominence now is because the web platform has grown sufficiently mature to deliver such experiences. HTML5 has become advanced enough to support features such as push notifications, geolocation, and offline experiences. These are all features that previously would have been found only in native apps. Several key HTML5 APIs make PWAs possible:

- **Service Workers API**: For offline and network challenges conditions, as well as handling push message notifications
- **Push API**, and **Notifications API**: For delivering asynchronous push messages
- **Web App Manifest**: Defines a mechanism for adding metadata to a web app, which helps with indexing and adding to the home screen of devices

PWA minimum requirements

Shortly, we'll discuss how AMP and PWAs can work together. We won't go into too much detail on building PWAs; that's a topic that could fill a book by itself. Instead, we'll demonstrate the AMP and PWA concepts by providing simple working examples. Before we jump in, it's worth pointing out that the absolute minimal PWA has a **web app manifest** file, which makes it installable, and a **service worker**, which helps deliver features such as offline functionality and push notifications. Let's briefly look at these two things.

What is a service worker?

Service workers are central to PWAs. A service worker is a script that the browser runs in the background. It can act as a proxy to a web page, intercepting requests and controlling responses, and this means it can implement advanced browser features, such as offline capabilities, background syncing, and push notifications. All major browsers currently support, or are building support for, service workers.

There are a number of libraries that can be used to help with common service worker tasks, such as the sw-toolbox (`github.com/GoogleChrome/sw-toolbox`) and workbox (`github.com/GoogleChrome/workbox`) libraries. We're only going to write a simple service worker here, so we won't be using them, but they might be useful if you plan to write your own service worker.

What is a web app manifest?

A web app manifest is a JSON file that publishes metadata about a web app that enables it to be installed on a device's home screen, and configures how it will be launched. It includes things such as the web app name and description, icon URLs and sizes, and launch configurations (for example, whether it should be launched full screen and in what orientation). A web app manifest helps to bring a more native app-like experience to the web.

In the examples in this chapter, to ensure we have a (minimal) PWA, we'll include a basic web app manifest. We'll use a similar manifest for all the examples, and it will look like this:

```json
{
  "name": "The AMP Book | AMP to PWA",
  "short_name": "AMP to PWA",
  "description": "The AMP Book | AMP to PWA Pattern",
  "icons": [
    {
      "sizes": "192x192",
      "type": "image/png",
      "src": "icon-192.png"
    }
  ],
  "display": "standalone",
  "background_color": "#fff",
  "theme_color": "#005689",
  "scope": "https://theampbook.com/ch11/ampaspwa/"
  "start_url": "index.html"
}
```

The main difference between the examples will be the `scope` property, which restricts what pages can be viewed as part of the web app; for each of the examples that follow, we'll use the folder containing the example files as the `scope`.

You can add a web app manifest to a web page, whether it's an AMP page or not, like this:

```html
<link rel="manifest" href="/path/to/manifest.json">
```

Adding a PWA to the home screen

When both a manifest and a service worker are detected, the browser may prompt the user to add the PWA to the home screen, as shown in the following image:

Typical add-to-homescreen prompt for PWAs (left), homescreen icon (middle), and autogenerated splash/loading screen (right)

When added, the icon and app name defined in the manifest will be added to the device home screen. When the app is launched, a splash screen generated from the manifest data will be displayed, and the app will then be loaded with the specified orientation and screen configuration.

AMP and PWAs - three approaches

The AMP team suggests three AMP-PWA patterns:

- **AMP as PWA**: In which the AMP page *is* the PWA
- **AMP to PWA**: In which the AMP page *bootstraps*, or warms up, the PWA
- **AMP in PWA**: In which the AMP page *serves as content* within the PWA

Let's explore these patterns.

AMP as PWA

In this approach, the AMP page *is* the PWA. It's a step up from the simple canonical AMP approach mentioned earlier. In common with the canonical approach, AMP is used for the entire range of web experiences for desktop, mobile, and anything else.

It differs from canonical AMP in that when the page is served from the source domain, its behavior can be augmented using a service worker. When served from the source domain, and not the AMP cache, the service worker can step in and handle requests and responses. This means the PWA page can do things that normally wouldn't be possible in AMP, such as adding custom components and behaviors. Since these features are delivered by the service worker, the AMP page will still be valid.

There are many ways in which we could augment an AMP page. We'll consider the following two:

- Offline access: With the service worker we can cache any content we want to make it available offline. Then, even when the network is absent, users can browse and interact with the app.
- Custom JavaScript: Likewise, with the service worker, we can add JavaScript functionality that wouldn't otherwise be allowed in AMP.

To set these things up, we need a way to install a service worker from an AMP page.

Installing a service worker with AMP

So how can an AMP page install a service worker? Conveniently, there's a dedicated component, `amp-install-serviceworker`, for exactly this purpose. It's imported with the following script:

```
<script async custom-element="amp-install-serviceworker"
src="https://cdn.ampproject.org/v0/amp-install-serviceworker-0.1.js">
</script>
```

We can now use the following code (/ch11/ampaspwa/index.html) to install the service worker:

```
<amp-install-serviceworker
  src="https://theampbook.com/ch11/ampaspwa/sw.js"
  layout="nodisplay">
</amp-install-serviceworker>
```

The src attribute here points at a file /ch11/ampaspwa/sw.js. This file contains the JavaScript code for the service worker. Let's see how it works.

Writing a service worker to cache resources

For this example, we want the service worker to cache a few resources--some pages and assets--so that the site can be used offline. The service worker API defines an install event that can be used to define what should happen when the service worker is installed. Typically, at this point, we'd want to cache all the pages and resources that will be needed when the user is offline. When the service worker is installed, we can open a cache (pwa-cache) and add items to it like this:

```
self.addEventListener('install', e => {
  e.waitUntil(
    caches.open('pwa-cache').then(cache => {
        return cache.addAll(['index.html', 'amp.html', 'extra.js',
'manifest.json'])
      })
    )
});
```

We can then intercept page requests by listening for the fetch event, and we can check whether we have the requested item in the cache, like this:

```
self.addEventListener('fetch', e => {
  e.respondWith(
    caches.match(e.request).then(response => {
      return response || fetch(e.request);
    })
  );
});
```

If there's no match for a request, then the request is fetched via the network, if it's available. You can confirm that this is working by opening the Chrome developer tools on the **Application** tab. Then visit the page /ch11/ampaspwa/index.html. You should be able to see that the cache has been populated:

Chrome developer tools showing service worker cached resources

If you open up the developer tools **Network** tab and load the page again, you should be able to see that the resources were loaded by the service worker:

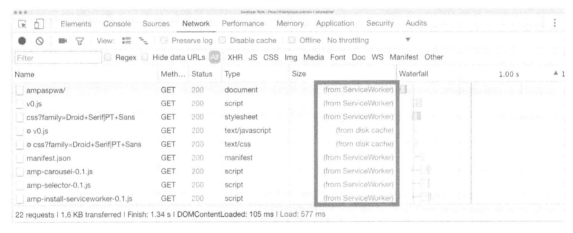

Chrome developer tools showing the service worker loading resources

If you disable the network and visit /ch11/ampaspwa/amp.html, this page should load via the service worker, even without a connection.

The important thing here for offline access is to make sure that all required resources are cached--what resources are needed will depend on the application. It's also a good idea for the PWA to *gracefully degrade*, that is, to have a catch-all fallback for when resources aren't available, rather than showing an error page. And finally, it's also a good idea to have the service worker update any cached items when there is a network connection. Check out *Jake Archibald's Offline Cookbook* to learn about caching strategies. You can find it at `jakearchibald.com/2014/offline-cookbook/`.

Injecting JavaScript with a service worker

As well as just caching pages and assets for offline use, we can add things that AMP doesn't normally permit, such as custom JavaScript. The following is a very basic example of how we could inject custom JavaScript into an AMP page with the service worker. We modify the service worker fetch block to include the `extra.js` file in any URL path that matches `*amp.html`:

```
self.addEventListener('fetch', e => {
  var url = new URL(e.request.url);
  if(url.pathname.split('/').pop().endsWith('amp.html')) {
    e.respondWith(
      fetch(e.request).then(response => {
        var init = {
          status:     200,
          statusText: "OK",
          headers: {'Content-Type': 'text/html'}
        };
        return response.text().then(body => {
          body = body.replace('</body>', '<script src="extra.js" async
></script></body>');
          return new Response(body, init);
        });
      })
    );
  }
  // Check the cache as before...
});
```

When loaded, the `extra.js` file simply pops up an alert dialog, something that is not normally allowed in AMP. You can test this by visiting `/ch11/ampaspwa/amp.html` twice:

- On the first visit, the service worker will be installed, and the resources cached (you might also be prompted to add it to your home screen)
- On the second visit, the service worker handles the request, and injects the JavaScript, and so you should see a JavaScript alert dialog, as shown in the following image:

 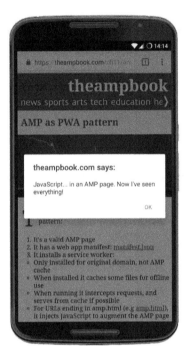

First and subsequent visits to AMP as a PWA page

If you test the page in the AMP validator, you will see that it is still valid. You can also visit the AMP Cache version of the page (prefix the URL with `theampbook-com.cdn.ampproject.org/c/s/`); there's no alert this time because the service worker only runs in the original domain.

Developing service workers can get complicated, but the developer tools in Chrome have great support under the **Applications** tab, where you can stop, start, and update service workers, clear out caches, view the app manifest, and so on. You can also use these tools to verify that the service worker is active when you visit via the original domain, but not when you visit the AMP cache URL.

AMP to PWA

In this approach, the AMP page bootstraps or *warms up* the PWA. The AMP page installs a service worker on the device and the service worker caches resources that will be used by the PWA. When the user subsequently visits the main PWA website, most of the resources are already loaded and the PWA can be rendered quickly.

This type of deployment thus capitalizes initially on the speed, efficient loading, and performance of the lightweight AMP page, and subsequently on the richness of the PWA page. It differs from the previous approach in that the PWA pages don't explicitly use the AMP library--they're not AMP pages and can include whatever technologies and features you like, such as JavaScript or anything else you might fancy.

So the main difference between this example from the previous one will be the inclusion of a separate non-AMP PWA page. The service worker we'll use will be very similar to the previous example, this time caching any resources needed by the PWA page.

We'll also use this example to show another nice feature of `amp-install-serviceworker`: the ability to install the service worker from the AMP Cache.

Caching PWA assets with a service worker

Starting with the service worker from the last example, there's not too much to do here. We just need to specify the PWA resources that we want to cache. Since the PWA page won't be an AMP page this time, let's also cache a JavaScript file that the PWA uses. To do this, we can just modify the previous service worker code like this (`/ch11/amptopwa/sw.js`):

```
return cache.addAll(['pwa.html', 'style.css', 'pwa.js']);
```

Installing a service worker from the AMP Cache

Now let's see how to install the service worker and the AMP page when it's served from the cache. We'll change our `amp-install-serviceworker` tag to look like this:

```
<amp-install-serviceworker
  src="https://theampbook.com/ch11/amp2pwa/sw.js"
  data-iframe-src="https://theampbook.com/ch11/amptopwa/sw-install.html"
  layout="nodisplay">
</amp-install-serviceworker>
```

This time, note the `data-iframe-src` attribute. When AMP files are served from the cache, they're served from a different domain, so we need a way to install the service worker from a domain other than the one it will be used on. This can be achieved via an iframe. When a user visits the original domain, the `src` attribute is used to install the service worker. When the user visits the AMP cache page, the `data-iframe-src attribute` is used. This attribute should point to a script on the origin domain that will install the service worker.

The service worker iframe installer

The iframe installer is a simple HTML page that will be loaded into an iframe by the `amp-install-serviceworker` component when the AMP page is loaded via the cache. It uses JavaScript to install the service worker (`/ch11/amptopwa/sw-install.html`):

```
<script type="text/javascript">
  if("serviceWorker" in navigator) {
    navigator.serviceWorker.register('/sw.js').then(function(reg){
      console.log('ServiceWorker scope: ', reg.scope);
    }).catch(function(err) {
      console.warn('ServiceWorker registration failed: ', err);
    });
  };
</script>
```

That's it! We use the same service worker file, but by using an iframe when needed, `amp-install-serviceworker` can install the service worker whether the user arrives via the cache or the source domain.

The PWA page

To complete the example, we need a page that will be the PWA itself. Strictly, to qualify as a PWA, it needs a `manifest.json` file and a service worker. We have both of these already.

The PWA itself will be a non-AMP HTML document. It will contain JavaScript code to install the service worker (for users that don't arrive via the AMP page), and we'll link to the manifest. Because it's not an AMP page, we'll also include some custom JavaScript (`pwa.js`) and some external CSS (`style.css`), just because we can! Other than that, for the purposes of this example, it doesn't really matter what's in this page. The important bits are shown as follows, while the full file can be found at `/ch11/amptopwa/pwa.html`:

```html
<!DOCTYPE html>
<html>
  <head>
    ...
    <link rel="stylesheet" href="style.css">
    <link rel="manifest" href="manifest.json">
    <script type="text/javascript">
      if("serviceWorker" in navigator) {
        navigator.serviceWorker.register("sw.js").then(function(reg){
          console.log('ServiceWorker scope: ', reg.scope);
        }).catch(function(err) {
          console.log('ServiceWorker registration failed: ', err);
        });
      };
    </script>
    ...
    <script src="pwa.js" async></script>
  </body>
</html>
```

So now we're ready to test. With your developer tools open, first load up the AMP page (`/ch11/amptopwa/amp.html`). As we saw earlier, under the **Applications** tab you should see that the service worker was installed and that the cache was populated:

AMP to PWA pattern: developer tools showing the service worker's caching of PWA resources

Now, click through to the PWA page (`/ch11/amptopwa/pwa.html`). You should notice that it loads quickly! On the **Network** tab, you should be able to see that the assets were loaded via the service worker. That is, they didn't need to be fetched from the network because the service worker had already downloaded them in the background. Mission accomplished: We just built an AMP page that bootstraps a PWA.

In fact, you can even use the PWA offline now and the service worker will handle the requests:

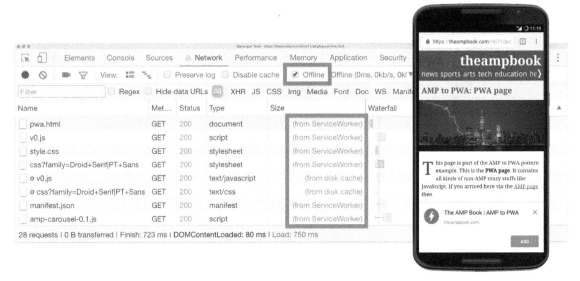

AMP to PWA pattern: developer tools showing service worker loading PWA resources in offline mode

Additionally, you may be prompted to install the PWA onto the home screen of your device. If you add it, when you tap the icon to load the PWA, you should see the splash screen that was generated automatically, and then you should see the PWA loaded full screen.

AMP in PWA

In this approach, AMP content is embedded and used as a data source in the PWA. This setup relies on the use of a special AMP runtime called **Shadow AMP**, which is designed to run AMP within a non-AMP page. When the Shadow AMP script is included in your main page, it doesn't convert your page into AMP. Rather, it's used to load and run AMP content within that page.

A common PWA architecture is to have an *app shell* that performs XHR content fetching--often via a JSON content API--and which then processes and displays the fetched content. The use case for AMP in PWA via Shadow AMP is that you can just reuse your AMP pages with very little work, rather than having to build a JSON content API separately.

While this method is described as **AMP in PWA** on the AMP project website, as with all of these approaches, the non-AMP part doesn't *have* to be a PWA, that is, to meet all the requirements of a PWA. The approach will also work in any non-AMP, non-PWA page, so long as the Shadow AMP library is imported. Let's see it in action.

Loading AMP with Shadow AMP

First, we'll create an HTML page that will be our PWA (`/ch11/ampinpwa/pwa.html`), and we'll include the Shadow AMP library like this:

```
<script async src="https://cdn.ampproject.org/shadow-v0.js"></script>
```

 It's not possible to use the Shadow AMP runtime in an AMP page--it's used to load AMP content into a non-AMP container or shell page.

We can check if Shadow AMP is ready to use with this code:

```
(window.AMP = window.AMP || []).push(function(AMP) {
  // Shadow AMP is now ready to use
  showAMPContent(url);
});
```

So we'll need to write the `showAMPContent()` function. But before we do, we'll set a few things up. First, we'll add a container element to hold the AMP content:

```
<div id="container"></div>
```

Next, we'll add a function to fetch the AMP document to be included in the PWA page. We can use an `XMLHTTPRequest` to return a `Document` object, which the Shadow AMP will then render for us:

```
function fetchDocument(url) {
  var xhr = new XMLHttpRequest();
  return new Promise(function(resolve, reject) {
    xhr.open('GET', url, true);
    xhr.responseType = 'document';
    xhr.setRequestHeader('Accept', 'text/html');
    xhr.onload = function() {
```

```
      // return a Document object
      resolve(xhr.responseXML);
    };
    xhr.send();
  });
}
```

Now that we have a way to fetch the AMP documents, we can write the showAMPContent function that will fetch and display them:

```
function showAMPContent(url) {
  fetchDocument(url).then(function(doc) {
    ...
```

Once we have the Document object we create a container for it, and then we can add it to our page with the attachShadowDoc() method like this:

```
      var newDocContainer = document.createElement('div');

      // Let Shadow AMP render the doc
      var ampedDoc = AMP.attachShadowDoc(newDocContainer, doc, url);

      // Remove old AMP doc if there is one
      var ampContainer = document.getElementById('ampContainer');
      if(ampContainer) container.removeChild(ampContainer);

      newDocContainer.setAttribute('id','ampContainer');

      // Add content to our main container
      container.appendChild(newDocContainer);
    }
```

The AMP content will now be included and rendered within the main document, along with its header and footer. If your PWA page also has a header and footer, you might want to remove the AMP header and footer to avoid duplication. This can be achieved with normal JavaScript DOM manipulation. In our example, before calling attachShadowDoc(), we could remove the header and footer like this:

```
      var header = doc.querySelector("header");
      if(null!=header) header.remove();

      var footer = doc.querySelector("footer");
      if(null!=footer) footer.remove();
```

Next, let's consider what happens when a user clicks an AMP link within the context of the PWA.

Navigating within the PWA

When we load the AMP content, there's another task we need to do to ensure a good user experience. If the user clicks a link to an AMP page within the AMP content, the AMP page will be loaded directly, and they will navigate away from the PWA context. However, the desired behavior is that the AMP page should be loaded into the PWA shell to replace the current content.

To achieve this, we can add a click handler that will prevent the default browser action that navigates to the linked page, and instead, we'll call the showAMPContent function again to repeat the process of fetching the AMP document and passing it to the Shadow AMP runtime to render.

To achieve, this we need to target the links within the AMP content that we wish to hijack. In this example, we've added the amp-link class to any link that should be loaded into the PWA. External links, for example, shouldn't be loaded into the PWA, and they will be ignored by the following code:

```
newDocContainer.shadowRoot.querySelectorAll("a.amp-link").forEach(function(el) {
  el.addEventListener("click", function(e){
    ampedDoc.close();
    ampedDoc = null;
    container.textContent='';
    e.preventDefault();
    showAMPContent(el.getAttribute('href'));
  }, false);
})
```

Note how we access the elements in the attached AMP document with newDocContainer.shadowRoot. We also perform some cleanup of the old content that we're about to replace with ampedDoc.close() and container.textContent = '';.

Navigation and the HTML5 History API

There's another issue to consider here. When the user clicks a link, we are essentially loading a new document into the PWA shell, but the URL hasn't changed: We've lost the navigation history. If the user clicks the browser's back button, they'll be brought to the last URL they visited before the PWA, rather than the most recent content they visited within the PWA. Equally bad, if the user tries to share the URL of the current page, they'll end up sharing the default `pwa.html` URL, rather than linking directly to the content they want to share.

We can fix this by using the HTML5 History API. This API allows us to manipulate the browser URL. We can use the `history.pushState()` method to:

- Change the browser URL to reflect the AMP document we've just loaded
- Store any data needed to restore the content at that URL

When the user clicks the back button and goes back to a previous URL, we can then replace the current content with the appropriate content for that URL. So anytime we add new AMP content into the PWA, we'll call `history.pushState()` like this:

```
history.pushState({ampUrl:url}, null, url);
```

Now, we just need to hook into the `popstate` event, which will be fired when the user hits the browser's back button. When this happens, we can access the URL that we pushed onto the history earlier with `event.state.ampUrl`. So, the following code will fix the browser navigation buttons for our PWA:

```
window.onpopstate = function (event) {
  showAMPContent(event.state.ampUrl);
};
```

You can see the full code at `/ch11/ampinpwa/pwa.html`. If you click any of the related content links at the bottom, they'll be loaded into the PWA shell:

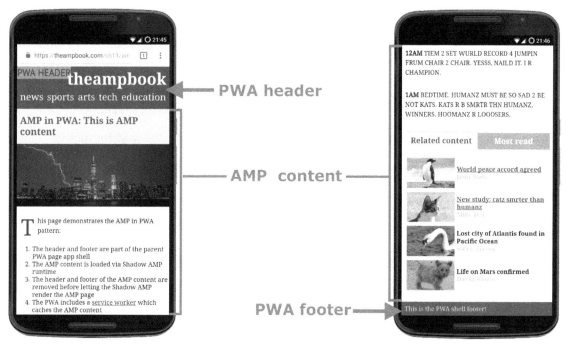

AMP in a PWA pattern: AMP pages are loaded into a PWA app shell

We've built a very simple vanilla JavaScript version here. If React's your framework of choice, then you can see a React version at: `github.com/ampproject/amp-publisher-sample/tree/master/amp-pwa`. Or if Polymer's your thing, you can find a Polymer version at: `github.com/Polymer/news/tree/amp`. Paul Bakhaus from the AMP team also has a great tutorial and demo implementation at: `paulbakaus.com/tutorials/html5/building-a-pwamp-0-introducing-the-shadowreader`.

Serving AMP pages to all mobile visitors

If you've set up your AMP pages as described in Chapter 1, *Ride the Lightning with AMP*, that is, with a `<link rel="amphtml" ...>` tag in your non-AMP pages pointing to your AMP pages, then unless you specifically set something up, the only way to get to your AMP pages is by clicking through a Google search result, or perhaps clicking on a Twitter or LinkedIn link. The point is, you're reliant on third-party services to decide which version of your page will be served to any particular visitor. But what if the user visits your website directly on a mobile device? They will still get your non-AMP, desktop page.

Since you've gone to the trouble of creating an AMP page that's optimized for mobile, wouldn't it be better to get as much value as possible from your AMP investment and serve it to all your mobile visitors, whether Google sent them or not?

To do this, you need some way to determine which visitors are mobile and which are not. This is essentially what Google and Twitter are doing when they decide to send a visitor to an AMP page rather than a desktop page. This can be achieved by using a device detection solution, such as DeviceAtlas (`deviceatlas.com`) or Wurfl (`scientiamobile.com`).

 This could also be done with client-side JavaScript, but then the browser has to load a page before this logic can even run, so you'd lose some of the speed advantages of AMP

As an example, let's see how we'd set this up using the DeviceAtlas device detection solution.

Using device detection to serve AMP

The details of how to set up device detection will vary depending on how your web server environment is set up. DeviceAtlas has a Cloud version and an Enterprise version. In some scenarios, the device switching logic can be included at the application layer using one of its language-specific APIs, such as JavaScript, PHP, or Java. In other cases, it could be included at the web server layer, for example, as an Apache, NGINX, or IIS module. In this example, we outline a simple desktop-mobile switching solution using the PHP Cloud API at the application layer.

Note that DeviceAtlas is a commercial solution that offers a free trial. You can set up this example using the free trial. The example here can easily be adapted to other device detection solutions.

The first thing to do is sign up with DeviceAtlas for a Cloud trial here: `deviceatlas.com/signup-cloud`.

Next, download the PHP API from: `deviceatlas.com/resources/download-cloud-api`.

Now we're ready to get coding. We can include the DeviceAtlas API like this:

```
require_once dirname(__FILE__).'/da/Api/Client.php';
```

Then we define constants for our desktop and AMP page templates:

```
define('DESKTOP_TEMPLATE', 'desktop.html');
define('AMP_TEMPLATE', 'amp.html');
```

Now let's use the DeviceAtlas API to identify the user's device. Behind the scenes, DeviceAtlas uses the browser's UserAgent string to identify the device:

```
$result = DeviceAtlasCloudClient::getDeviceData();
if (isset($result[DeviceAtlasCloudClient::KEY_PROPERTIES])) {
  $properties = $result[DeviceAtlasCloudClient::KEY_PROPERTIES];
}
```

Now all the properties that DeviceAtlas knows about for this device are stored in the `$properties` array. In this example, we're going to use the `isBrowser`, `isMasqueradingAsDesktop`, and `mobileDevice` properties to decide which page template to show the user. There are many more properties, such as `isTablet`, `screenWidth`, and `screenHeight`, which could just be used to optimize content in various ways.

First, let's check if it's a desktop browser (or pretending to be one); if it is, we'll include the desktop page template:

```
if ((isset($properties['isBrowser']) && $properties['isBrowser']) ||
    (isset($properties['isMasqueradingAsDesktop']) &&
$properties['isMasqueradingAsDesktop'])) {

  include(DESKTOP_TEMPLATE);
  exit;
}
```

Then let's check if it's a mobile browser, and show the mobile template if it is:

```
if (isset($properties['mobileDevice']) && $properties['mobileDevice']) {
  include(AMP_TEMPLATE);
  exit;
}
```

Finally, if a choice hasn't been made yet, just show the default page. We've chosen to show the AMP page by default, but you could as easily show the desktop page:

```
/* If we got here just show AMP page (or desktop if you prefer!) */
include(AMP_TEMPLATE);
```

Now we just need to set up the `desktop.html` and `amp.html` pages, and that's it:

Serving AMP pages using device detection: mobile devices get the AMP version (left), and non-mobile devices get the desktop version (right)

You can see this in action at `/ch11/switcher/index.php`. On a desktop browser, you will get the desktop page, otherwise, you will get the AMP page.

This is a fairly basic example that shows how device-detection-based routing works. There are a few things you could do to improve it:

- Route all page requests through the switcher. That is, include the switching logic in every page so that the user will be routed correctly no matter what their entry point.

- Once you've determined a user's device and the appropriate page routing, you can set a cookie to store this information so that subsequent requests in the session can skip the device lookup.

- Always provide a link to the alternative page template for the user: On the AMP page, include a link to the desktop page and vice versa. If the user chooses to *override* the device detection routing like this, then set this preference in the cookie so that they don't get routed back to the other version on the next page request.

AMP and WordPress

Deployment of AMP alongside WordPress is worthy of a mention here because of the popularity of WordPress. There are several plugins to choose from that create an AMP version of your site, such as the AMP plugin from Automaticc (`wordpress.org/plugins/amp`), and they generally require you to do very little, apart from installing the plugin.

However, it's a little disappointing to see that many WordPress site owners, including major site publishers, simply install the plugin and leave it at that. This leaves the default blue template in place, and so when the AMP page is reached via Google or Twitter, the site's brand identity is lost and many WordPress sites using this plugin look the same.

But it doesn't have to be this way! At the very least, the branding colors can be customized in the WordPress Admin under **Admin** | **Appearance** | **Design**. Even better than this, it's straightforward to modify the AMP template so that the branding matches the non-AMP pages. You can do this by following these steps:

1. Copy the AMP plugin template file `single.php` from the plugin folder (`/wp-content/plugins/amp/templates/`) to your theme folder. Save it as `single.amp.tpl.php`. Also copy the file `style.php` and save it as `style.amp.php`.

2. Add the following to the `functions.php` file in your theme directory:

```php
add_filter('amp_post_template_file', 'mytheme_amp_custom', 10,
3);

function mytheme_amp_custom($file, $type, $post) {
  if ('single' === $type) {
    $file = dirname(__FILE__) . '/single.amp.tpl.php';
  }
  else if ('style' === $type) {
    $file = dirname(__FILE__) . '/amp.style.php';
  }
  return $file;
}
```

3. Now you can make HTML and PHP changes in the `single.amp.tpl.php` file, and you can make CSS styling changes in `amp.style.php`.

4. If you need to modify the header or footer too, then copy the header and footer files (`header-bar.php`, `footer.php`) from the plugin folder to your theme folder, as in step 1. Then add the following lines to the `mytheme_amp_custom` function before the `return $file` line:

```php
else if ( 'footer' === $type ) {
  $file = dirname( __FILE__ ) . '/footer.amp.tpl.php';
}
else if ( 'header-bar' === $type ) {
  $file = dirname( __FILE__ ) . '/header.amp.tpl.php';
}
```

Now you can modify `footer.amp.tpl.php` and `header.amp.tpl.php` to suit your needs.

Summary

In this chapter, we've seen that there are quite a few options for deploying an AMP site. For some, AMP will be the whole solution, while for others, AMP is just one part of a larger web presence. Before you deploy AMP, you should consider how it will fit in with the rest of your web properties. Just how you integrate AMP will depend on your needs. However, the range of possibilities should be taken as a positive because it means that AMP, as a publishing format, is flexible enough to be used in pretty much any web publishing scenario you can think of, while still delivering the benefits we've seen throughout this book.

At this point, we've covered as much of AMP as we can within a volume of this length, and what remains in the next chapter is to ponder where AMP will go from here, and what else it might have to offer in the future.

12
AMP - Where It's At and Where It's Going

We've covered a lot of ground in this book and now it's coming to a close. In these final few pages, we'll reflect on what we've covered and where AMP is going. In particular, we'll

- Review what we've learned
- Discuss the AMP project's current trajectory
- Revisit the main criticisms of AMP

From zero to AMP

We started off this book in the programming tradition of building a simple *"Hello World!"* example. This allowed us to introduce the AMP boilerplate code that forms the backbone of every AMP page.

After this, we quickly built up more practical examples, with article and e-commerce pages being the main focus. We saw a variety of layout and presentation techniques, we learned about monetization through ads and analytics, and we saw some advanced deployment techniques. We built some nice prototypes!

We also considered the driving force behind AMP, namely performance on the web, or the lack of it in general. Performance is a good goal to have. Having performance at its heart, driving all design decisions in AMP, benefits users and publishers alike. In Chapter 1, *Ride the Lightning with AMP*, we saw plenty of statistics about how AMP increases conversions. Poor performance is bad for user experience.

A bad user experience is bad for conversions since users don't engage as much with slow, poorly performing pages. It's really that simple! AMP solves performance issues for publishers who don't have the time, resources, or inclination to do this themselves without AMP.

Keeping up with AMP - the AMP roadmap

While we've gone into great detail on many aspects and features of AMP, it would be impossible to cover everything in a book of this length, and, undoubtedly, there will be some feature or topic that you might have expected to be included but that is missing.

The AMP project is an active and well organized open source project. It publishes and updates its roadmap here: `ampproject.org/roadmap/`.

The roadmap is updated twice per quarter (mid-quarter and end-quarter), and lists quarterly goals and priorities for the current and next quarters. It lists the activities and development status of items that fall into certain categories. Those categories are as follows:

- Planning and design
- Intent to implement (feature descriptions)
- Coding started
- Pull request

With this setup, it's easy to track the progress of a feature from inception to release date.

Since AMP is a very active project, it does not make much sense to go into too much detail here on upcoming features; it's probably better just to go direct to the roadmap itself to review the current status of the project.

Contributing

AMP is an open source project, hosted on GitHub, although, ultimately, design decisions are approved by the AMP project team, which is mostly made up of Google employees. However, the team is extremely receptive and responsive to feedback. Where functionality is lacking, users are encouraged to make feature requests. You can open issues directly on the project page and someone from the AMP team normally responds within hours. Perhaps conscious of the perception that it is a Google project, the project is open to new contributors and members.

There is a dedicated document outlining how to get involved at `ampproject.org/contribute`. There's another document that outlines how to make your first Git code contribution, and a list of *Great First Issues* has been created for issues specifically deemed suitable for newcomers to work on.

During the course of writing this book, I was able to make minor contributions back to the project by reporting bugs and issues when I found them, and by improving the documentation where I found it to be unclear or lacking. Getting involved is easy!

AMP - from web pages to web apps

At the first AMP conference (in March 2017), many features and prototypes were demonstrated. Among them was a full messaging client, complete with live messaging and push notifications, built by AMP team member Sebastian Benz. This example was particularly interesting since it uses AMP to build what can be described as a relatively complex messaging app. By using AMP components creatively, in ways beyond what they were originally designed for, it was possible to build such an application. This was built on a framework that--as you will know by now--doesn't support custom JavaScript or programming. This was a real eye-opener. It demonstrated the flexibility of AMP--by using and combining AMP components creatively, complex behaviors and applications could be built.

Another point that this example drove home was that AMP is not just about *pages*. It's clear that AMP has moved well beyond the article-type page that it was originally designed for. We are now living in an age of *AMP Web Apps*!

As an active project, new features are being added to AMP regularly. Thus, the capabilities of AMP web apps will increase over time. At some point, you might be faced with having to decide which framework to use for your next web project. So, if in the future you are faced with the decision of what framework to use for your next project--AMP or something else--what might tip the decision in favor of AMP, assuming that it meets the project requirements?

User-friendliness

We've seen in this book how we were able to build quite complex prototypes with minimal coding and without too much difficultly. Of course, *difficulty* is subjective. However, in the grand scheme of the programming projects I've experienced, on a pleasure-pain spectrum of web development, working with AMP has been decidedly at the pleasure end of the spectrum: it's a fun, user-friendly technology to work with.

The AMP Cache

Love it or hate it, the AMP Cache is a differentiator. Choosing AMP over another technology could come down to the difference in accelerated page loading due to the AMP Cache. The AMP Cache puts the A in AMP; it's what delivers instant-loading pages.

If you are one of the many who shares concerns about the AMP Cache--we'll come back to these concerns shortly--but can still appreciate it for the components that it offers, what if there was a way to opt out of the cache? Wouldn't it be great if the AMP team built that?

Well, you can already do this! All you need to do is leave out the lightning symbol in the `<html>` declaration at the top of your document. Then it's not technically an AMP page, and it won't be added by Google to the AMP Cache; it will be a just another web page, but one that uses the AMP framework. When people complain about AMP, one of the biggest complaints is about the cache. Well, you can have AMP without the cache if you like, but you will, of course, be losing the benefits that it offers.

Flexibility

You don't necessarily need to treat AMP as a competing technology, of course! As we saw in `Chapter 11`, *AMP Deployment and Your Web Presence*, AMP is extremely flexible--it works well with other technologies. In that chapter, we saw many different ways that AMP can be deployed to complement other web technologies, and we implemented several different solutions. We saw that AMP can be integrated with Progressive Web Apps; CMSes, such as WordPress; and server-side device detection solutions, as well as with frameworks such as React and Polymer. The point is that you don't need to view AMP as a competing technology--it can complement an existing project or stand on its own. How it fits in will depend on any particular project, but AMP is flexible, so it's likely that it *can* fit in with your project, whatever the web technology you're using.

Criticism of AMP

It would be remiss not to briefly revisit the main criticisms of the AMP project here. Since its launch, there have been three main criticisms leveled at the AMP project. These criticisms come from open web advocates who believe certain parts of the project are incompatible with a distributed and open web. These criticisms are:

- The AMP Cache URL
- The AMP lightning symbol in search results
- The SEO benefits of the AMP Top Stories carousel

AMP Cache URL

As we saw in `Chapter 1`, *Ride the Lightning with AMP*, when an AMP page is served from the AMP Cache, which sits on a Google domain, the original URL is obscured, and the address bar shows a URL that starts with a Google domain. The original URL is buried in the AMP URL, but most users won't see it. This can dilute your brand.

When the source URL is obscured, it's not hard to see how the content of a domain might be attributed incorrectly. When an AMP page is displayed with `google.com` as the domain in the address bar, a user unfamiliar with AMP could easily attribute that content to Google, which might lend it some authority. In this age of propaganda and fake news that we find ourselves in, knowing the true source of the content we consume is crucial. Unfortunately, the AMP Cache URL can cause confusion in this regard.

The AMP team is painfully aware of these issues. They argue that it's a necessary evil, however. Back to the A in AMP. The only way that AMP can guarantee that the pages are indeed *accelerated*--that is, that they load quickly or even instantly--is by hosting only **valid AMP pages** in the AMP Cache. Then--and this is how AMP can achieve instant page loads--AMP pages can be pre-rendered in the background, even before a user has decided to visit one.

This only works at scale because of AMP validation. If a page is valid, then it has a provable baseline performance--because performance dictated how AMP was built, such a page won't be doing anything that causes the performance to drop below this baseline. And the only way that the project can guarantee that a page is valid at request time is by serving that page from the cache. If the page is served from the original domain, then there's no guarantee that it will be available or that it hasn't had invalidating changes made to it in the meantime. That's the whole point of validation.

The AMP team has said that it's committed to displaying the original URL wherever technically possible, and Malte Ubl, the project lead, has hinted that they're working on a solution. This would be a welcome development since the AMP Cache URL is probably the biggest valid criticism of AMP. Without this issue, it would be harder to find fault with the project. However, it's difficult to see how it can provide the AMP Cache *and* guarantee instant page loads without it.

The DNS solution

One approach to resolving the AMP Cache URL issues would be to allow users to use their own domain with the AMP Cache. Sure, there would be some technical overhead for the user in setting this up, but if you've already got a website, then you either have the skills, or have employed somebody who has the skills, needed to perform the required DNS changes. It's somewhat puzzling that Google doesn't offer this option to those who want it, since it would certainly dilute the criticism.

AMP lightning badge of trust in search results

The AMP performance guarantee is symbolized in search results with a lightning badge that's displayed next to AMP results, and this brings us to the next major criticism of the project. The AMP lightning symbol indicates to the user that they will experience a fast or instant page load if they click a link. Critics argue that Google is using its dominant position in search to promote its own technology. Why not, after all, just display the symbol beside *any* fast page, not just AMP pages?

This brings us back to the performance guarantee again. Google can't guarantee that a page will be quick at request time unless it's hosted in the AMP Cache. A page might have been quick the last time Google crawled it, but anything could have changed in the meantime. If you try to pre-render pages from the original domain, then you quickly run into trouble. At least this is what the Bing team that was working on its own AMP Cache had to say. They basically confirmed Google's approach to implementing the AMP pre-render. Back to square one! (You can watch this panel discussion on YouTube here: youtu.be/oRobCzJPihY)

De facto SEO benefits of the AMP carousel

One last criticism worth a mention here is the AMP *Top Stories* carousel. We saw this in `Chapter 1`, *Ride the lightning with AMP*, where AMP pages can be promoted to the AMP Top Stories carousel when relevant to a search query. The Google search team has said that AMP is not a ranking signal. However, regardless of whether there is an explicit ranking bias in the indexing or retrieval algorithms, there is a definite SEO benefit to having your pages appear in the Top Stories carousel.

This is the problem. If you don't embrace AMP, then your web pages and your business are at a disadvantage. It's different to other Google products in that, for example, you can decide whether or not you want to share traffic data to a service such as Google Analytics. If, however, you are competing for positioning in search results, you can't afford to be outside the AMP tent. Once again, this is seen by some as Google's abuse of its dominant position in searching.

Summary

Is AMP for you? If you've read this far, then the answer is probably yes! It's true, however, that certain aspects of AMP are not ideal, but for many, the benefits outweigh the costs. For users, AMP pages load perceptibly faster. For publishers, AMP pages convert better. We noted earlier in the book that AMP pages are currently being exposed to over two billion web users, there are over one billion AMP pages live, and publishers are happy with the effects AMP have had on their bottom line. Right or wrong, users have voted for AMP with their taps and their touches.

Of course, AMP is not an all-or-nothing affair. It's a component framework after all, and it's not intrinsically tied to the AMP Cache; you can use AMP as a framework without needing to use the AMP Cache at all. Whether it works for you--if the benefits do indeed outweigh the downsides--is something you must decide for your own project.

This brings our journey to an end. We've seen what AMP can do, and we were able to build up relatively complex applications without too much pain! Whatever else you might think about AMP, having made it this far, I hope that you'd agree it's a versatile, capable, and user-friendly framework, and that you'll consider it for your next project.

AMP Components

Ads and analytics

Component	Description
amp-ad	Displays an ad
amp-ad-exit	Defines behavior for ad exits for A4A (AMP for Ads)
amp-analytics	Captures analytics and integrates analytics providers
amp-auto-ads	Inserts ads using remote configuration file
amp-call-tracking	Replaces phone numbers with click-to-call links
amp-experiment	For conducting UX experiments
amp-pixel	Simple pixel-based pageview analytics
amp-sticky-ad	Displays a sticky ad at bottom of page

Dynamic content

Component	Description
amp-access-laterpay	Integrates with LaterPay micropayments
amp-access	Offers login and paywall support
amp-bind	A programming layer for AMP
amp-form	Form support and enhancements

amp-gist	Displays a GitHub Gist
amp-install-serviceworker	Installs a ServiceWorker
amp-list	Fetches content from server and displays with mustache template
amp-live-list	Live content polling and updating
amp-mustache	Renders mustache.js templates
amp-selector	UI control for choosing options
amp-user-notification	Displays a dismissable notification
amp-web-push	Lets users subscribe to web push notifications

Layout

Component	Description
amp-accordion	Displays content in collapsible sections
amp-app-banner	Displays app-install banner
amp-carousel	Displays multiple content items in a horizontal slider or scrollable list
amp-fx-flying-carpet	Full-screen container that shows fixed portion
amp-fx-parallex	Displays 3D scrolling perspective on an element
amp-iframe	Embeds an iframe
amp-lightbox	Displays content within a lightbox
amp-position-observer	Tracks position of an element as user scrolls, and dispatches events
amp-sidebar	Displays sidebar content

Media

Component	Description
amp-anim	Display animated image such as GIF
amp-audio	HTML5 audio tag replacement
amp-image-lightbox	Specialized lightbox component for images
amp-img	HTML5 img tag replacement
amp-video	HTML5 video tag replacement

Presentation

Component	Description
amp-animation	Displays an animation
amp-dynamic-css-classes	Adds dynamic CSS classes to an HTML element
amp-fit-text	Sizes text to fit its container
amp-font	Triggers and monitors font loading
amp-timeago	Formats dates in "hours|days|months ago" style
amp-viz-vega	Displays Vega visualization

Third-party media

Component	Description
amp-3q-player	Embeds 3Q SDN videos
amp-apester-media	Displays Apester content unit
amp-brid-player	Embeds Brid.tv player
amp-brightcove	Displays Brightcove Video Cloud or Perform player
amp-dailymotion	Displays Dailymotion video
amp-google-vrview-image	Displays a VR image
amp-hulu	Embeds Hulu video

`amp-ima-video`	Embeds IMA SDK video ad
`amp-imgur`	Displays Imgur post
`amp-izlesene`	Displays Izlesene video
`amp-jwplayer`	Displays cloud-hosted JW Player
`amp-kaltura-player`	Embeds Kaltura video player
`amp-nexxtv-player`	Displays nexxOMNIA media
`amp-o2-player`	Displays AOL O2Player
`amp-ooyala-player`	Displays Ooyala video player
`amp-playbuzz`	Displays Playbuzz content
`amp-reach-player`	Displays Beachfront Reach video player
`amp-soundcloud`	Embeds SoundCloud audio
`amp-springboard-player`	Displays Springboard Platform video player
`amp-vimeo`	Embeds Vimeo video
`amp-youtube`	Displays YouTube video

B
Actions and Events

Events

Event	Element(s)	Description	Data
`tap`	`*`	Fired when element is tapped or clicked	

`change`	`input, select`	Fired when element value changes and is committed	`event.min`
			`event.max`
			`event.value`
			`event.valueAsNumber`

`input-debounced`	`input, select`	Same as change event	
`slideChange`	`amp-carousel` `[type="slides"]`	Fired on manual change of current carousel slide	`event.index`
`select`	`amp-selector`	Fired on manual selection of option	`event.targetOption`
`submit`	`form`	Fired on form submission	`event.response`
`submit-success`	`form`	Fired on success response of form submission	`event.response`

submit-error	form	Fired on error response of form submission	
valid	form	Fired when form is valid	
invalid	form	Fired when form is invalid	

Actions

Action	Element(s)	Description
hide	*	Hides the element
show	*	Shows the element
toggleVisibility	*	Toggles element visibility
scrollTo(duration, position)	*	Scrolls element into view. duration (optional, default: 500 ms) specifies length of scroll animation. position (optional, default: top) specifies end position in viewport, is one of top, center, bottom
focus	*	Give focus to target element
goToSlide(index)	amp-carousel [type="slides"]	Advances carousel to slide index (integer)
open	amp-image-lightbox amp-lightbox amp-sidebar	Opens the component
close	amp-image-lightbox amp-lightbox amp-sidebar	Closes the component
toggle	amp-sidebar	Toggles the sidebar state

dismiss	amp-user-notification	Hides the notification
submit	form	Submits the form
play	amp-video amp-youtube amp-3q-player amp-ima-video amp-brid-player amp-dailymotion	Plays video
pause	amp-video amp-youtube amp-3q-player amp-ima-video amp-brid-player amp-dailymotion	Pauses video
mute	amp-video amp-youtube amp-3q-player amp-ima-video amp-brid-player amp-dailymotion	Mutes video
unmute	amp-video amp-youtube amp-3q-player amp-ima-video amp-brid-player amp-dailymotion	Unmutes video
fullscreen	amp-video amp-youtube amp-3q-player amp-ima-video amp-brid-player amp-dailymotion	Expands video to fullscreen

C

amp-bind Whitelisted Functions

JavaScript whitelisted functions

The following is a list of whitelisted JavaScript functions that can be used in `amp-bind` expressions.

Object type	Function
Array	concat
	filter
	includes
	indexOf
	join
	lastIndexOf
	map
	reduce
	slice
	some
Number	toExponential
	toFixed
	toPrecision
	toString

String	charAt
	charCodeAt
	concat
	indexOf
	lastIndexOf
	slice
	split
	substr
	substring
	toLowerCase
	toUpperCase
Math	abs
	ceil
	floor
	max
	min
	random
	round
	sign
Object	keys
	values
Global	encodeURI
	encodeURIComponent
Custom	splice
	sort

D

amp-bind Permitted Attribute Bindings

Component/Element	Attribute binding(s)

`<amp-brightcove>`	`[data-account]`
	`[data-embed]`
	`[data-player]`
	`[data-player-id]`
	`[data-playlist-id]`
	`[data-video-id]`

`<amp-carousel type=slides>`	`[slide]`
`<amp-iframe>`	`[src]`

`<amp-img>`	`[alt]`
	`[attribution]`
	`[src]`
	`[srcset]`

`<amp-list>`	`[src]`
`<amp-selector>`	`[selected]`
`<amp-state>`	`[src]`

`<amp-video>`	`[alt]`
	`[attribution]`
	`[controls]`
	`[loop]`
	`[poster]`
	`[preload]`
	`[src]`

`<amp-youtube>`	`[data-videoid]`
`<a>`	`[href]`

`<button>`	`[disabled]`
	`[type]`
	`[value]`

`<fieldset>`	`[disabled]`

`<input>`	`[accept]`
	`[accessKey]`
	`[autocomplete]`
	`[checked]`
	`[disabled]`
	`[height]`
	`[inputmode]`
	`[max]`
	`[maxlength]`
	`[min]`
	`[minlength]`
	`[multiple]`
	`[pattern]`
	`[placeholder]`
	`[readonly]`
	`[required]`
	`[selectiondirection]`
	`[size]`
	`[spellcheck]`
	`[step]`
	`[type]`
	`[value]`
	`[width]`

`<option>`	`[disabled]`
	`[label]`
	`[selected]`
	`[value]`

`<optgroup>`	`[disabled]` `[label]`

`<select>`	`[autofocus]`
	`[disabled]`
	`[multiple]`
	`[required]`
	`[size]`

`<source>`	`[src]` `[type]`

`<track>`	`[label]`
	`[src]`
	`[srclang]`

`<textarea>`	`[autocomplete]`
	`[autofocus]`
	`[cols]`
	`[disabled]`
	`[maxlength]`
	`[minlength]`
	`[placeholder]`
	`[readonly]`
	`[required]`
	`[rows]`
	`[selectiondirection]`
	`[selectionend]`
	`[selectionstart]`
	`[spellcheck]`
	`[wrap]`

Index

B

Box Model 60

C

canonical AMP pages 298
carousel ads
  creating 294
checkout process
  building, with Payment Request API 264
  HTML5 Payment Request API 265
collapsible content
  building, with amp-accordion 88
  expandable top stories category list, building 89
components
  about 15
  AMP Cache 16
  AMP URLs 17
  AMP-HTML 16
  AMP-JS 16
criticisms, AMP
  about 327
  AMP Cache URL 327
  AMP carousel 329
CSS3 flexbox
  using, for layout in AMP 60
CSS
  using, in AMP pages 39
custom CSS, in AMP pages
  custom fonts, adding 77, 79
  custom fonts, using for improving page design 79
  SVG graphics, adding 83, 84, 85
  text layout, with amp-fit-text component 82, 83
  text layout, with CSS and HTML 80, 82
  using 76

D

device detection
  setting up, for serving AMP pages 316
DeviceAtlas
  URL 316
  URL, for Cloud 317
Disqus
  about 261
  amp-iframe, adding 263, 264

  comments, in AMP 261
  configuring, for site 261, 262
  iframe, resizing 263
  reference link 261
dynamic content
  AMP cache, complications 198
  JSON data, fetching on page load 178

E

e-commerce
  analytics, applying 286
  item addition to cart, tracking 286
  item removal from cart, tracking 287
elements, AMP pages
  laying out 52
Event model
  about 114
  event handlers, attaching with on attribute 115
  events 115
  multiple events, handling on single element 115
expandable top stories category list
  accordion, improving with expanded state
    indicator 91, 92, 93
  amp-accordion, styling 90
  building 89
  example accordion content 93
expressions, amp-bind component
  about 209
  arithmetic expression 209
  if...else expression 209
  linking, to element state 210
  text manipulation expression 209

F

fallbacks
  about 76
  used, for improving user experience 76
flex-item layout
  flex and non-flex items, mixing 73
  flex items with specific proportions 72
  full width flex item container 71
  horizontal flex items 69, 70
  using 69
  vertical flex items 70
Flexible Box Model (flexbox) 60

197

M

mobile web performance, measuring
  about 44
  PageSpeed Insights 46, 47
  remote debugging, with developer tools 47, 48, 49
  waterfall charts 45
  WebPagetest 45, 46
mobile web performance
  optimizing 23

N

navigation menus
  building 95
  building, with amp-carousel 97, 98, 99
  horizontal navigation menus 95
  scrollable horizontal navigation 95, 96
  side navigation, adding with amp-sidebar 99
newsletter sign-up form
  building 152
  custom form validation 157, 158
  UX improvement 159
  visual feedback on submission 159
  XHR AJAX forms, submitting in AMP 153
  XHR responses, handling with amp-mustache 154

P

PageSpeed Insights 46
Payment Request API
  used, for building checkout process 264
performance optimization 24
placeholders
  about 74
  used, for improving user experience 74, 75
product image carousel
  improving, with amp-bind component 225
product image gallery
  building 126
  code, reducing with amp-selector 129, 130
  jumping to specific image, with goToSlide() 128
  selected thumbnail, highlighting 128, 129
  with thumbnail previews 126, 127

product images
  lightbox, closing 140, 141
  lightboxing 138, 139
product options
  advanced configuration 232
  configuration 227
  configuring, with amp-bind component 227
  image preview thumbnails, with amp-selector component 235
  price, tracking 237
  product carousels, creating 233
  product data, initializing with amp-state component 232
  selecting, with amp-bind component 229
  selecting, with amp-selector component 228
  selection options, binding to shopping cart 230
  size option, adding 234
  thumbnails preview option, syncing 236
  tracking 237
product search form
  building 160, 161
  caveat 167
  JSON data, iterating over with amp-mustache 163, 164, 165
  JSON list of products 162
  search icon, animating 166
  search status, displaying 165, 166
  server response 162
  styling 161, 162
product search
  autosuggest, adding 222
  improving, with amp-bind component 218
  improving, with amp-list component 218
  JSON response, modifying 220
  results, displaying with amp-list component 219
  results, filtering 219
  results, sorting 219
  results, updating 219
product SEO
  improving, with metadata 147
products, promoting with social media
  about 144
  default share text, setting 145
products
  carousel, building 120, 121

www.ingramcontent.com/pod-product-compliance
Lightning Source LLC
Chambersburg PA
CBHW080613060326
40690CB00021B/4683